# YOUTH WORK

## Improving the Lives of Young People and Communities

Tracie Trimmer-Platman

I0136005

P

First published in Great Britain in 2026 by

Policy Press, an imprint of
Bristol University Press
University of Bristol
1-9 Old Park Hill
Bristol
BS2 8BB
UK
t: +44 (0)117 374 6645
e: bup-info@bristol.ac.uk

Details of international sales and distribution partners are available at policy.bristoluniversitypress.co.uk

© Bristol University Press 2026

DOI: 10.51952/9781447368670

British Library Cataloguing in Publication Data
A catalogue record for this book is available from the British Library

ISBN 978-1-4473-6864-9 hardcover
ISBN 978-1-4473-6865-6 paperback
ISBN 978-1-4473-6866-3 ePub
ISBN 978-1-4473-6867-0 ePdf

The right of Tracie Trimmer-Platman to be identified as author of this work has been asserted by her in accordance with the Copyright, Designs and Patents Act 1988.

All rights reserved: no part of this publication may be reproduced, stored in a retrieval system, or transmitted in any form or by any means, electronic, mechanical, photocopying, recording, or otherwise without the prior permission of Bristol University Press.

Every reasonable effort has been made to obtain permission to reproduce copyrighted material. If, however, anyone knows of an oversight, please contact the publisher.

The statements and opinions contained within this publication are solely those of the author and not of the University of Bristol or Bristol University Press. The University of Bristol and Bristol University Press disclaim responsibility for any injury to persons or property resulting from any material published in this publication.

Bristol University Press and Policy Press work to counter discrimination on grounds of gender, race, disability, age and sexuality.

Cover design: Lyn Davies

# Contents

# Introduction

This book is unique in many ways, not least because it introduces research which took place in Hackney Wick in East London during and after the 2012 Olympics and enabled the development of a model of practice for open access youth work. It aims to discuss the challenges which youth workers encounter generally, as well as specifically in urban areas undergoing regeneration. The chapters provide insight into the key issues which emerged as residents, in particular young people, began to navigate the shifting landscape and search for a space of their own.

Open access youth work is a provision for young people to access regardless of their background, needs and societal status (Robertson, 2005) and is based on their voluntary participation. Young people engage in safe, enriching, non-judgemental activities overseen by qualified youth workers who encourage them to develop personal, social and educational skills. Once available in almost every neighbourhood across the country, the service is now a victim of cuts in government funding by billions in the last ten years (Children and Young People Now (CYPN), 2023).

Youth work has a distinct set of principles and practices (which are highlighted specifically in Chapter 4) and focuses on the needs, interests, equity and justice as it applies to young people aged between 13 and 19. There are certainly crossovers with community work, which at its core is about 'addressing inequalities to enable full and meaningful participation of communities and individuals in any and all aspects of their lives' (McArdle, 2024, p 50). However, youth work aims to empower young people with the skills, knowledge and awareness to actively arrive at adulthood and positive community citizenship.

The catalyst for this study was the Games, but what transpired was a research case study about the small and isolated community of Hackney Wick and how groups and individuals managed to make 'wishing for space' for young people a reality. It outlines the obstacles, objections and opportunities encountered along the way and how fears, attitudes and hopes for young people were identified and how professional youth workers negotiated and navigated a way through this, which benefited young people primarily, but also the wider neighbourhood, leading to the creation of the Hub67 model of practice.

The Hub67 model offers some strategies and theory about including young people in community change and what can be encouraged in areas undergoing regenerative development. When neighbourhoods are suddenly gentrified, it can often be alienating for young people who have no choice but to watch as new communities rise around them. Utilising provisions such as open access youth work and the Hub67 model enables long-term improvement of the developmental process for all concerned.

## The chapters

Chapter 1: 'Understanding youth work in changing urban environments' provides a view of what youth work is and how I came to understand it through theories, dilemmas and education in the context of urban regeneration. It encourages you to understand how young people and youth work are perceived and the impact this has on individuals and groups.

Chapter 2: 'Social capital: a commodity for young people?' aims to demystify the idea of social capital and discusses its potential for young people as they navigate the regenerative process and gather confidence in their communities.

Chapter 3: 'The lived experiences of young people and other residents' introduces and describes the experiences of young people, their families and other residents as the research case study emerged. Drawing on the research interviews, focus groups and other data, you are led through the concerns and opportunities which emerged.

Chapter 4: 'Young people and community' offers background and context to the research and identifies the working principles that were adopted for working with young people and the wider neighbourhood through outreach, networking and community engagement.

Chapter 5: 'The co-creation of Hub67' explains how the hub was co-created as a space for young people and how difference was managed when navigating change in the neighbourhood. This chapter shares the obstacles and dilemmas which practitioners faced during the case study and how these were resolved.

Chapter 6: 'The Hub67 model' presents the model for best practice, its aims, attitudes, values and beliefs and how these were and can be applied in the context of open access youth work, and how it is implemented.

Chapter 7: 'The impact and potential of open access youth work' draws on the findings and observations from the case study to discuss the impact that participating in the hub had on young people, their families and the community.

Chapter 8: 'What now for young people and youth work?' concludes the key learning from the study and makes recommendations for future consideration and practice in open access youth work in changing urban contexts.

This book will take you on a journey – one which was part of my lived experience as a youth worker, a researcher and a resident of Hackney Wick.

You will be introduced to the area and the people who lived through this period with me, and especially to the young people who were otherwise ignored by ensuing regeneration and change following the injection of millions into the neighbourhood. How they were given a voice, a space, social capital and respect is discussed and intended to provide a model for good future practice. This book foregrounds the development of self-awareness, agency and citizenship, highlighting how youth work can foster these attributes and promote both individual wellbeing and social change. These concepts are present throughout the chapters. In the context of urban regeneration, where marginalisation and exclusion limit opportunity and belonging, these attributes become critical tools of resilience and resistance.

There is some discussion in this book of the gradual destruction of the youth service, silencing of young people and disregard for open access youth work; a distinctive 'open door' provision for young people in youth clubs over 35 years. Throughout the book, I consider the impact that the reduction of funding, resources and acknowledgement of youth work practice has had on youth workers both psychologically and professionally, and the ways that youth work became hesitant to collaborate and have sometimes retreated into practice silos. I hope that it provides a vision for change and renewed advocacy for young people as community members, neighbourhood participants and self-aware citizens.

The research that underpins this book was a case study which aimed to determine whether the lived experiences of young people and their community could be improved if an open access youth work provision were to be positioned in the neighbourhood. The following chapters are presented chronologically to provide a case study narrative in the order in which it developed and materialised.

## My background

In this chapter, I will talk about how and why I became a youth worker and how I developed my professional attitudes and values. I will provide some insight into what youth work is, why it is important and why I champion it. My experience as a youth work practitioner over the past 30-plus years began rather late, after I had done a variety of jobs in retail and drama, and was desperately looking for something satisfying. As a newly qualified teacher in the early 1990s, I transitioned from head of department in a church school in south London to a full-time youth and community worker in west London – almost overnight.

I didn't discover youth work because of my ideals though – at the time I didn't know much about it – instead I made a financial decision to take on a bit of extra work on top of my role as an art, textiles and home economics teacher (which probably tells you something about teacher salaries!).

I set up 'needlework' sessions at the youth club attached to the school. For two nights a week, I took it on, sitting and chatting with the young people who came along, rarely doing any sewing at all. I soon realised that 'needlework' was unimportant for the young people, but the space, the camaraderie and the opportunity to simply hang out were huge. I learnt so much about these young people over the weeks that followed – far more than I could ever have done in the classroom. I learnt about their lives, in all their diversity, their troubles, motivations, aspirations, stresses and much more. Their narratives became richer, and my concern equalled my admiration for them. In this setting, I met young people who were considered 'troublesome', 'disruptive' and 'difficult' in school, as well as some who would not attend my lessons in school, permanently referred to alternative provision. My developing relationships with them encouraged them to go back into school.

In the classroom, I was keen to create an informal but structured atmosphere for workshop sessions, while practical work was being done, the radio played. I decorated the walls and shelves with youth-oriented news, themes and artwork that I hoped were inspirational images and ideas. I did this without thinking too much about it, but realised that young people felt comfortable in the space. They respected the times when the radio was off, usually when there were instructions, demonstrations and sharing of important information. Creativity flourished, and they made everything from shoes to wall hangings. My classroom became a referral space for young people excluded from other lessons, and soon I had to open an adjoining classroom to accommodate the extra bodies. I enjoyed seeing them develop, interact, invent and assert themselves. It was obvious to me that most of them thrived where they were not judged, monitored or forced into academic achievement that they were unready for. I had unexpectedly encountered informal education for the first time, and I recognised that I could engage with young people, listen to them, hear them, and motivate and empathise with them. But I could also work with them to identify their skills, qualities, aspirations and energies.

I had turned a corner, quite by accident, in my understanding of young people and decided quite quickly that I preferred working in an informal arena. I applied for a full-time youth work post in West London – a huge community school with a purpose-built youth centre attached, where I was appointed Assistant Head of Centre. As I arrived outside on my first day, I found the Head of Centre – my manager – unloading phones, photocopiers, cash boxes and an array of sports equipment from his car, which, he explained, he had taken home over the weekend for safe keeping because it was 'almost impossible to trust anyone'. I remember my mouth dropping open and words similar to 'Are the kids that bad?' falling out. But his response indicated that the 'kids' were fine; it was the staff who needed watching. Baffled and rather anxious, I followed him into the building. By the end of that week, he stated that he was 'done' and resigned, leaving me Acting Head of Centre.

The challenges I faced over the first 18 months in this post presented me with completely new experiences. The 'youth workers' who had previously spent their evenings behind the coffee bar, drinking Guinness and playing cards with each other, had moved on. The administrator had marched out, and a new and invigorated youth and community work team had been recruited. The new team had been hand-picked as they showed an interest in young people, shared the same ethos and values, and their personal and professional values were embedded in empowerment and respect. In my second year, the young people were designing graffiti for the gym walls and enjoying a host of activities of their own invention. The centre now had young people at the heart, offering them the space to explore, question, challenge and reinforce their place in the world, free to be 'young people' in a non-judgemental environment which challenged behaviour, attitudes and values in ways that encouraged reflection, consequence and growth. They became tolerant of others, assertive, interactive and creative. They had a stake in the centre, owning and embracing it. They were proud of it and saw it as a key part of their community, as did their parents, social workers, teachers and neighbours.

In around three years, the centre was fully accessible, had opened the first lesbian, gay and bisexual sessions for young people in the area, and was running controversial but vibrant and well-attended cultural awareness programmes. Our crime diversion projects took young 'offenders' away for intense residential soul searching. Partner organisations and teams worked with us to provide holistic services to young people, including health and social care, sexual health teams, employers and careers services. The local police and youth justice teams were regular visitors and often got involved in activities with young people for fun. Sponsors supported various projects, and faith groups trusted us enough to offer sessions to their young people. The centre had been renamed as a 'resource centre', and it certainly had become one.

I recount this to demonstrate how (and why) I became a youth worker. I had been managed by supportive managers with healthy budgets and local authority approval at a time when youth clubs were part of the community fabric, well known for after-school activities and community engagement. This was where my professional ideologies and philosophies were formed. Although I had an undergraduate degree in teacher education, I had no training and very little experience in youth work – I was technically naïve and unfamiliar with policies and procedures, but my underlying belief in young people's capacity for change, their energy for experience and how they so often lacked a voice or place in their communities had motivated me. It was clear to me that open access youth work offered young people, neighbourhoods and communities important opportunities.

As I enthusiastically hurtled through my career, this period never left me. My early experience proved what an impact an open access youth centre could have on the lives of young people and communities. As the centre was moved and squashed into ever smaller buildings over the following few years after successive funding cuts, I began to witness the theoretical and literal shrinking of the youth service across the UK. Over the next 20 or so years, I worked in a variety of roles, witnessing youth work change significantly. Resources and priorities altered as roles, responsibilities and landscapes shifted – I witnessed a gradual deconstruction of traditional youth work, especially in local authorities. Buildings were repurposed or sold off, funding was withdrawn or became competitive, and grants were allocated to specialist and time-limited projects. These changing tides encouraged uncertainty and instability in all areas of service delivery to young people across the country (Robertson, 2005; Davies, 2024a).

In the late 1990s, I embarked on an MA in youth and community work where I began to understand the values, history and intentions behind the work. I had successfully managed to work with young people for many years, developing some skills as I went, and my understanding and appreciation of the work had grown thanks to mentors, managers, colleagues, funders and young people. However, over time, subject to a fluctuating climate in which youth work was popular one minute, unpopular the next, well-funded at times, and others ignored, I realised I needed to know more.

I learnt a lot about what is needed to ensure that a system will support youth work for the genuine benefit of young people themselves. In subsequent years, I would see ways that youth work was being sold to funders and donors that ultimately, and unfortunately, undermined its real value.

## What is youth work, and why is it important?

Youth work in the early 00s had begun to focus on young people's employability, their achievements in school, and their potential roles in the workforce (Belton, 2009; Jeffs and Smith, 2010; Batsleer, 2012). Youth workers delivered targeted 'products' rather than considering the 'process'. Expectations were more corporate (Smith, 2002a, b), and the process of youth work (reflection, empathy and relationships) was gradually undermined by both social and political needs over the next few decades (Jeffs and Smith, 2010; B. Davies, 2012, 2019). Youth work was required to focus on how young people should be worked with, as opposed to their needs (Ord, 2012a; Bradford and Byrne, 2010; Batsleer, 2012; B. Davies, 2019, 2012). Targeted provision was more 'cost-effective' and measurable than any other kind of work, diluting both open access youth work and the local youth club almost completely.

Youth workers, in my experience, find it difficult to articulate what young people achieve through youth work, making it something of a mystery to outsiders. From the late 90s until 2015, one youth work organisation, Kids Company, mastered their messaging around this and created a narrative that the public understood: young people were problematic because they were bereft of what I best describe as 'love', and this could be remedied with sufficient funding. However, their popularity unfortunately detracted from traditional youth work and smaller organisations, as government and donor funding was diverted away from them and directly to Kids Company. The charity boldly claimed to be solving society's problem with young people, and its CEO (Batmanghelidjh) became the media's 'go-to' spokesperson on all things young and troubled. Kids Company encouraged everyone – from politicians to celebrities to the woman on the street – to believe that 'love' was the answer to the 'dangerous' and 'feral' young people they claimed as their client group. This 'love' (which was what Kids Company claimed was missing from these young people's lives) became a tangible commodity – a feasible way of making a difference (Dean, 2020). For once, the nation seemed to understand what young people needed. Donors were endless and generous in responding to the problem of young people, and were thrilled to be able to pay for some love for these young people. Kids Company used aggressive language to describe young people and their needs. They were presented as dangerous, feral and knife-wielding – an unruly challenge and a threat to others – there was tension as we watched this organisation become a giant in the youth work world. On the one hand, they put young people firmly on the agenda, in the news and on TV. On the other hand, they were demonising them and telling the country to fear them. The fear, according to their narrative, could rapidly remedy this scary dynamic by sponsoring the charity, which would give all young people the love that they so obviously lacked. It was interesting and shattering to see donations in the millions directed at an organisation that made spurious and aggressive claims about young people.

I often wonder whether more traditional youth workers have suffered from a professional psychological trauma, given that youth work has been perpetually undermined and undervalued over the years. On a personal level, I spent some time throughout my career being a little sheepish about open access youth work (youth clubs and so on), not because I didn't believe in them, but because others (government, funders and so on) encouraged me to believe it had no value. I am delighted to say that my recent research and reflection have encouraged a robust belief in the potential and importance of open access youth work, and I am about to shout about it.

Services and workers – wherever or whatever they are – commit to the rights of young people and uphold these through their work. At the same time, they reflect the multiplicity of needs that young people have (Bauman, 2003;

Bunyan, 2009; Furlong, 2009; de St Croix, 2018). It is important to me that I attempt in this book to describe exactly what youth work is and how it might be articulated. This is how I began to build the Hub67 model that I will discuss in the following chapters.

Hackney Wick was a postindustrial, low-rise community, housing a thriving creative community in old factory buildings and warehouses in huge numbers, with artworks and graffiti being commonplace on walls and in doorways across the ward. It was also the community in which I lived and in which I began to develop the model presented in this book. What happened was a merger between my personal and professional self, all thanks to the London Olympics.

When London won the bid for the Olympic Games in 2005, Hackney Wick, a ward within the borough of Hackney, remained a relatively segregated and largely unexplored area of the East End of London. This changed when Hackney was chosen as one of five Olympic boroughs alongside Newham, Tower Hamlets, Barking and Dagenham and Greenwich. With the arrival of the development for the Olympics in 2012, I was among many (mostly from the creative and hospitality businesses) who saw potential and opportunity to benefit from the forthcoming event in Hackney Wick. I became interested in whether it was possible to revitalise community support for young people and to establish opportunities for youth work provision in the area.

Youth work often takes place in regenerational contexts (although of course, not exclusively) where young people are more likely to be underresourced, socioeconomically deprived and struggling for self-identity in these areas. Over the period which covered the announcement of the event and beyond, I became focused on identifying opportunities and ways to implement open access youth provision in Hackney Wick. I was determined that young people should not be overlooked and that all of the hype, finance and construction meant something to them, as well as being rewarded in some way for the inconvenience of it all.

The original research which enabled the model to emerge took place in Hackney Wick on the edge of Hackney, an unloved and shabby part of the borough. The area was not well served by youth and community work because activities for young people tended to be focused on youth centres and sports venues outside of the Wick Ward, on the Marshes or around housing estates, targeted at the needs of specific communities.

Hackney Wick parents were vocal about their concerns for the safety of their children while young people enjoyed the green spaces in the area (Hackney Quest, hackneyquest.org.uk). Though young people at the time recognised a sense of community, they were aware of inequality in the area and able to see the gap between rich and poor and the ongoing gentrification and regeneration in the area as it grew. Young people were seemingly positive about the 'creatives' in the area but felt that they were perceived negatively by them, and that the divisions between social background and lifestyle were pertinent (Hackney CVS, vchackney.org). The 'creatives' referred to are the extensive and vibrant creative community (artists, musicians, designers) that reside in warehouses and converted factories in the Wick at this time.

Young people in East London were facing significant challenges in almost every aspect of their lives and were more likely than adults to face discrimination and crime, as they still are to this day (ONS, 2019; ONS, 2021). Waiting lists for social housing, along with steep rises in housing costs, have impacted these communities (Woodcraft et al, 2024).

Hackney Wick has a history of poverty, deprivation and disadvantage compared to the rest of London, which has driven policy makers and philanthropists to support needs for over 200 years (Moore and Woodcraft, 2019). Regeneration programmes, such as the 2012 Olympic Games, promised to 'narrow the gap' between the wealthiest and poorest residents (Kynaston, 2011, p 12), but the criticism was that for long term residents, situations had declined further (Woodcraft et al, 2024).

I began to seize the opportunity to respond to the threats and opportunities that were likely to arise because of the Games and accompanying projects. Recognising the void between school and home for young people in the Wick, it provided an opportunity to address these inequalities, to engage with the community, particularly of young people and to understand and advocate for changes in the local landscape that could benefit them.

Although the research is rooted in youth work practice, many of the themes are likely to resonate in broader practice where young people are involved. Many practitioners work in areas which are affected by poverty, change and conditions outside of their control. This book draws on a world of practice which aims to be theoretically and empirically inspiring, reflective and creative, and to prompt discussion in an underrepresented environment. Given the necessity for more consensus about what youth work is and what it does, the need for more research and development in the field is apparent (Ord, 2004; Davies, 2003; Batsleer and Davies, 2010; de St Croix, 2016; B. Davies, 2019).

What this book aims to do is set the scene for the future of open access youth and work, particularly in line with regeneration and development. To offer practical and theoretical ideas to encourage and enable practitioners and communities to include, celebrate and empower young people.

# 1

# Understanding youth work in changing urban environments

This chapter offers a review of what is currently understood about youth work, particularly in changing and contemporary environments. I aim here to provide an overview of what is understood about youth work (as well as what is not) and how it is contextualised in current thinking. I have provided some emphasis on how young people and youth work is perceived, and consider the role that regeneration plays in the lived experiences of young people and communities. I aim to identify the key issues, dilemmas and challenges encountered by youth work professionals working in the current and changing landscape and how we have navigated political and social influences. I will consider a range of theories which underpin youth work and how they influence the aims and values of practice. The chapter draws on the concept of social capital as a potential for offering a different (or additional) approach to making sense of open access youth work, but particularly as it relates to Hackney Wick, the area in which Hub67 was established.

*The Guardian* newspaper (The Guardian, 2024) claimed that teenagers are 'crying out' for the return of youth clubs in England indicating that steep cuts have left three quarters of 16- to 19-year-olds unable to get support. With the election of a new Labour government a few months later, promises have been made to develop 'youth hubs' offering support to all young people. According to the new Secretary of State for Work and Pensions, young people will be given opportunities to 'earn or learn' (Davies, 2024b), resonating rather well with the policy intentions of the previous government for those not in education, training or employment (NEET). We await the outcomes and prospects provided (or not) by this over the coming years

In 2014, I wrote about youth work lacking recognition and value in the eyes of other professionals and suggested that a 'rebranding' might be helpful – this, as you might imagine did not change anything, but I was completely serious when I said:

> Advertising agencies encourage us to believe that rebranding is a process and not a project – it is in fact a 'fundamental cultural shift' (Cheinman, 2014, p 47). It could be seen to be the tool with which new positioning and platforms meet desired objectives. It could be the way in which youth work reconnects with its audience and inspires action. (Trimmer-Platman, 2014, p 37)

Youth work takes place anywhere it is practically possible, but can be especially relevant in urban environments where identifying key issues around young people's participation and experience can be important. Youth work has developed over time, with particular emphasis on how open access youth work has been challenged and compromised by target-driven provision, cuts in budgets, priorities and provision. The generic function of youth work is to develop voluntary and informal relationships with young people, conducive to the provision of opportunities and support to help with positive personal and social development (Mason, 2015). We might wonder then why it is contested ideologically and pedagogically, and why identifying the parameters of youth work helps to appreciate its boundaries, opportunities and limitations. We also need to know how and why it operates in so many different ways, sometimes within complex and conflicting applications. Unsurprisingly, this has led to tensions historically existing in the field.

## What is it all about?

This book is concerned with how youth work can foster self-awareness, agency and active citizenship in young people. These three interlinked concepts are essential not only to young people's development but also to meaningful inclusion in processes of urban regeneration. Across the chapters, I draw from young people's lived experiences at Hub67 to explore how these themes are supported or challenged as the model for Hub67 emerges.

Having been involved with youth work for over three decades, most practitioners will be familiar with misunderstandings around its purpose and potential, which partially provides a rationale for this book. In my lifetime, youth work has been known, among other things, as social and personal education, youth leadership, informal education, youth participation, personal and social education, youth empowerment and youth action. With each shift in government, the labels and social concerns around young people have influenced funding and understanding of youth work (Batsleer, 2011; Davies, 2024a; Robbins et al, 2024). Historically associated with volunteering (Ord, 2007; Jeffs and Smith, 2010; Davies, 2024a), assumptions are often made about the nature of youth work as a profession because of this (Davies, 2024a). Voluntary and informal approaches to youth clubs and organisations have traditionally been founded in concern for the welfare of those young people deemed needy in impoverished societies (Batsleer, 2009; Batsleer and Davies, 2010) or with those most 'at risk' in some way. Local authority budgets for youth work have been largely eliminated, leaving it practically nonexistent since 2010 (Davies, 2024a).

Driven by concerns about how young people's actions might impact communities, youth work has almost always responded with immediate and long-term problem-solving interventions. Some practitioners suggest that youth workers 'provide information' and 'support to effect changes in attitudes and practice within young people, services, communities and society as a whole to enable young people to have a say in the issues that affect them' and 'support young people to become responsible adults' (Sapin, 2009, p 11). Failure to adequately justify the effectiveness of the work or validate what young people achieve through it leads to ambiguity (Batsleer and Davies, 2010; Jeffs, 2011; Davies, 2012; Wiley, 2012).

Attempts at defining what youth work is have included Eichsteller and Holthoff (2011), who claim it is pedagogical, related to non-formal education and informal learning. Corey (2021) maintains that it is dependent on the complex needs of young people and, as a result, is difficult to define. Many agree that it is a 'perennial problem' (Kiilakoski and Kivijärvi, 2015, p 56) and that it is virtually impossible to pin down. I often ask students to prepare for an elevator pitch in which they have an opportunity to approach all of the world's decision makers – they have to, on the journey from ground floor to first floor, explain what youth work is. Although their attempts are excellent in themselves, they rarely describe the work in a way which is easily understood, often containing lists of features and potentials, written in several sentences, but certainly nothing concise.

Youth work in the UK has always claimed it is based on a robust set of principles, including encompassing young people's voluntary participation, embracing their world view, establishing and maintaining mutual trust and respect and encouraging the development of skills, positive attitudes and values difference. Key to this is reducing notions of problematic youth and encouraging their voices to be heard (Alldred et al, 2018). Practitioners assert that the work is relational (Batsleer and Davies, 2010; Jeffs and Smith, 2010; Davies, 2012). There is generally agreement that traditional youth work is based on a voluntary relationship (association) in which young people choose to engage (Batsleer and Davies, 2010; Bradford, 2012; Seal and Frost, 2014; Cooper et al, 2024; de St Croix, 2016). When young people invest in something (like a relationship), they are more likely to do so with positivity and interest in the outcomes, as in most relational dynamics, when someone is 'getting something out of it', they will continue to engage.

So, in a way, youth workers somehow deviate from being 'part of the establishment', aiming to create relationships with young people which are different from other professional adults such as teachers, social workers, faith leaders and so on. Knowing about the boundaries between youth work and other types of work with young people could help to understand political, public and professional perceptions and remove youth work from what some have claimed is 'dubious practice' (Butters and Newell, 1978, p 17; McKee et al, 2010; Williamson, 2015). Unlike teachers, youth workers do not have the same contextual or institutional relevance. Irrespective of their individual effectiveness and approach, the role of a teacher is universally understood; generally located in schools, colleges and institutions recognised as places of learning. Youth work, on the other hand, is delivered in a variety of settings, and most adults have little, if any, experience of it. Youth work can take place wherever young people are – literally making the contexts diverse (Batsleer and Davies, 2010). Youth workers are found in clubs or centres, on the streets, in parks and other public spaces where young people tend to gravitate. Unlike teaching, youth work cannot easily be defined by location or how it is funded. Formal education has a recognised structural framework used to monitor and measure efficiency and effectiveness, but there is no comparable structure for youth work.

## Framing youth work theoretically

In seeking to develop the Hub67 model, I drew explicitly from multiple theoretical perspectives to offer an approach that is grounded in theory and reflection. Theory itself is not 'good, bad, true or false, but often just more useful for one application or another' (Mintzberg, 2009, p 356). The theory explored in this chapter helps to develop a framework that does justice to the lived experience of young people in relation to Hub67. Throughout this chapter, several theoretical frameworks are drawn upon – some of which have long influenced traditional youth work practice and others which provide insight into contemporary challenges. These include:

- **Rogerian person-centred theory (Rogers, 1961)**, which promotes the concept of *unconditional positive regard*, empathy and support. This underpins approaches to youth work that emphasise emotional intelligence and positive relationships.
- **Radical youth work (Freire, 1972)**, which frames youth work as a form of social pedagogy and empowerment, viewing education as a political act and youth work as a way of promoting social justice.
- **Non-formal and informal education theory (Kolb, 1984)**, which positions learning as participatory, flexible and situated within real-world contexts, and promotes peer-led and relationship-based learning.
- **Social capital (Putnam, 2000)**, which explores the networks, norms, and social ties that enable individuals and communities to thrive and is particularly relevant to the role of youth work in rebuilding social ties in the context of urban regeneration and exclusion.

These theoretical frameworks offer richness and depth to our understanding of youth work – particularly as applied to the Hub67 model. The remainder of this chapter draws on these theories to critique and explore the context and realities in which youth work operates.

## Is there a history behind this?

The Victorian 'deserving poor', which led to the creation of Ragged and Sunday schools, provided welfare as part of state services and 'association', working with poor and underprivileged communities following wartime fallout. By the 1980s, the voluntary sector was stimulated by privatisation, when most local authorities contracted out youth work services (Batsleer and Davies, 2010; B. Davies, 2019), at a time when youth clubs were a common feature of local communities. With the rise of local authority youth services and the decline of the third sector, the relationship between non-profit organisations and the government proved complicated and contractual provision emerged to supplement government activities (Salamon, nd). This presented competition or adversity (Anheier, 2005) or substitutions for what was already on offer (Weisbrod, 1988). A reduced recognition of the contribution of the third sector began to include youth work which had traditionally been in clubs and centres with a focus on informal relationship-based engagement in which youth workers interacted with young people, encouraging social and personal development by addressing young people's attitudes and values.

Since 2000, policies and practice directives (from government) have led youth work to focus on particular groups of young people, who are socially or politically perceived as being most 'in need' (Batsleer, 2011; Ord, 2011; B. Davies, 2019). 'Need' is determined by social problems, such as risk of failing in school, gang involvement, criminal activity and anti-social behaviour. As a result, tensions in practice exist about how young people are 'labelled' and how those who are not can be worked with. This highlights for many the need for a discussion about whether traditional (open access) practice is diluted in favour of targeted provision. The 'deserving poor', as previously described, sounds judgemental and 'worthy'- difficult, historically, to separate from youth work – suggesting that it is only for those most deprived and less privileged. As practitioners, we are tied to the constraints of funding priorities, which rarely deviate from government rhetoric, how we label the work that we do and ultimately the young people we do it with has long-term resonance.

As this example demonstrates:

> I used to think I was poor, then they told me, I wasn't poor, I was needy. Then they told me it was self-defeating to think of myself as needy, I was deprived. Then they told me deprived was a bad image, I was underprivileged. Then they told me underprivileged was over-used, I was disadvantaged. I still don't have a dime, but have a great vocabulary. (attributed to Jukes Feiffer, Walker et al, 2009)

## How can youth work establish credibility?

Youth work has endured some complex and contradictory criticisms, as it strives to identify itself credibly within a professional context. It is difficult to articulate what it is. The fact that young people participate voluntarily in youth work relationships is one of the most prominent values used to explain the uniqueness of the work (Batsleer, 1994; Davies, 2001; Smith, 2012; Jeffs, 2011). However, in the last 20 years, a significant increase in the delivery of youth projects skilling young people for life, funded by authorities or trusts requiring evidential and accredited 'proof of purchase' targets has forced a shift in the relevance of associational relationships (Chauke, 2024; Cooper et al, 2024; Davies, 2024a; Robbins et al, 2024). Youth workers are often expected to address concerns around all types of anti-social or risky behaviour, aiming for pre-determined outcomes – usually based on target-driven financial reward (to the youth services). In a sense, such projects could deem 'association' and voluntary relationships redundant when young people are *required* to take part (Smith, 2012; Bradford and Cullen, 2014; Davies, 2024a). As you might imagine, this encourages youth services to leave behind a rich history and philosophy based on young people's choices (Davies, 2013; Bradford and Cullen, 2014).

Rogerian principles often underpin youth work (and my style of youth work) theory and practice in applying the notions of 'unconditional positive regard' (Rogers, 1961, p 42) and person-centred participation, which is compromised when there are changes in the direction of the work. Open access youth work embraces Rogerian theory, making a distinction between the individual and their behaviour, encouraging the isolation of bad behaviour from the young person and what they did (anti-socially) and their ability to make changes for themselves. In targeted work, it is often young people's actions which become the core focus, with a desired change and most likely by a particular deadline (for example, someone not attending school would hopefully end up re-entering education in one way or another). Although the outcomes can be the same, open access approaches are led largely by the young person and their capacity for self-development (Murphy and Ord, 2013; Batsleer, 2021).

Applying unconditional positive regard allows for a reduction in tensions, judgements or assumptions, focusing on working directly on the immediate needs of the young person, as opposed to their perceived needs. Some thinkers maintain that actions deserve punishment without question and that poor behaviour cannot be changed (Bradford, 2007; Smith, 2009; Davies, 2011). However, most youth workers agree that positive, non-judgemental relationships can be fundamental in identifying young people's troubles, stresses and mental health awareness, as well as encouraging them to make significant changes to their attitudes and values. When a young person does not feel trusted or respected by their youth worker, change is unlikely (de St Croix, 2018). The tensions between open access and target-driven ways of working have become fundamental characteristics in the task of understanding and utilising youth work as a method for practice.

## Dilemmas in practice – identity crisis

In a changing social environment, it would be helpful to have a professional understanding of youth work that practitioners could universally articulate so that we might have a better standing in political and educational discussions and decision making. Not only would this encourage appreciation in communities but also a strong positioning in professional arenas – not least to avoid overlap or service confusion. Davies and Merton explained that 'anecdotal evidence over many years has suggested that many youth workers and their managers live permanently with a professional identity crisis' (Davies and Merton, 2009, p 42). Research into the nature and purpose of youth and work, compared to other themes, is relatively sparse, not least because of the difficulty in securing a youth work definition (Ord, 2012b; Bradford and Cullen, 2014). Bright described youth work as 'a somewhat polymorphous activity, which has taken, and continues to take on various shapes and expressions' (Bright, 2015, p 3) – sustaining the confusion. Unsurprisingly, practitioners feel conflicted – and have been known to question whether what they are engaged in is youth work at all (Bradford, 2011).

On the other hand, directing young people to attend youth projects prompts compulsion (Ord, 2009a; Davies, 2012; Bradford and Cullen, 2014) and can be a concern for youth worker motivation to support such programmes within the given constraints. The identity crisis, which Davies and Merton refer to, has encouraged significant debates in the field about contradictory roles between expectations and intentions in practice. The In Defence of Youth Work (IDYW) campaign, born in 2009, aimed to 'defend and extend youth work as a distinctive educational practice founded on a voluntary relationship with young people and shaped by their agendas' (IDYW, 2009, p 11). Youth work as a democratic process includes the importance of the voluntary relationship, harnessing a young person's autonomy, agency, uniqueness and ability to make choices. Voluntary participation has been one of the most controversial issues in contemporary youth work, particularly as workers are increasingly requested to work in situations 'when young people do not access the provision voluntarily' (Ord, 2009a, p 45). The similarity between formal and non-formal relationships when targeted work is prioritised has led to uncomfortable conversations (de St Croix and Doherty, 2024; Howard, 2023). In comparing the two modes of practice, when young people are not joining in voluntarily, the purpose of the relationship alters, making the work about problem solving as opposed to informal and personal development. Relationships between young people and youth workers must be built on trust, respect, sincerity and authenticity. It is also claimed that authenticity can only exist when the adults are familiar with what is important in the lives of young people (Fyfe and Mackie, 2024). Target-driven outcomes, despite their potential for productivity, imply the undermining of the philosophical fabric of traditional youth work by diluting the intensity and respectful relationships enabled by young people's voluntary and active participation in the process. In other words, targeted outcomes can move youth work away from the non-formal methods that it has thus far been determined to hang on to. In a profession that struggles to position itself, it is frustrating when the foundations and principles (albeit updated to respond to current trends and needs) are only applied to ensure existence. It is rather like taking a driving test in a computer-driven car.

The importance of community in youth work is fundamental since young people are members of their communities (Marsiglio, 2008; Coburn and Gormally, 2017). To redress the concerns and problems that young people manifest in neighbourhoods, youth workers tend to engage cooperatively and consultatively with communities to encourage investment in young people (Marsiglio, 2008). When I first became a youth worker, most schools had their own after-school provision with youth clubs and projects in local neighbourhoods, on housing estates and in faith groups across the country – youth clubs were physical community assets.

Those who blame neoliberal thinking for the dissolution of the youth service and for normalising the volunteer spirit were not in favour of outsourcing services and education, measuring outcomes or working to targets, but they were often driven reluctantly by non-profit contracts which were designed to look and feel like youth work (Hookway, 2013; de St Croix, 2016; Taylor et al, 2018).

There are claims that the neoliberal 'moral collapse' (Giroux, 2009, p 691) and shifts in cultural attitudes and institutional mismanagement have redefined policy and practice, which appears to have reimagined the meaning of youth (Smith, 2017; Howard, 2024). As a result, there are considerable practitioner concerns around the focus of targeted youth work and, in particular, around those young people who fall outside of the targeted net. Further, conflicts exist for practitioners between the ideology of tangible outcomes and accountability agendas guided by government policy. Youth work has had little choice but to align itself with the business sectors, that in turn determined how financial support was allocated, requiring a shift toward corporate identities (Taylor et al, 2018; Smith and Seal, 2021). These operations force youth work to sell and market itself as a commodity that other businesses understand (Moustakim, 2012; Williamson, 2015; Taylor et al, 2018; Smith and Seal, 2021).

Youth workers have claimed that neoliberalism offered services as an 'exemplar par excellence of the corrosive influence exerted by this latest manifestation of capitalist ideology upon an emancipatory and democratic youth work practice' (IDYW, 2009, p 3). It is also widely thought that the National Citizens Service (NCS), a national social action programme established in 2011, effectively led to youth work being privatised, as another radical consequence of the neoliberalist agenda. Many argued at the time that targeted projects were rarely designed to incorporate the ideas and aspirations of young people, but this had become commonplace in the youth work sector (de St Croix, 2018; T. Davies, 2019). Focussed on the desire for a volunteering nation and a sense of community, the government, via the NCS, directed youth work away from an individual values-based framework at its traditional core and thrust third sector youth providers into a competitive and results-driven environment (Davies, 2015; Taylor, 2017; Davies, 2024a). The NCS scheme aims to create young civil activists who would notionally be more likely to become and remain volunteers throughout their lives. It highlights the social and personal benefits of volunteering and civic responsibility, advancing the message that young people have civil obligations. Unsurprisingly, around 60 per cent of those who participate in the scheme do go on to volunteer further (NCS, 2018). However, youth workers have observed that young people who are independently motivated would probably volunteer anyway. For this reason, there seems to be a good number of young people who would not and do not benefit from the NCS (Chapman, 2015; Dean, 2016). The Centre for Youth Social Action (CYSA) suggest that 'Youth social action refers to activities that young people can do to make a positive difference to others or their environment, such as getting involved in campaigning, volunteering, fundraising or advocacy' (CYSA, 2013). To fund the NCS, cuts to local authority youth services were made, causing the loss of 139,000 youth service places between 2012 and 2016 (UNISON, 2016). Continuing with the programme they claim 'the NCS experience exists to engage, unite and empower young people, building your confidence so you can go out there and achieve your dreams, no matter where you're from or what your background is' (Gov.uk, 2022). The scheme has received billions in funding to create a volunteering generation. In the long term, it is a service which appeals largely to young people from families with better resources, leaving other young people bereft of any particular youth work experience at all. NCS creates the need to reconsider how youth work reaches more vulnerable (excluded/disadvantaged) young people.

Models of youth work exist and change over time, often responding to social and political movements (Forrest and Dunn, 2010). The promotion of social action programmes by the coalition government (2010–15) claimed to encourage the development of connections between individuals and groups, harbouring trust and reciprocity, healing exclusion and community decline (Putnam, 2000; Packham, 2008), and uniting dissimilar people (Tyler, 2009). Some argue that the greater the number of projects, the higher the levels of social capital in communities (Putnam, 2000; Granot and Tyler, 2024) because such projects address a range of complex factors affecting lived experiences. However, such projects rarely targeted young people. Previously, the Department of Health maintained: 'Neighbourhoods where people know each other and trust each other and where they have a say in the way the community is run can be a powerful support in coping with the day-to-day stresses of life. … And having a stake in the local community gives people self-respect and makes them feel better' (DeVilbiss, 1921, p 11). Whether projects which critically engage young people with community issues can help tackle some of the most critical social ills is for ongoing debate, and some practitioners think social action is heavily reliant on social class, relying on the committed middle class who support social causes (Chapman, 2015; Dean, 2016). Research has shown that a young person's choice to volunteer can be predicted if their parents are professionals (Dean, 2016).

Reducing state support for the most vulnerable young people provided a social template for regressive youth provision and reverted to historical models of youth work designed to 'appease middle England' (Kennedy, 2014, p 3). In 2024, it seems history could be repeating itself. Youth workers are best placed to help transform young people as they critically face and change their world (Batsleer, 2011; Kennedy, 2014; Sheridan, 2018). Cooper says that 'relevant models of Youth Work can help Youth Workers to develop clear answers to all of the questions [asked of them by policy makers], but presently, Youth Workers do not have such models that will perform these functions' (Cooper, 2012, p 40) and this seems not to have changed. Keir Starmer's government has promised to create and fund Young Future Hubs (YFH), which will 'intervene earlier to stop young people being drawn into crime, creating a new network of hubs reaching every community. These hubs will have youth workers, mental health support workers, and careers advisers on hand to support young people's mental health and avoid them being drawn into crime' (Gov.uk, 2024). Led by Yvette Cooper as Home Secretary, the focus is on crime diversion and employment.

For youth workers, government perceptions and strategies to support young people often lack fundamental values and approaches that are utilised in practice. Young people are regularly stereotyped and labelled according to current trends in fashion, education, music and recreation, and youth workers are seen as do-gooders. Youth workers are professionals who crave much-deserved recognition and status, but in recent years, this has been as much of a challenge as working with young people themselves.

## Youth work in theory

Theories of youth work are developed in response to the tensions and challenges of the time, rather than being abstract ideas. Youth work practice evolves in response to wider social and political themes, such as neoliberalism and individualism. Over the last three decades, youth work has been positioned in increasingly contradictory ways, not least due to responding to significant change. On the one hand, practitioners may be influenced by emancipatory aims and drawn to theories such as Freire's *praxis*, which calls for reflection and action to transform the world (Freire, 1974). On the other hand, practitioners may be constrained by capitalist ideology and individualism that focus on performance and results, while operating at the expense of the common good (Davies, 2017; Ord and Davies, 2022). This is not merely theoretical but instead impacts everyday youth work practice, such as the design and delivery of projects. Ultimately, this has put youth work in a difficult position, having to consider the interests and motivations for social change and how the work should be situated. Many academics and practitioners feel that the traditional roots of the service have been compromised in favour of supporting and delivering political targets (Corney et al, 2024). As a result, some workers may feel that they are the 'good cop that enables the bad cops to get on with their work' (Taylor, 2017, p 3), which is demotivating for most but is recognised as a technique today.

At Hub67, this tension was particularly apparent. The youth work model deliberately positioned itself in opposition to this outcome-led, neoliberal approach. Instead, Hub67 adopted non-formal and informal education models as a foundational lens. This approach conceptualises learning as something that occurs through everyday life rather than within formal institutions (Kolb, 1984). This can be likened to a 'continuum which explains varying degrees of response to situations and relationships' (Buchroth and Parkin, 2010, p 4). Some think about youth work as operating against the status quo as it offers access to resources and opportunities not readily available in the young person's social circle, particularly those most marginalised (IDYW, 2011; Ord, 2012b, 2007; Davies, 2015). It is also thought that youth workers act as agents of social change and enjoy the dual role of making resources available and encouraging the development of key strategies for empowerment and democracy (Cooper, 2018). We continue to attempt to define and clarify what youth work means (Seebach, 2008; Sercombe, 2010; Cooper, 2012):

Youth workers have always been keen to communicate the distinct benefits of their professional interventions with young people. They have done so in formal and non-formal settings, yet they seem generally unconvinced that their work is fully understood by policy makers, fellow professionals, or the general public. Whether or not their perceptions are accurate, anxiety among workers is evident by their need to constantly explain and justify their practice. This 'betrays a' defensiveness which implies that despite their verbal dexterity the problem of communication in the public sphere is real enough for them. (Spence, 2008, p 3)

In the case of Hub67, informal learning occurred through experience, social connection and group activity and allowed young people to engage on their terms. The model also consciously incorporated Rogerian principles, particularly *unconditional positive regard* (Rogers, 1961), allowing practitioners to focus on respect and acceptance, rather than on challenging behaviour. At the same time, the project drew inspiration from radical youth work traditions (Cooper, 2017), which positions youth work as a 'force against the reproduction of social inequalities which the mainstream education system magnifies' (p 5). Practitioners who favour radical youth work and support Marxist ideology consider a five-step approach which includes character building, working with cultural adjustment, institutional reform, community development and self-emancipation (Jeffs and Smith, 2021; Belton, 2017). This thinking has certainly influenced youth work terminology and practice (Smith, 1988). Hub67's open access model and emphasis on belonging and voice can be seen as modes in which young people were supported to develop skills that challenge social structure and effect change.

## Is youth work educational?

Perhaps instead of trying to identify what youth work is, we should attempt to understand young people and their complexities, considering the process of youth work as holistic and unique to everyone and how they have responded to the contextual delivery of their experiences. Cooper (2018) thinks that proving conceptual definitions of the youth work process or processes is what is needed. In response to this, Davies (2018) announced that youth work is a 'distinctive educational process', rather like Jeffs and Smith (2021), who sees youth work as a pedagogical undertaking which is about the process rather than the product, and is undertaken in non-formal and informal relationships. Non-formal education refers to that which takes place outside of formal settings, and informal as that which is directed by young people. Whichever way we look at it, youth work should be adaptive and creative (Ord, 2016). Informal learning is experiential and is more about participation than social activity (Kolb, 1984). Concurring with this, Jeffs and Smith (2021) agree that learning should emerge through experience as an alternative to formal education.

Youth work as informal education, some say, 'occurs as results of direct participation in the events of life' (Smith, 1988, p 9), and is a 'dynamic process, which leads to action' (Batsleer, 2014, p 101) or 'to be meaningful, learning needs to be tested in reality' (Young, 2006, p 79). However, youth work seems to 'oscillate between liberal and radical models of social action' (Bradford, 2004, p 23), largely with policy makers demonstrating a preference for the former and practitioners choosing the latter (Davies, 2005). Non-formal education, which for a while was how youth work was described, is perceived as being inferior to formal education (Coffield, 2024; Batsleer, 2013) and is supported accordingly. In many ways, we realise that young people from disadvantaged communities are less likely to participate in informal education and are likely to require more help than those from wealthier backgrounds (Chapman, 2015; Dean, 2016; Wick, 2018).

Despite these theories and debates, youth work is lacking in educational theory and requires a theoretical framework around social pedagogy more than ever (Williamson, 2020). This should include a focus on holistic development and empowerment in theoretical terms (Corney et al, 2024). In addition, Freire discussed theories of 'praxis' which have influenced radical youth workers in advocating for 'reflection and action upon the world to transform it' (Freire, 1970, p 36). 'Praxis' means continual reflexivity (Duncan-Andrade and Morrell, 2008) and practitioners who support the notion of praxis work with a 'learning from doing' approach or 'learning in life as it is lived' (Jeffs and Smith, 2005, p 4). In much earlier times, Dewey referred to this way of working as a 'person-centred curriculum' (Dewey, 1916, p 9).

A model called the Cycle of Courage was developed by Brendtro (1990), and it encompasses the empowering and social educational elements of traditional youth work. The model focuses on attachment, achievement, autonomy, altruism and adheres to youth work values and attitudes (Brendtro, 1990). Basic youth work theory holds 'a generous view of human capacity and potential' (Silbereisen and Richard, 2007, p 93) and thrives because each young person is a resource in themselves, owning their possibilities. Profound learning can take place in group participation and relationships with others (Smith, 2003; Batsleer, 2000; Eraut et al, 2000; Davies, 2005), but this is often undermined by educationalists who struggle when this takes place outside of schools. Non-formal education is part of our everyday lives if we embrace it – young people learn from peers, families and people they encounter in everyday life, in literature, film, music and social media, yet it remains one of the most contested topics when trying to define youth work (Smith, 2003; Henze, 1992; Davies, 2005; de St Croix, 2016).

Most youth workers agree that their role is about supporting young people's self-education (Batsleer, 2000; Davies, 2005). More specifically, they argue that 'education is a moral enterprise that needs to be judged as to whether it elevates and furthers well-being' (INFED, nd). There is concern about youth work practice in societies where association and sociality appear to be dying notions (Smith, 2001; Jeffs and Smith, 2008), especially since the COVID-19 pandemic, there have been proposals and examples of how digital youth work in the new age can be effective and current (Ord and Davies, 2022; Robbins et al, 2024). This, of course, changes the relationship-building element of youth work dramatically.

Emerging social tensions and boundaries around gender, sexual health, sexuality and mental health pose challenges that most youth workers seek training for. The complexities and diversity of young people's personal and social challenges have probably never been greater than they are now. Young people's learning through youth work is often underpinned by conversational relationships founded on mutual trust and respect in support of their 'transition' from child to adulthood. Youth work can do this through what can be described as 'conversation, as the basis of practice, links young people's personal agendas to wider social and political agendas and forms the bond between informal learning and informal support in practice' (Batsleer, 2008, p 6). Informal support engages with a young person's social situation, their rights, needs, emotions and personal development.

## Young people in contemporary contexts

The complexities of understanding and identifying how youth work can best be practised should be followed by an understanding of young people and their needs in the changing and challenging environments that they find themselves in. How young people see themselves and how they are seen by others is always contentious, as social and generational interpretations of youth culture and what it means to be young differ. The socialisation of young people into social norms takes and lasts longer than ever (Zuchowski et al, 2022). However, in Western societies, there is consistency in 'youth' being a sociocultural period between childhood and adulthood (Marshall and Bottomore, 1992; Cieslik and Simpson, 2015). Young people are generally physically healthier, better educated, with better mobility and cultural options than their parents were at the same age. Improved opportunities for young people are emerging in many places, and more opportunities exist generically for young people than those afforded to older generations. This seems positive, but opportunities have changed, as life and society have. How they communicate, with whom, what we have access to, how we apply it and what we want to achieve, socially, emotionally, educationally and financially, impact young people's decision making. Young people are familiar with technology, fashion, music, travel, environmental issues, gender and identity issues, relationships, politics, faith, education, employment, housing, benefits, racism, food banks, terrorism, safeguarding, mental health, bullying, abuse, feminism and suicide in open media. Many of these issues would rarely have been discussed in previous decades.

Historically, communities have been troubled by youth culture, as witnessed in film, music, literature and particularly in the fabled forms of mods and rockers, punks, ravers and, more recently, gang members and radicalised youth. Nostalgically, young people thought of as 'folk devils' (Cohen, 1972, p 12) were, in fact, simply members of their unique youth culture. All generations are identified by their specific cultural references – we now have generic yet socially acceptable labels emerging for this, such as Millennials, Gen Z and so on.

Young people's culture, attitudes and actions over the last 50 years have often led to moral panic (Cohen, 1972), resulting in state intervention via education, leisure time and training for young people. However, concerning youth knife and gang crime in recent years, some politicians and high-ranking officials have openly condemned moral panic around young people and crime, as it is unhelpful. History has revealed that moral panics about so-called hooligans, gangs and uncontrolled youth has focussed attention on young people and crime long before we recognised the teen age. As long as we continue to create folk devils of our children and young people, we will view them as a threat to the moral fabric of civilised society while at the same time being consumed with protecting their innocence (McAra and McVie, 2022).

This raises the point about where we 'sit' in relation to young people being one or the other. Young people navigate a very different landscape today, spending longer in education, gaining higher qualifications (some of them), and most view their prospects negatively (Zuchowski et al, 2019), particularly around employment. Unemployment rates for young people have been more sensitive to the economic roller coaster than those of other age ranges. Decent homes at affordable prices are few and far between, which, according to some commentators, is the symbol of barriers to life choices and intergenerational decline (Zuchowski et al, 2022). Increasing intergenerational inequalities exist in this century. Youth transitions are key to sociological perceptions of development, and the transition to adulthood has always been a marker in time, establishing the young person as an achiever, emerging as an individual with responsibility and maturity. Transitions to work have been a concern for decades (Setty, 2023), and unemployment rates globally signify that only half of the youth population is in work. It was once thought that transition from school to work 'involves inevitable stresses and strains [it] does not normally create problems' (Ashton and Field, 1976, p 34) yet we know now that youth unemployment has reached a new point of crisis (Newlove, 2022) and is delaying young people's ability to enter the workplace. However, these interruptions for today's young people should also take into consideration their significance concerning the need for societal change (Setty, 2023).

Youth is historically viewed as a period of biological, social and physiological change in preparation for independence and socialisation. Most young people are involved in social interactions of various kinds in groups, networks and sociocultural worlds that may include family, friends, gaming, school, community and other institutional organisations and support services of their choosing. Generally, their socialisation will include learning to navigate, negotiate and participate in a variety of different identities and systems with shared or contested values, beliefs, aspirations, perceptions and motives. Working-class and minority young people often frequent worlds which are culturally differentiated, each embodying distinct ways of existing in the world (Bourdieu and Passeron, 1977; Salazar, 2011). They pursue this by learning 'on the job' via 'social practices and scaffolding supported by people who have already mastered the course' (Gee, 1989, p 292). Young people learn from what they know about and how they experience the world, often learning what it is to be restricted in opportunities and choices. Social structure, historical change and individual experiences suggest that life is not lived cyclically but that newness emerges out of what is no longer appropriate, possible or acceptable (Mannheim, 1952; Mills, 2000). In other words, times change. Young people's sociological imagination maintains *generational units* in which groups live with opposing views and differing experiences (Mannheim, 1952, p 282).

Despite living unequal lives, determined by a distinct set of political, economic and cultural struggles to which they have little choice but to orientate, experiences in youth and young adulthood manifest a distinct set of dispositions and ways of being which can be built on and changed over time (Woodman and Wyn, 2015). Evidence of this is seen in how young people now communicate with each other – often via social media platforms and forums. Some think that adult financial burdens, precarious and fewer full-time employment opportunities have encouraged young people to develop resilience (Zuchowski et al, 2022), adjusting their expectations, reducing investment in many aspects of adult life, even, in some circumstances, their relationships (Caban et al, 2023). Young people, who begin from a place which is underresourced are most likely to be excluded from provision and services (Lamb et al, 2015; Woodman and Wyn, 2018). However critical these acknowledgements may be, it is important to recognise that transitions are extended or delayed for everyone in this world where boundaries are becoming blurred and securities diluted. Longer transitions disproportionately impact more disadvantaged young people (Furlong and Cartmel, 2012). Structural barriers which exist and prevent young people from making successful transitions to adulthood require young people to reimagine and mitigate adverse effects with agency and social identity

(Dryden and Greenshields, 2020), highlighting the need for self-awareness and resilience.

## Young people in the context of regeneration

Youth workers have an important role in normalising transitions, through supporting and encouraging agency in young people (Côté, 2014). In current contexts, this frequently involves the impact of urban regeneration, it is important to understand how young people navigate trajectories into adulthood, or how they might be excluded.

Most societal notions of youth work suggest that young people are either at risk or a risk to society (Bradford and Cullen, 2014; Newlove, 2022), are deficient in some way (Muncie, 2006; Pitts, 2013; Zuchowski et al, 2022) and more vulnerable than any other generational group. More recently, we have focused on young men, in light of concerns about gang association and related tensions and violence, as well as the rising incidence of youth suicide and mental ill health, which has engendered fear and distrust of young people, but young men in particular (Petrocchi et al, 2024). Where young people have been seen to be deviant or 'at risk', youth work has been expected to work as a treatment or remedy for this, acting to reduce the risks (Lunneblad et al, 2024). At other times, it aims to raise consciousness, anti-oppression and advocacy to empower young people (Batsleer and Davies, 2010; Axford et al, 2023). Youth work is rarely understood by all people (as I will keep saying), maintaining ambiguity and confusion about its role and purpose. Academics have claimed that 'the result is a distinctive way of approaching and responding to young people and of prompting them to reach for more than they might otherwise have considered or even thought possible for themselves' (Batsleer and Davies, 2010, p 23), and as 'having some of the same contradictory qualities as great jazz. It is well prepared and highly disciplined yet improvised' (Batsleer and Davies, 2010, p 29).

In regeneration policies, young people and their parents are welcome new inhabitants to affected neighbourhoods, and conversely, urban problems and undesirable social concerns are not. Such double standards create tension (Lee, 2008; van den Berg, 2013) with young people being seen as 'illegitimate subjects' (Watt, 2006, p 777) in designers' images of 'instant gentrification' (Rose and Shevlin, 2004, p 156). It is often thought that young people are the cause of urban decay, where middle-class, nuclear families with 'potential' are drawn into advertising panoramas of prosperous and vibrant upgraded cities (Rose and Shevlin, 2004; van den Berg, 2013; Schinkel, 2019). Like many areas, Hackney Wick had been abandoned socially, politically and economically throughout the 20th century (Hsieh and Pugh, 1993; Daly and Wilson, 2001; Elgar and Aitken, 2011; Schlichtman and Patch, 2014) yet, when the opportunity arrived, the proposed regeneration heralded a dramatic shift in the demographic. Unsurprisingly, gentrification would welcome wealthier residents. The subsequent displacement of poor and working-class families had political, racial and economic consequences for families, young people and neighbourhoods at the time.

Shifts in space, place, mobility and wealth are negotiated by 'desirables' (Pattillo, 2008) who demand improved services and amenities, indicating that previous residents were unworthy of such things. When visible in local communities, young people in urban settings are very often 'managed out' of sight, moved on as they are seen as unwelcome and problematic (Kavanagh and Lewis, 2024; de St Croix, 2018). New urban spaces are advertised on hoardings and marketing materials with images which present idealistic spaces, often featuring mainly white faces and nuclear families (Oscilowicz et al, 2020).

When regeneration began in Hackney Wick, marketing images appeared to remove all trace of the rich and diverse communities already living there, with no youth-oriented spaces. Unsurprisingly, young people felt excluded. Youth workers often encourage the use of communal space to encounter and work creatively with young people (Hughes and Batsleer, 2014), yet many adults identify young people 'hanging out' as undesirable, particularly in open spaces (de St Croix, 2018). 'These places can provide opportunities for social interaction, social mixing and social inclusion, and facilitate the development of community ties' (Worpole and Knox, 2007, p 5). Often, however, adults do not appreciate the 'hanging out' and are concerned or threatened by it (Heath et al, 2023). Gentrification is a metaphor for upgrading (Hamnet, 1983; Butler and Lees, 2006), encompassing middle-class sociospatial habitus, where years ago assumptions about 'positive gentrification' (Lees et al, 2007, p 34) and the potential for benefits to trickle down to the lower classes (Lowry, 1960; Altshuler, 1969; Smith, 1970) were upheld despite perhaps an 'uneasy cohabitation' (Rose and Shevlin, 2004, p 280) between gentrification and social mix. Regeneration has gained traction despite it being 'constructed as a threat of social and spatial exclusion' (Cahill, 2007, p 300). Providing services for new residents can be perceived as neglecting previous residents (Baldridge, 2020), and once gentrification begins, community ties are lost, and connection to place is shifted from one to another. Radical landscape redesign loses cultural vibrancy when it becomes an area of suffering for poor residents, and spaces of wealth and opportunity for those with the means to live there (Pattillo, 2008; Baldridge, 2020). The impact of gentrification and the production of urban space from a cultural perspective is highlighted by the desires of middle-class people to experience 'authentic' urbanist design, public space, and transport (Zukin, 2010; Ocejo, 2011). On the other hand, the displacement of the lower classes, in particular people of colour, devastates and segregates neighbourhoods (Kavanagh and Lewis, 2024). For young people in particular, their communities become both alien and alienating, and the model that is described in this book remains mindful of this and faithfully redresses this.

The Hub67 model was a deliberate response to these dynamics. Theoretical perspectives on social capital, belonging and spatial justice informed the project's commitment to creating a space where young people could feel valued, visible and safe. As gentrification led to increasing exclusion – and even erasure – of young and working-class people, Hub67 countered this by maintaining a consistent physical presence, promoting community and relationships between young people. The space was co-designed with young people and embedded in local partnerships, aligning with theories of community capital and youth empowerment (Putnam, 2000; Batsleer, 2013). This visible presence served both a practical and symbolic purpose.

## Summary

This chapter has identified youth and community work as a profession and method of working with young people which is contested. It has outlined the diverse theoretical perspectives that help to make sense of the shifting context in which youth work operates. From person-centred and relational approaches to radical pedagogy and social capital theory, these frameworks offer powerful insights into youth work's potential and its ongoing challenges. Yet theory alone is not enough; it must be lived, practised and made relevant. Marginalised young people are underresourced and poorly supported. Youth workers are conflicted about where they locate themselves politically and socially, and how youth work receives funding and recognition. The lack of professional institutional oversight of the work leads to differing values in response to social and economic changes and in whether to problematise young people. Discussions around the value of target-driven work as opposed to open access provision continue to present themselves, and there is a strong desire among colleagues to interrogate this, particularly as it relates to regeneration.

Contemporary youth work often takes place in a regenerational context where young people are likely to be underresourced, socioeconomically deprived and struggling for self-identity. In identifying opportunities to implement open access youth provision, embedded in the traditional and ethical practice of youth work, social capital could be seen as a helpful concept to underpin current youth work theory and practice. In the development of Hub67 and the subsequent model, it was important to use an approach that was founded in traditional, open access, voluntary engagement, associational youth work. The Hub67 model incorporated the theories discussed in this chapter – grounding its approach in voluntary participation, relational trust and embedded community presence. The overall aims of the model developed and adopted are to make a significant contribution to the young people's personal, social development and wellbeing. The model, therefore, attempts to encourage an understanding of how youth work can help to improve young people's lived experiences and whether this too can improve their communities.

# 2

# Social capital: a commodity
# for young people?

This chapter explores how two key theorists – Bourdieu and Putnam – have shaped thinking on social capital and how their ideas apply to youth work in contexts like Hackney Wick. While their theories offer useful lenses for understanding belonging, trust and resources in communities, both have limitations. This chapter reflects on how these frameworks intersect with my own lived experience as a youth worker and resident. Social capital is a critical resource in urban areas, where some people struggle to earn a living and others can purchase anything they need, it is claimed as an intrinsic part of urban culture (Wesselow et al, 2024). Since Hub67 developed amid urban development, it was necessary to examine how this concept related or not to the lived experiences of the young people involved.

Social capital is a multidisciplinary concept discussed widely in social sciences. Bourdieu imagined social capital as an estimation of potential or actual resources that exist because of social connections (Bourdieu, 1986), and Putnam described it as a sum of social networks and their associated norms of reciprocity (Putnam, 2000). However, it is also important to consider that Bourdieu's account has been critiqued for being overly deterministic. When applied to youth, it could risk underestimating young people's agency in negotiating or resisting social structures (Dean, 2016). His emphasis on the reproduction of class can downplay the significance of resistance, emotion and relationship in shaping young people's choices. In the context of Hub67, young people often demonstrated forms of social mobility and resilience that cannot be fully explained by acquiring status or capital. Bourdieu's theory arguably reinforces elite power, whereas youth work practice – particularly in open access models – can offer unique opportunities to interrupt dominant social patterns in other ways. Nevertheless, as will be shown, the concept of social capital is an important lens through which to understand youth work practice. There are many theories of social capital and how it manifests in communities, but most of these originate from three key schools of thought, those being of Bourdieu, Putnam and Coleman. I will introduce each of these in relation to Hub67.

## Do young people need social capital?

Young people are rarely allowed to be involved in discussions that impact their lives and they feel powerless to change their situations. It may be that young people gain power when their voices are heard (Giroux, 1997). It is interesting to consider the benefits of social capital for young people, especially when they feel isolated. Young people who report having a supportive, significant adult in their lives also claim better psychological wellbeing, academic success, employment opportunities, school completion and fewer problems with peers (Brewis, 2024; Dean, 2016). The idea of 'institutional agents' (Salazar, 2011, p 10) helping young people to find their way through socialisation and personal development fits well into youth work ideology. Youth workers naturally become the agents, able to guide young people in managing and understanding the social structures and systems they encounter. An institutional agent (or youth worker) might mobilise and support young people within an environment that they claim some control over (Quintanar, 2007; Dean, 2016). Marshall studied young people and social capital globally and found that the variables of the social capital of vulnerable urban groups of young people included having a caring adult at home, a caring teacher or adult at school or one caring friend (Marshall et al, 2014). Two parents living in the same home were significant indicators that young people were more likely to engage socially than those living in single or blended families. Significant in all cities of the study was that all young people considered their 'self-reported health' improved as a result of gathering social capital (Marshall et al, 2014, p S29). Socioeconomic factors impact young people's access to social capital opportunities, and studies have found agreement that the mainstream global economy impacts social resources, which affects young people's resilience to poverty (Campbell, 2011; Cooper, 2011; Marshall et al, 2014). Marshall explains: 'surprisingly similar levels of social capital across sites [Baltimore, Delhi, Shanghai, Ibadan and Johannesburg] underscores how the structural constraints of urban poverty and exclusion impact social resources which effect [sic] young people's resilience across a diverse set of vulnerable environments' (Marshall et al, 2014, pp S27–28).

Young people using public space is often discussed by adults in criminalising or accusatory language. In the context of oppression and inequality, young people are psychologically damaged by this as their sense of worth, dignity, respect and place in the world are criticised (Prilleltensky, 2008, 2014; Hunter and Greenberg, 2016; Case and Hunter, 2012). Some practitioners might suggest that such experience encourages young people to take positive action against the status quo (Freire, 1993) and youth work can be a vehicle by which young people might push against or challenge the system in this respect. Bourdieu would argue that there is always potential to challenge the status quo for marginalised young people through the reform of institutions (Bourdieu, 1986, 1990). Bourdieu's conceptualisation of social capital is based on the recognition that capital is not only economic but that social exchanges gain 'capital and profit in all their forms' (Bourdieu, 1986, p 241).

Acknowledging inequalities in access to resources based on race, gender and class, Bourdieu emphasises social capital as the property of an individual rather than any given group. This enables young people to exert power over those who mobilise the resources. The significance of this in youth work is that Bourdieu saw social capital as not uniformly available to members of a group but available to those who make efforts to acquire it by achieving positions of power and by developing and showing goodwill (Bourdieu, 1986). Bourdieu framed social capital as accrued resources acquired by individuals or groups through the possession of 'more or less institutionalised relationships of mutual acquaintance and recognition' (Bourdieu and Wacquant, 1992, p 119). What this means is that social capital depends on how much a person invests in it, irrespective of their status. In youth work, social capital can also refer to effective relationships with adults with whom to challenge social norms.

Bourdieu (1973) and Goffman (1978) share similar ideas about how young people are understood in communities. They suggest that adults constitute, embed and reinforce negative images that young people are not fit or ready to join the adult world. This is done through our education systems, for example, by insisting young people remain in formal education until a specified age. Bourdieu's approach is based on his wider sociological theories of what he calls habitus and field (Bourdieu, 1984a) in which the fluidity and specificity of objects of study are emphasised, meaning that social capital is reliant on the context of a particular social space – in most cases where you live and where you learn.

Using a triad of concepts, habitus, field and capital, Bourdieu introduced ways of understanding the dynamics of social inequality by using social, cultural and capital as tools for recognising the complexities of neighbourhoods and their ability to create vastly different social and economic capacities. A 'system of dispositions' (Bourdieu and Nice, 1980, p 231) refers to the ways that individuals tend to approach their lived experiences via habitus. This requires young people to actively invest in their success, or not, depending on their early experience in adult negotiations and judgements – and what they make of it. Bourdieu maintains that the cultural capital acquired at birth, which is reflective of an individual's, class, gender and race, is incubated into the habitus and invested into social institutions outside of the home. Habitus reveals how human capacity can be embodied, corresponding directly to social worlds via 'multiple correspondence analysis' (Bourdieu, 1998a, p 111) that makes dispositions such as class and status obvious to others. The idea is that correspondence can be used to assess the relationship between habitus and field as understood by young people (Savage, 2000; Alanen, 2012). Correspondence can be assessed by viewing young people in the context of their school, family and social lives and their sense of belonging in each.

Most young people in urban neighbourhoods make social networks and friendships with others who live and study in the same place (Weller and Bruegel, 2006), making the 'fit' between habitus and field feasible and offering opportunities for increased self-awareness (Bourdieu, 1990). Young people, comfortable in their field and habitus are less likely to notice social divisions and exclusions or what he calls a habitus field clash (Bourdieu, 1998b). Those who travel outside of their neighbourhood to school do tend to notice a clash (Maton, 2008; Sweetman, 2009; Alanen, 2012). The clashes mean that young people might change their behaviour to interact socially with those with different habitus and field (behaving differently with friends at school and those at home, for example).

Bourdieu was probably the first to begin talking about social capital and was influenced by Marxist theory. As a result, he described and applied notions to it in a rather utilitarian way – namely in terms of actual or potential resources. In his summaries, he claimed that the volume of someone's social capital depends on the size of the network of connections they can mobilise and the number of connections they have in their own right. The networks Bourdieu refers to are established and maintained through what he says are like chains of exchanges, such as gifts, favours and material resources as these are 'the essential element that ties people together' (Bourdieu, 1986, p 62). He also claims that 'exchange transforms the things exchanged into signs of recognition, and through the mutual recognition of group membership – which it implies, re-produces the group' (Bourdieu, 1986, p 63). He further said that social capital was an individual resource that consists of two inseparable dimensions; social networks and exchange – the latter being what builds and sustains the former.

These ideas are linked to the concept of a social network – this can be described as a set of socially linked or interconnected discrete individuals or groups, as well as the structure, number and character of the relationships that link members of the network (Wasserman and Faust, 1994; Lin, 2001). Coleman researched high school pupils' education achievement and drop-out rates and discovered that for those who attended Catholic schools, where the religious community formed a protective resource, young people's social capital was high. (Coleman, 1973). With a gentler lens, Coleman sees social capital as a network of relationships incorporating 'closures' where members know and interact with each other and form a closure where older and younger generations share the same values, norms and sanctions, calling this 'functional community' (Coleman, 1973, 1990). Coleman describes social capital in terms of obligations, expectations and trust all delivered through various information channels, but with trust and obligations encouraging repayment of gifts or favours. When young people have present parents interested in young people's lives, Coleman claims they are more likely to have good social capital with teachers and peers as they would if they had interested community networks or closures. A good closure, as far as I can see requires reciprocal kindness and interaction.

In contrast to Bourdieu, Coleman sees social capital as an outcome of social structures, not so much of individual behaviours. Putnam on the other hand considers social capital as connections between individual social networks and the norms of reciprocity and trustworthiness that arise from them – these, he says are overall social norms. The way this makes sense to me is thinking about being invited to a friend's house for dinner – you might take a bottle of wine or a box of chocolates as a way of reciprocating the gift of dinner – or there might be an expectation for you to reciprocate by an invite to yours in due course. Putnam talks about this as being the norm of reciprocity. Putnam says that social networks almost always entail reciprocity – two-way interactions – where a favour is done and evokes an expectation and a moral obligation to return the favour at some point. This, he says is how it becomes a norm. Conversely, generalised reciprocity is about helping a person without expecting anything directly in return – trusting that there will always be people to help when needed. Social trust is linked to active citizenship and participation in social networks and is concerned with social good rather than individual gain – what we might call social action or, simply, kindness. By participating in this way, we will likely feel better about ourselves and our self-worth and feel greater happiness. Young people thrive in environments where people trust each other and frequently interact.

If social capital is about the resources and support that can come from social networks - friends, family, neighbours and communities (Richardson et al, 2022) - it is easy to see why it relates so well to the development and outcomes of Hub67. Putnam's work has been criticised for being too positive and for failing to account for the exclusions and inequalities that social capital can reproduce (Portes, 1997; Farrell, 2007). His framing often assumes a shared cultural norm, which may not reflect the lived realities of diverse urban youth populations like those in Hackney Wick. In the case of Hub67, it became apparent that bonding capital could both support young people's confidence and, at times, limit their networks to those who were already similar in background and experience. Further, it may unintentionally overlook other important dynamics, such as how social trust and cohesion may be unevenly distributed across race and class, which is particularly relevant to Hackney Wick.

However, Putnam's theories seem to fit strongly with the lived experiences of young people in the development of the Hub67 model. Putnam's notions of youth work were focused on recreation and companionship with advocacy being of great significance. He defined clubs (for adults and young people) as 'societies where social intercourse, innocent amusement, mental improvement and mutual helpfulness embody the conception of brotherhood' (Jeffs and Smith, 2010). He also believed in self-help and the full participation of young people in the organisation of their clubs. On the other hand, as a practitioner involved in the development of Hub67, I was often struck by how theories like Putnam's failed to fully capture the complexity of trust-building among young people experiencing exclusion. While the notion of reciprocity was present, it was often through everyday interactions and informal acts of support that didn't neatly fit into Putnam's ideas of structured civic engagement.

There is thinking which suggests the dynamics of social support in neighbourhoods are best placed for effective social capital for all its members (Vonneilich, 2022). Youth, and in particular adolescence, is a time when we consolidate our social selves – or aim to, and our interest in others and peer relationships begins to be more important than any other (Terrion, 2006). Young people between the ages of 0–19 who have relationships with trusted adults (who are not their parents) are more likely to find socialising easier and have fewer behavioural and mental health problems than those who do not.

A sense of community might be considered a type of social capital when it promotes prosocial behaviour and social wellbeing that helps individuals understand the link between civic engagement and happiness and could be seen as an essential determinant of social wellbeing among young people (Sharbatiyan, 2011).

## How social capital existed and emerged in the Hub67 model

Social capital can also be seen as intellectual currency for understanding social networks and individual and community resources which can inform practice or policy development (Hawkins and Maurer, 2010). As a concept, it could be an effective construct for seeking to interpret the separate aspects of social networks and support to analyse the 'by-products' of social relationships and access to resources and opportunities. This resonates rather neatly with youth work in low-resourced communities (Lin, 2000). By-products of social interactions are accessed via the formal and informal social relationships developed with individuals and communities, and in this case, via interaction with and for Hub67.

Social capital was once oversimplified but made applicable to the structural, economic, racial, ethnic, gender and geographic disparities in society. Indeed, where social connections exist, life can be good (Putnam, 2000). This can have positive power in capturing the complexities in social relationships and nuanced interactions in youth work practice, particularly if we believe youth work is about young people's wellbeing and social justice for all. While Bourdieu's framing of social capital as contingent on networks was useful in conceptualising the role of youth workers, it did not always align with the grassroots nature of relationship-building that occurred at Hub67. Many young people were more motivated by feeling emotionally safe and in an inclusive and familiar environment rather than strategically seeking social capital. Arguably, the emotional labour of youth work was its own form of capital outside of this theoretical framework.

Field argues that social networks are linked to the development of several assets such as the 'capacity to trust', cooperation, communication, organisational skills, tolerance, self-worth and willingness to take the initiative (Field, 2008, p 29), and I am tempted to add here self-awareness, helping decision making and making judgements. Rhodes et al (2014) noted that high-quality mentoring (such as in youth work) leads to improvements in other relationships. Social capital from friends, family and others is apparently 'bonding' capital that helps people 'get by' (Field, 2003a, p 31), while bridging capital, from looser connections to people in different social circles helps us to 'get on' and is rather like a 'magic wand' for unexpected opportunities (Putnam, 2000, p 362). You can see that in applying these theories to youth work, social capital can make some practical and significant differences in the developmental lives of young people.

For the young people in Hackney Wick, the impending impact of the Olympic opportunity was a mystery, if it was imagined at all. There were TV and news alerts about the changes the community might expect as well as 'marketing talk' about the new and exciting developments which were to be experienced, such as the Olympic sports venues, the park and walkways, and the job opportunities that all of these elements would offer. The volunteering and paid posts were consistently mentioned as huge benefits to the local community and in this, opportunities for young people in full-time employment. The sense of aspirational options and places potentially available to young people were the subject of presentations and notifications from developers and organisers across the five boroughs. This certainly gave some hope for residents despite the angst and tensions that ensued over the years of building, designing and excluding locals in favour of wealthy newcomers and investors. In the case of Hackney Wick, resident families, in general, are attached to the neighbourhood by families, with parents and grandparents being historical residents or by social placement of housing associations or support groups. The images presented on planning brochures and consultation documents did not depict families – but they were single business types and couples on bicycles or dog walking. The target groups for the new developments were not impoverished families or families at all, but those with healthy leisure times and salaries to match.

In applying Putnam and Bourdieu to the Hub67 context, it became clear that each offers insights but also leaves gaps. Putnam's emphasis on trust and reciprocity resonated with the aspirational aspects of the project – fostering social bonds and community engagement. On the other hand, Bourdieu's attention to structural power dynamics was more helpful in understanding why some young people accessed networks easily while others continued to struggle against their exclusion. The challenge in practice was in reconciling these two views: one hopeful, one more critical – it was important to remain focused on the agency and creativity of the young people themselves. I was also struck by how the everyday realities of young people – such as challenges with schooling, housing and institutional exclusion – demonstrated inequalities in terms of access to social capital. My role was not only to help build networks but also to notice the complexities of how relationships and opportunities are built in the shifting context of Hackney Wick.

## Social capital in context

Having established that social capital would be beneficial to the young people of Hackney Wick, it is helpful to look at how this might manifest and in what ways young people might utilise and develop it as a commodity. Social capital in research has demonstrated positive elements which promote community cohesion and a lack of social conflict in neighbourhoods (Wesselow et al, 2024).

Saying 'hello' to people on the street who say 'hello' back is a positive and encouraging interaction that we can take for granted – and perhaps we might only realise the impact it has when it is taken away. Think about how you might feel when you go to a new neighbourhood and you don't know anyone who you can speak to. When someone acknowledges you, they have seen you, registered your presence and validated your existence. Hearing 'hi' from someone can also suggest that they are looking out for you (and vice versa).

The more people you recognise in your local area, the more likely you are to feel welcomed into local places and venues, except restricted areas, such as pubs, for young people. Also, there is reduced stress and anxiety when you and others are aware of what is going on in your neighbourhood and who is involved. These simple acquisitions are available through social capital and can lead to further and wider relationships, belonging, membership, social support, shared values, influence, participation and safety as confidence and networks develop. Social capital for young people in Hackney Wick can encourage their confidence and competence as community members and citizens who feel like they belong, and who can benefit from and exchange local knowledge, culture and values.

## Summary

Social capital is often viewed as more complicated than it is. We understand that young people in urban neighbourhoods seek their own space and sense of place, as well as ways they can identify with and connect to the place they live and the people who live there. This is not unique to young people; all humans want to belong somewhere.

Social capital offers a valuable lens for understanding young people's connections, opportunities and sense of belonging. There are benefits in accruing social capital since it can demystify an area, make it accessible and encourage individuals and groups to feel less isolated or excluded within it. This study shows how young people can change their attitude toward their area, engaging in political decision making, as well as interacting with residents that they might not have previously known. Social capital as a concept could be understood as a 'shorthand term guiding us towards and encapsulating the types of processes and practices that are important for understanding family and community lives, and the connections between the micro and macro social' (Hollands, 2008, p 315). Another way of seeing social capital is as a specific resource which can both enable and constrain. Young people develop resilience from positive relationships and accrue social capital from their relationships with peers, youth workers, parents, teachers and other residents, sharing and gathering skills, knowledge, connections and resilience. This helps them to collaborate and communicate within an environment in which they have a sense of belonging and connection. However, while the frameworks of Bourdieu and Putnam helped to shape the approach at Hub67, it is important to consider that the lived realities of the young people and practitioners often required stepping beyond theory. It was in the complexities of building relationships, navigating exclusions and creating shared meaning that social capital came to life – not always as predicted.

3

# The lived experiences of young people and other residents

## The research

An experiential case study approach was adopted to capture lived experiences and neighbourhood narratives in the context of considerable change. I aimed to identify and understand the perceptions and experiences of the residents in a time of considerable disruption. Neighbourhood perspectives and lived experiences are subjective and reflect various localised values and emotions. The study was not devised specifically as an ethnographic study, but being able to interrogate my experiences (values and emotions) throughout the study was provided via an ethnographic lens (Palmer, 2001; Shipway and Jones, 2007; Ervasti et al, 2012) which represented both my practitioner and research roles (Shipway et al, 2013).

It is important to acknowledge the multiple roles I occupied throughout this research: as a youth worker, academic, researcher, local resident and community activist. These positions were not static – they shifted throughout the project and at times were in conflict. While I shared cultural ties with other residents, I often found myself in opposition to their assumptions about young people, particularly around issues of safety, responsibility and belonging. These tensions shaped how I was perceived, how the project unfolded, and how I engaged with the data, and therefore deserve transparency within the analysis. My role as a researcher could have been described as one as a research activist, trying to affect social change. Considering my multiple roles, an experiential case study and learning in the research context led to the evolution of the study and the development of the hub. Throughout the study, the research process, my reflections, actions, activities, research subjects, my lived experience outside of the topic and in the youth work field, plus my embodied characteristics, were all significant (Jamal and Hollinshead, 2001; Phillimore and Goodson, 2008; Coghlan, 2012). It was necessary to acknowledge my lived experience in the research as well as my centrality to it and my desire to shape the acquisition of knowledge and space (Botterill and Carruthers, 1999). I was influenced by emotional and relational aspects outside of the research. Family relationships provided opportunities and created constraints, yet my family were also members of the studied community located in the neighbourhood amid the ongoing developments. Yamagishi (2011) undertook a similar exploration of relationships that influenced her research and concluded that this can provide a more critical and richer reflexive assessment. As a researcher, my life would inevitably be affected in similar ways as theirs by the unfolding changes associated with the Olympic Games and development and as a result, the role of participant became more relevant and the observational role less realistic. Hennigh (1981) identifies the difficulties in remaining detached in long-term research, suggesting that an activist role is more ethical because it means that the researcher invests time and energy in the community. My long-term engagement indeed established common experiences and connections as the project progressed.

As the instrument of data collection, I was aware that I needed to ensure sensitivity, reflexivity and intuition, and to remain receptive (Leedy and Ormrod, 1980; Quinn Patton, 2002). Continuing field notes enabled me to reflect on my experience and findings in aiming to develop an understanding of local perceptions and experiences of the rapidly changing area. Endeavouring to establish 'practical wisdom' (Flyvbjerg et al, 2012, p 1) about how to act on social problems in the study context (Flyvbjerg, 2001; Flyvbjerg et al, 2003), a focus on the knowledge grew from intimate familiarity needing to be contextualised.

The research into the outcomes of young people's participation in Hub67, was negotiated by way of open access youth work practice in Hackney Wick. I aimed to discover how young people and the community experienced it, what the pros and cons were and how obstacles and opportunities were navigated. Relationships were key in this process between young people and peers, adults and the wider community as well as between various community groups. Social capital was considered as one way to measure what young people gained from participating amid ensuing urban regeneration and whether there was a greater sense of community and belonging following the creation of Hub67.

I was aware from the outset that my personal investment in youth work – and my frustration at its absence in Hackney Wick – would shape my perspective and engagement in the project. As someone with long-standing beliefs about the value of informal education, I had to be conscious of how this might produce bias, for example, by being ideologically motivated or by being influenced by my professional identity. There were moments when I had to ask myself whether I was interpreting events based on my expectations rather than on the realities. However, this offered essential insights and helped me to navigate the interplay between practice and perception. My motivation and interest in the development of Hub67 emerged rather organically from my experience as a youth worker and a resident of Hackney Wick. It will be helpful to understand how the study developed and how my personal and professional narrative, beliefs and values influenced the process. My task here though is to present and explain the Hub67 model as well as how I managed reflexivity within the process. With the arrival of the Olympic development leading to the 2012 games, it became apparent to me and other members of the community that the disruption and diversions which were about to begin might offer opportunities to redress inequalities in the borough. I began to watch, listen and read what was taking place and how if at all, any of it focused on young people's non-formal education and development. Under the umbrella of regeneration and change, I wondered what could be learnt outside of formal education about what was about to take place and how this might be beneficial to young people. These are reflected in the research approach.

The application and belief in reflection as a developmental tool is central to my working philosophy of youth work development and I use it (and advocate for it) as an educational tool, which when utilised encourages enhanced understanding of the world and those who live in it. Reflection can also be significant in learning to understand ourselves on both personal and professional levels. I have, over my years of practice endeavoured to create as a fundamental pillar to my thinking, the nature and necessity of reflection (Hammersley and Atkinson, 2019).

Primarily, while researching the neighbourhoods in Hackney Wick I understood that communities have a 'tendency to fight to remain the same' (Schön, 1983, p 30) but with reflective learning methods, we can recognise that 'to permit change of state without intolerable threat to the essential functions the system fulfils for the self. Our systems need to maintain their identity and their ability to support the self-identity of those who belong to them, but they must at the same time, be capable of transforming themselves' (Schön, 1983, p 57).

This study used research methods located in the realm of the practitioner and tied closely with self-reflection, where practitioners

> marshal evidence or data to expose unjust practices or environmental dangers and recommend actions for change. In many respects, it is linked into traditions of citizen's action and community organising. The practitioner is actively involved in the cause for which the research is conducted. For others, it is such commitment is a necessary part of being a practitioner or member of a community of practice. (Bogdan and Biklen, 1997, p 223)

I was mindful that I had dual roles and responsibilities in this research and was careful to articulate this when and where it became necessary, but I must admit that I always prioritised the youth worker in me and not the resident. However, as a resident, the absence of youth work in the area demonstrated a deficit for young people that had remained, until now, unchallenged.

It is impossible to be part of the social world and escape from it for research. Relying on 'common sense' knowledge and affecting the phenomena researched is a challenge to be embraced (Hammersley and Atkinson, 2019). Rather than viewing reactivity as a biased source, it can be exploited as a data form. Certainly, noting how people react to your presence as an observer and how they respond to other situations can be informative (Hammersley and Atkinson, 2019). I applied common sense as one of my barometers. In situational research (such as the case study) it was necessary to consider the 'basic social process' (Clarke, 2013, p 55) as the situation became the unit of analysis. I needed to be close enough to the social life and culture of the research group to be able to demonstrate accurate accounts of the real world; in this case, the world in which young people, youth workers and community met. This did not seem to be too much of a problem. Although the having the roles of resident, practitioner and researcher were challenging and sometimes conflicting, they enabled me to be 'close enough' to document and experience the study. Inevitably, qualitative tensions emerged between relevance and importance as I experienced the points of reference which were unique to me. Aiming to practice critical reflexivity, I remained mindful of my researcher 'situatedness' (Spry et al, 2001, p 1406). Certainly, I have found myself to be self-critical in my analysis of practice, beliefs and understandings in a way that I am clear would not have been possible had I not undertaken this process – leading me to appreciate fully this methodology and its capacity for observation, change and education.

As with most qualitative research, I wanted to explore the 'phenomenon' or case study using a variety of data sources. Being close to the project as it developed reminded me of the notion of the 'life cycle of innovation' (Chen, Yin and Mei, 2018, p 6) in which they explore whether unique findings can be described, explained and evaluated credibly and congruently in line with the lived experience of those involved when the research and the researcher are so closely connected. Adopting a realist approach meant that I relied on the premise of a social construction of reality (Searle, 1995). An advantage of this approach is the close collaboration between the researcher and the participants, enabling them to tell their stories (Crabtree and Miller, 1999). Their stories describe their views of reality and enable the researcher to better understand the participants' actions (Lather, 1992; Robottom and Hart, 1993). You might see why this worked well as a position.

## The case study unit

Yin's (2003) assessment of case study design focuses on answering 'how' and 'why' questions. The behaviour of the participants could not be manipulated, and covering contextual conditions was important because I believed in the power of youth work (the phenomenon) studied. Gathering data came from my journal, interviews, focus groups, meeting minutes and conversations recorded throughout the study, and the unit of analysis was Hub67 itself.

Several community groups were significant in this research and I needed to be closely connected to them. These groups included creative networks, neighbourhood groups, cultural groups, corporate and development teams and, of course, young people and families. Over a short period, I introduced myself to these groups, shared my ideas and intentions and was generally welcomed. All groups were happy to include me in their meetings and wider actions and I became a regular visitor to projects and activities. The agendas and actions from these meetings were recorded in my journal as were conversations and observations as and when I encountered them around Hackney Wick. I carried with me a generalised consent statement which meant that all participants were assured of confidentiality and anonymity. When it came to interviewing or including young people in focus groups, I was diligent in obtaining consent from them and their parents or guardians. I was heartened by the willingness of participants to take part and by their enthusiasm. I considered that my identity as a resident of Hackney Wick was welcomed and that those who shared their stories did so because they had something to say about issues we both cared about. However, that welcome also came with expectation. People made assumptions about me – expecting agreement, familiarity or shared grievances. I had to navigate these assumptions carefully, balancing the need to maintain rapport with the need and responsibility to challenge views that reinforced negative stereotypes about young people. This tension between advocacy and diplomacy was a defining feature of my role as a researcher.

## Semi-structured interviews

Semi-structured interviews were one of the most important ways of interviewing in case study and case study research generally (Brinkmann, 2014), so these needed to be done well. Semi-structured interviews were undertaken with young people participating in Hub67 at two stages of the centre's development: after one month of opening and again six months later. The rationale was to encourage the participants to feel as relaxed as possible and for them to share as much as possible about how they experienced Hub67. I wanted to encourage a sense of the interviews being naturally occurring conversations, so I would not necessarily lead the dialogue but prepare to include elements when topics were left out or prompts were needed (Brinkmann, 2014). I asked open questions but ensured that the key issues relevant to the research were covered in each interview. My role was to facilitate and guide rather than dictate exactly what would happen. The interviews were either individual or in small groups, covering similar ground, but I found that as I went along most of the young people preferred to be interviewed in pairs or small groups. I considered this was positive rather than anything else as they seemed to enjoy the sharing of stories and talking about each other. My style was flexible and responsive to my participants and recording them was the most effective way of ensuring that all of the content was stored and there was an opportunity to discern more at a later time.

## Focus groups

Focus groups are not uncommon in research as an effective way of collecting qualitative data, which involves engaging small numbers of people in an informal group discussion focused on a particular topic or set of issues (Williamson et al, 2015). A common misconception that people are inhibited from revealing intimate details in the context of a group discussion is undermined by my previous experience with young people and communities. Focus groups are well suited to exploring 'sensitive' topics, and the group context can sometimes actually facilitate personal disclosures (Farquhar and Das, 1999). I was careful that the discussions that took place in the focus groups were based on a series of questions (the focus group 'schedule') that moderated the process. I posed the questions, kept the discussion flowing and encouraged people to participate fully. Sometimes referred to as 'group interviews' it was not about asking questions of each participant in turn, but rather facilitating group discussions, actively encouraging the group members to interact with each other. Compared with interviews, the focus groups were 'naturalistic' (closer to everyday conversation) in that they typically included a range of communicative processes such as storytelling, joking, arguing, boasting and even teasing (Breen, 2006).

## Fieldwork journal

Maintaining a fieldwork journal is something which many youth workers are familiar with, as this as a practice allows for educational development. As a method of deep reflection, it enables improved practice and understanding through interpretation, knowledge production and reflexivity. In research, it has been argued that this is rather like 'navel-gazing' and self-indulgent (Kobayashi, 2003; Sultana, 2007), but it can add to the richness of relationships between researcher and participants and what can be utilised in the context of institutional, social and political realities. Journal writing is recognised as an important element of qualitative research (Etherington, 2006) and, as such, I found it integral to conducting ethical research (Trotz and Peake, 2000). My fieldwork journal enabled me to focus on my internal responses to being a researcher and encouraged me to capture a changing and developing understanding of the world in which I was studying. In many entries, I reflected on moments where my internal reactions – especially frustration, loyalty or protectiveness toward young people – threatened my ability to analyse objectively. As a practitioner, my instinct was to defend, advocate and explain. As a researcher, I had to observe, document and sometimes sit with discomfort. This required continuous reflexivity to avoid projecting my own narrative onto theirs. My journal became the space where I could critique myself, examine my values and biases, and ultimately strengthen my analysis.

I was able to reflect on my role, the impact of the research on my personal and professional life, my relationships with participants and my perceptions about how the research was impacting others. By creating a private 'space' to process my thoughts and feelings, I was able to consider and reconsider whether I may have become stuck or blocked or be able to notice and critique my biases and weaknesses (Ely et al, 1999). My biases were discussed in my journal as 'enabling biases' (Bernstein, 1983, p 65) as opposed to blinding ones. This enabled my local analysis to look more broadly into social justice, equity and democracy as the development proceeded (Nagar, 2002). I kept the journal over the entire period of the study.

## Data analysis

I chose thematic analysis (Braun and Clarke, 2006) as my chosen method as it would provide a framework and process compatible with my research and style of working. Thematic analysis is a method of identifying, analysing and reporting themes within data (Braun and Clarke, 2006) and is one of the most used methods for analysing qualitative data (Riessman, 2008; Bryman, 2016). Thematic analysis, like any data method, has weaknesses and limitations. It has been criticised for having a less theoretical approach than other methods, but it enables the researcher to organise and describe data sets in rich detail by identifying, analysing and recording themes that emerge (Boyatzis, 1998).

It was important to think about themes throughout, particularly in analysing the data and what constitutes a theme. For example, if road safety came up as a neighbourhood concern in one data set (minutes) unless it came up in other areas, it is unlikely to be considered a theme.

Undertaking the analysis, I wanted strong thematic data that adequately described the research journey. The predominant and important themes became an accurate reflection of what was experienced. I coded the data without a preconceived framework to ensure the data were realistic. I adopted Braun and Clarke's (2006) six-stage model of thematic analysis. First, I read through the data several times in considerable detail, aiming to identify themes by coding responses and comments as they came up in my gathered data. I listened to audio tapes of focus groups and interviews and read and re-read field notes and minutes, checking these alongside the respective transcripts and texts. This was useful in gaining a wider context of comments when coding the transcripts and in noticing potential themes. I highlighted sections or words in the texts and applied a code to them. Matching codes to the same or similar words and comments made up the second stage of the model.

The data came from recordings and notes from 18 interviews, 15 focus groups, 80 journal entries and 120 sets of minutes from various meetings, overall, making up 250 A4 pages. I searched for themes by grouping codes, noting codes that linked together to create a 'level of patterned responses or meaning' (Braun and Clarke, 2006, p 82). The themes central to my research were coded as they appeared and developed key thematic identities. The research design, methods and assumptions were based on realism and enabled a robust and critical account of the lived experiences of young people in the urban context of Hackney Wick amid rapid regeneration. The research analysis enabled me to articulate the role of youth work in this urban setting and to consider how the findings, observations and recommendations were realised in the development of the Hub67 model.

## Working in the community

Beginning work with the community is usually about striving for change (McArdle, 2022), yet in this scenario change was rather being forced onto the neighbourhood of Hackney Wick. However the community is viewed, there will be significant numbers of those living in stressful, chaotic and underresourced families where austerity and wellbeing collide, and resilience is essential but difficult. In terms of my role, despite being a resident, I was often positioned as an outsider – particularly by long-term community members who assumed my involvement in youth work aligned me with institutional agendas or middle-class regeneration values. I encountered assumptions that I 'must' agree with their views on young people, or that my engagement with young residents was misplaced. I was reminded that being 'local' does not mean sharing one perspective or set of values.

It was inevitable that the Games would bring some attention to Hackney and the other surrounding boroughs, and it was becoming clear that the creative community in the Hackney Wick ward were keen to engage with the potential financial and environmental publicity that was about to hit the area that was previously 'abandoned entirely to the working class' (Saunders, 1989, p 191). The long-term resident community was less interested in the promotional element of the Games and more inclined to want to know how it would benefit them and to what extent their lives would be disrupted. Increasingly, references to young people's lack of after-school and out-of-school activities were becoming central to conversations, and rising concerns around youth knife crime and gang activity were cited frequently as being of major influence on how parents and young people felt about living in the area. It was unclear whether the concerns expressed by parents and young people in Hackney Wick were due to actual events or perceptions about the prevalence of violence in general, but an emerging theme in meetings was fear for the safety of young people and that a youth-orientated space or provision was required.

Hackney had featured frequently in news reports and headlines as being a high-risk area for youth crime. Indeed, Hackney had a negative, crime-related press image and was regularly featured in reports relating to youth crime and through the media, youth music, popular film and television. Turton implies this has been the case for all decades of teenagers universally (Turton, 2014). However, neighbourhoods across the UK in 2011 experienced four nights of 'mindless violence' at the hands of what many had come to believe were what Cohen (2011) described as 'folk devils'. It was argued that gangster culture had become 'fashion' (O'Carroll, 2016, p 7) thanks to clothing and record brands aligning themselves with it and rap music advocating for it (Hancox, 2011; Neate, 2011). Media reports on 24-hour coverage showed hooded young people burning buildings and looting in 'an explosion of hedonism and nihilism' (Lammy, 2011, p 17). Some evidence shows that these disturbances had a materialistic element to them (Evans, 2011; British Youth Council, 2011) yet others argued that a broken society, inadequate parenting, poor role models and ill-discipline were to blame (Matthew, 2011, p 233). Others presented the riots as an opportunity to address wider social inequality, decades of neoliberal social restructuring and cuts to community services, such as the closure of youth services, increased tuition fees and cuts to educational maintenance grants (British Youth Council, 2011, The Children's Society, 2011). These were cited by young people themselves as the cause of their 'authentic rage' (Zizek, 2011, p 5) and the lack of opportunity for 'self-definition and political interaction and representational status as active citizens' (Giroux, 2012, p 112). Young people had been opportunistic in seeking to be heard but socially and emotionally moved their communities to fear them.

The creative community, at least, were keen to 'work with' the residents and young people in the area – either by offering activities or opportunities to engage in creative skills and fun activities. A need to be clear and confident in communication was going to be key and establishing some knowledge about the community groups, their motivations, issues and endeavours was necessary in understanding and engaging them in this somewhat unknown but inevitable journey. Being tuned in to the community and individuals that fuel it was going to be essential and awareness of their differing agendas needed to be keenly acknowledged.

When I think about people's agendas or reasons for participating in something, I imagine them setting out for a meeting. There will be some who are wholeheartedly invested in the group's mission and would attend at any cost. Some will attend because they have nothing better to do at that time, some because they have something (not necessarily on the agenda) that they want to know about, others will attend because they feel they have something to contribute, and others who will because they fancy a cup of tea and a biscuit. Whatever their reasons, you will never completely know, but you can be assured of them having a diverse range of views on the rationale and outcomes for the meeting.

My job, in situations like this, was to appreciate and make room for it all – and not assume that all parties were of the same 'mind'. In the same way that I adjust and adapt my communication style in various settings; when talking to children or when trying to quiet a group down, I was mindful that I had to do this in meetings regularly to ensure that messages were not misunderstood, or my delivery misinterpreted. I have always referred to this as having a 'switch' which you can turn on and off, and so was delighted when I discovered that a linguist in the 50s had called this 'code-switching' (Poplack, 1988), as this seemed to make sense. The switching for me means being able to address other perspectives on issues without judgement or making assumptions but with fair and credible discussion. In this case study, many conversations materialised around older people's fear of young people, for example. Many times, accusing them of behaviour or attitudes which were not necessarily fair (not all young people are muggers or knife carriers), but beginning a conversation with something like 'that's not true' would hardly gain investment in where the discussion goes. I believe that as youth workers we need to be constantly mindful of the value of each person's point of view as it has been driven by or nurtured in what they deem to be true. Our role concerning young people is not to quash their ideas but to validate and then demystify them, to articulate and demonstrate that not all young people are violent. This is not only good for young people but for us as professionals.

In many of the groups I encountered, there were similar or mutually beneficial objectives or connections, and it was important in the development of this case study to identify where partnership or networking might be productive. There is some skill in having an umbrella view of community communication and the ability to make connections between them is useful in any developmental environment, particularly when the development is emerging. I was able to link groups who had similar issues, such as outdoor space, road safety, care for the elderly, sports resources and indeed young people. What this did was enable individuals (as members of the groups) to make connections with each other and discuss their concerns or ideas, leading to extensions in networks and knowledge.

## Networking

The more that groups were identified, and communication continued across the ward, the more networking became common and useful. Most people have social ties across different communities depending on their family, faith, education, work, and financial and personal interests, and we generally consider someone without such group links to be socially isolated. There was a growing concern for some elements of the community who were thought to be socially isolated and ageing and there were several special interest groups who worked together to facilitate a project to address this, one involving a community garden and gardening sessions which was eventually very well attended.

In drawing groups together, it was important that they could see the similarities in their ideas and dilemmas and that the pooling of resources would be positive, especially where funding or permanent change was required. If they could see that 'the more the merrier' motto applied to having a proactive assertion, the more they were likely to engage. Networks are generally based on shared values, interests and interpersonal relationships. A 'well connected community' (Gilchrist, 2019) pulls together, supports the most vulnerable and is resourceful. In the first stages of the case study, it was obvious that the Hackney Wick community was not a well-connected one and that extensive work was needed to make this possible.

## Motivating participation

Groups with shared interests needed to be encouraged to see the potential in working together and, in most cases, this meant assuring people that it would not mean they needed to participate more. In most cases, time was important in engagement. Encouraging and motivating residents to become involved was a challenge. Putting up posters, passing out leaflets, posting on Facebook pages, Twitter, newsletters, emails and door-to-door canvassing were almost fruitless. Very few residents responded and even those who did seemed to withdraw rapidly and become disinterested quickly. Language barriers led to producing news bulletins in Turkish and Urdu as well as French, Gujarati and English.

Young people were encouraged to engage their families as it would benefit them, but even this proved ineffective. There was a significant number of families who had been moved to Hackney Wick following violent or distressing experiences, seeking asylum or refuge, and they wanted to live with privacy and seclusion. I also recognised that many residents lived in blended households on low or state-supported incomes. Providing networking events and opportunities for the residents which had no financial cost was essential and meant that some small-scale fundraising was needed.

In the early stages, housing associations, the local authority, local businesses and trusts were forthcoming and enabled the curation of several whole days of activities on the 'village' green. A climbing wall, circus skills and local baked offerings were well attended and appreciated, and craft activities, historical talks and demonstrations were popular.

Canvassing for people to join in the community groups and consultations was a more challenging task. Those who showed any interest were crushed by commitment issues, a lack of confidence and questions about how and what they could contribute – excuses or reasons why they could not commit were endless. Limited time, many commitments and a genuine inability to see how they might contribute hindered many volunteers. It is congruent to say that in the first stages of the research, encouraging people to become involved, even in discussion, was a struggle. Most people felt that whatever happened, the decisions had already been made about changes in Hackney Wick and that these would be 'helicoptered' in as and when necessary. In the scheme of things, very few members of the community thought they could make any difference at all.

Reflecting on the case study, it became clear that my understanding of youth work, community tension and regeneration was shaped as much by my own biography as by what young people shared. My interpretations were filtered through years of experience, emotion and investment in Hackney Wick as both a home and a site of struggle. Rather than try to neutralise this, I leaned into it, allowing reflexivity to become a tool for strengthening my analysis. This approach helped surface difficult truths about community resistance, exclusion and the trust required to build anything collaborative.

## Summary

There was much to overcome in terms of attitudes and expectations over the coming months.

It was clear and somewhat daunting that the tensions in the community needed addressing. The task ahead was likely to be an unpredictable one which required community buy in and changes to resident's perceptions about young people. I began to prepare myself for the complexities that were ahead.

# 4

# Young people and community

You will have gathered from previous chapters that I am not alone in my concerns for more understanding and appreciation of youth work, youth workers and the outcomes that are inherent in the practice. Generally, a non-formal learning approach which is education- and relationship-focused, is often facilitated in some way by a professional and has unarticulated but desired outcomes. This chapter tells the story of the need, challenges and ethos that led to the creation of the hub, as expressed through the lived experiences of the young people who participated in the inception of the hub.

## Background to the research

Traffic in and out of Hackney Wick was negligible during the Games since the closure of the train station. This rendered new parking projects, shopping and eating opportunities for visitors redundant. The Olympic opening ceremony in 2012 was a major event. Residents of Hackney Wick watched what they could from various vantage points along the canal and riverbank pop up barbeques. The atmosphere was jovial and celebratory, with the sharing of food and drink and conversation. Residents brought various home cooked offerings, balloons and whistles while the creatives grouped themselves around sound systems, oversized paella pans and woks for sharing. Most residents watched the opening ceremony at home on the television. It was so close but could have been anywhere.

It was incongruous not to consider the hours and hours of meetings, discussions, reading and influencing that had taken place over the previous years. what they had all meant and achieved. For the creative community, the entrepreneurs and investors, there had been significant gain, but for the resident community and young people there seemed to be no evidence of any significant positive changes. The realisation that 'otherness' (Freire, 1995; Davies, 2005; Young, 2006; Healy and O'Prey, 2011) and power relations between residents and those 'across the canal' had been utilised negatively, creating an exclusive identity, extending difference more strongly than ever. The various community groups meeting regularly acted as gatekeepers in this experimental though manipulative game and, as a result, had gathered social capital, only visible and useful to themselves, leaving behind the community members who had less influence and fewer pieces of the proverbial pie.

There was a sense that the development companies, funders and government departments who ultimately held the power had spent time with the community, getting to know them, 'grooming' them, navigating their way through those elements of the community that were beneficial to them and deconstructing those which were not. Hackney Wick had been insignificant in the Games. It had been seen as an embarrassment on the global platform. The residents were torn between not caring and caring a lot.

Asking residents in the days after the event what they felt and experienced demonstrated that some were more enthusiastic than others.

Nelly, a 67-year-old resident of Hackney Wick for 40 years said:

[W]ell, it's like anything really, isn't it? You know they been and done their thing and now they will up and go like the circus. I'm not surprised, I was expecting it – we got to tidy up the mess now ain't we?

Brad, a 32-year-old father of four said:

I thought it was gonna make this place better, I thought it would bring in some jobs but there was none of that, they just wanted the land and the cred and now they're gonna take it all away again like they was never here.

Jade, a 35-year-old life-long resident explained:

You know, I was open-minded, I was pleased that Hackney was on the map in a positive way, and not for gangs and crime and poverty for a change, but you know, I can't tell you how disappointed I am that nothing has happened for us, as residents, for our children, for the older people, there has been nothing for the community. Ok so they've given bits of money here and there for improvements on the streets but that's all for show – so that we don't look like a ghetto, it's all a big fake. You know, it's all a big fake.

Young people were intrigued by the remaining park and felt that there could be more to attract them. Many appreciated the open space, but they were also registering negative experiences of being there.

Jack:       It'll be good but if we keep getting kicked out or moved on it will just get annoying.

Hamil:      Well, I will go over there but I can't afford the gym and that so it will just be to hang.

Joe:          I'll go there and take my sisters; they love running about and love the grass and all that. I don't know what else is there, I know there's a pool, but I think it's dear to get in.

Macca:     I wouldn't mind seeing what the potential is, you know for graffiti and skating, but I can't see me using it all that much to be fair.

Energy was low after the Games, and meetings were lacking in motivation, but there was a sense of wanting to 'keep the sense of community together' by working on community projects and activities as and when possible. Over the next few months, recycled wood planters, plants and trees became available to residents as did the newly structured but temporary canal-side garden. A low-rise orchard emerged along some of the pathways through the Wick and a 30-foot decorated Christmas tree was placed outside local shops. New shops opened including a bicycle shop, a curios market and a vinyl record and café emporium, all unlikely to appeal to the long-standing locals but more to the fresh newbies about to make the area their home.

There was no consultation about the new projects which emerged and certainly nothing had been generated for young people. There was, however, on the horizon, an opportunity for a grant from the Big Lottery to improve community services and secure funding for youth provision. There had been no ideas about where might be available to open access youth work and so a full outreach programme began.

## Hanging out and anti-social behaviour

The grant process had been advancing with enthusiasm and small grants were being offered to local groups, particularly to those who presented community ideas and improvements for local families and elders. As local outreach continued, feedback had determined that for most residents, young people were a key concern. They were aware that there was nothing for them to do outside of school hours and that they were either left to cause problems on the streets and estates or suffered boredom. Unsurprisingly, most people voiced their concerns about young people 'hanging out' in the area – although there was little evidence that they were engaged in anti-social behaviour. The fact that they tended to gather in larger than average groups and made noise seemed to unnerve people.

Mo, a senior resident said:

[I]f I see them all on the corner I just don't go out, even if I need milk or something, I wait until they are gone. I get too nervous about walking past them.

She explained that she lived on her own and was worried about being followed home. She said she had no experience of any anti-social behaviour but that she read the papers and knew what went on. Her neighbour, also in her 70s, added 'I don't go out on my own, I always go with my brother or my friend – I think if you are on your own you are a target'. As stereotyped as it seems, this was a common attitude toward young people in the area which was not unique to the elders.

In multicultural cities, young people are 'a generation of suspects' (Giroux, 2003, p 6), particularly those located in socially, ethnically and economically polarised communities. Public spaces are built with adults and children in mind, yet young people are rarely perceived as being entitled to use public space as much as others. This contributes to stigma, perceptions of loitering or threatening behaviour when they gather in groups. Despite their status as residents, young people's resourcefulness when it came to utilising space in the Wick was viewed with negativity.

Marginalised young people challenge what is acceptable (Lefebvre, 1991; Amin and Thrift, 2002; Harvey, 2003; Massey, 2005; McFarlane, 2011), having ambiguous attitudes toward public spaces. This can be empowering and demystifying around boundaries and territory but can prompt a 'mutual lack of understanding' (Pain, 2000, pp 910–11) around social and communal space. It is well known that young people test the boundaries of acceptable and unacceptable behaviour as part of their search for self (Giroux, 1996), yet when doing so in public spaces, they are viewed unfairly, as though they are aiming to cause disquiet or social harm. Some say that they test spaces as part of the process of change in everyday experiences. This, of course relates directly to the consequences of inequality and urban change (Lefebvre, 1991; Amin and Thrift, 2002; Harvey, 2003; Massey, 2005; McFarlane, 2011). In Hackney Wick, there was ample opportunity to do the testing.

Like everyone else in the Wick, young people experienced a disconnect between what outwardly appeared to be a celebration of change but intrinsically continued to challenge their status as community members. Tensions arose between young people hanging out on the streets and residents. Being moved on not only irritated young people but caused parents and carers concern. Power dynamics between adults and young people were played out in the dialogue around moving on and acceptable behaviour which only added to young people feeling they had no space of their own, and certainly no venue in which to formulate their cultural identity.

In 2015, *The Guardian* newspaper reported an article by the Chief Inspector of Cleveland police, Jacqui Cheer, who claimed that adults were becoming 'quite intolerant' of young people in public spaces and that to her what looked like kids growing up was too quickly labelled as anti-social behaviour. She said the police and public needed to understand that anti-social behaviour 'is not just being annoying or being in the wrong place at the wrong time or there's more than three of you' (The Guardian, 2015). She feared that we were beginning to treat 'childhood behaviour' as anti-social. Speaking further, she said 'What's anti-social to one person is just what I did and what many young people do. ... We've closed down a lot of places that people are allowed to go. We've fenced off school grounds, I get it, but where do people collect? When you're in a crowd of three or four it can get a bit noisy, is that anti-social? When you're walking down the street and might be having a bit of a laugh and a joke, is that anti-social?'

Hilary Emery, Chief Executive of the National Children's Bureau at the time, in the same article said that the anti-social behaviour bill had perverse and harmful consequences. She explained that young people would be getting into trouble for 'being annoying' and that to penalise them for doing what is part of growing up, such as playing on the street, kicking a ball around in a public space and hanging out with friends, threatened to increase the divide between generations and caused the alienation of young people.

These two seemingly lone voices said what the outreach team were thinking. Young people were aware that residents viewed them as 'anti-social'. Most were amused by it but also felt unfairly targeted. A group of 14-year-olds, regularly encountered by the outreach team told them:

Jam: We always getting moved on, man. It's how it goes, ya' know. The folks don't like us hanging and they can't handle it so we gotta move.

Jah: Yeah man, we always getting shouted at and told to go away – life innit.

Sash: It's not fair man, we ain't doing bad things, we just get moaned at the whole time, it's like we are stereotyped y'know, they just expect us to be bad.

Acknowledging that they are seen as being anti-social, young people in the Wick talked about gang and knife crime – either with specific information about gangs and activities or with assumption based on rumour. They were fearful about gangs in the area and, in fact, throughout this case study, media attention on young people as perpetrators and victims of knife and gang crime had become commonplace, with many being affected directly by incidents. Fifty per cent of young people London-wide identified a lack of safety and policing as the most worrying thing about living in London (London Youth, 2019). Young people in Hackney Wick were harsh about perpetrators of crime and showed deep concern for their own safety.

Amid the existing tensions around young people, a lack of space of their own and the unknown dynamics among the gang communities, a derelict space in the industrial area of the Wick became available as a skate park - Frontside Gardens. A successful bid was made by a skating entrepreneur and competitor, Andrew Willis, and he was allocated the space by the Legacy Company. Immediate work commenced to clear and make safe the derelict site. Young people watched intently as the space was flattened and an intense, rustic oasis emerged made from recycled and sustainable materials – there were ramps, runners and movable furniture. Equipment was robust and 'make-and-mend' and there was an urban garden feel with piles of tyres housing green and luscious plants, benches constructed from railway sleepers and tables from cable housing. When it opened, it offered an impressive and creative space which was welcoming and strangely comfortable. Young people flocked to the space with their skateboards, cycles and helmets and even brought plants along to fill the makeshift planters. Artists had created colourful graffiti backdrops and coloured the recycled furniture with unique colours and prints. There was a general sense of fun and creativity.

Funding for the project was limited and opening hours were organised around volunteer availability. Young people, in claiming the space took this on themselves, meeting in small groups, climbing over the fences whenever they could. This was of concern for several reasons but mostly around safety. If the space was unsupervised, it was thought that the young people were not only in danger but also in breach of the contractual agreement. More volunteers were sought and threats from the Legacy Development Company to close it down were strong. Young people were frustrated and became more determined to use the park as often as possible. Volunteers were not forthcoming and gradually, security from the Olympic graveyard patrolled the site to move them on. Very few young women attended the park and only those with an interest in skating and biking seemed bothered.

Over two months, young people disappeared from the skate park as it became overcrowded by adults aggressively using the ramps and runways to show off their skills, drink beer and smoke, creating an environment which parents felt unsuitable for their children. The limitations of the contractual agreement and the necessity within it for the space to be well used meant that little could be done to reverse this. The space became less accessible (and attractive) to young people. Without a doubt, the community was disappointed by this and encouraged more advocacy for a space uniquely for young people. What had seemed like a great opportunity in the first instance had been taken over by adults, again leaving young people bereft.

A centre at the Old Baths had been redeveloped into an impressive open space and they claimed that they wanted to open the space to young people. Discussions ensued to plan how sessions for young people might work, where they would be and how the youth workers would take this forward. We discussed in depth our working ethos, work in practice and how young people would benefit from the sessions. The centre was gifted a self-sufficient funding programme which would generate income and secure minimal costs in operation. The first hurdle was to ensure that any running costs were covered and that inconvenience to the centre staff and structure was minimised. However, the centre's board had concerns about young people being in the space and wanted us to explain how security would be employed in the evenings when we were engaged. By security, they envisaged a bouncer on the door who would search and monitor young people as they entered and left, first to ensure that nothing was being removed from the centre but also to prevent any 'gang members' from carrying weapons. The idea of searching young people, particularly without any reason to do so was against any values we had. We encouraged the board to consider the assumptions that this made about the young people who they had thus far not met. If they were having to be searched on entry while no one else was we could not see this being a space in which they felt anything other than judged. This was a non-starter and we moved on to pursue other venues.

The purpose-built Senior Citizens Centre was used twice weekly exclusively by resident elders for bingo and dances. It offered large internal and external areas, a fully equipped kitchen and a large open space. Meeting with the committee it became rapidly clear that they were unable to offer the centre to young people who would likely destroy and vandalise their already shabby equipment and resources. A sense of discomfort in these meetings about young people 'taking over' and assumptions about young people being 'loud', 'rowdy', 'ungrateful' and 'disrespectful' grew over the weeks. Some of the group highlighted examples of personal experiences with young people on their estate which coloured their view of them overall. There was something territorial about the way they discussed the space and the attitudes they held about it, which resonated with the research we had undertaken in the initial stages. There was a sense of admiration for their determination to maintain their right to space. It felt, despite our advocacy for young people's opportunities, that the community's elder people also needed advocacy and space.

As a team, we could reasonably envisage the possibility of sharing the space and the benefits of intergenerational dialogue and learning, but at the same time, understood the rationale behind the committee's hesitation to give it up. It seemed that their desire to maintain the centre as uniquely 'theirs' was, in fact, greater than their dislike or distrust of young people. Conversations about intergenerational conflict over space encouraged us to consider the potential of exploring this further. One study of East London, in 2009, about young people's claim to public space ranked opposition from elders as the highest factor affecting local liveability (Zukin, 2010). Others have found that tensions and conflicts over public space have generally intensified once motivations to regenerate are shared in localised areas and the dynamics of power are interplayed between the generations (Lees, 2003). This strengthens the disconnect between the generations and perpetuates the prejudice that elders have of their younger neighbours. 'This is not simply a smokescreen for vested interests, but also provides opportunities for expressing alternative visions of what diversity and the city itself should be' (Lees, 2003, p 615).

Young people have ideas about how their neighbourhoods could be improved, yet barriers to being heard include adults' perceptions of them and how decisions are made about them in the belief that adults know what is 'best for them'. We know that young people have social and emotional challenges to navigate during their transitional phases and adding stereotypical assumptions about their place or role in community proves daunting for them. Young people spontaneously select and appropriate space for their informal use. 'Slack space' (CABE Space and CABE Education, 2004) say there is a fine line between asserting ownership and anti-social behaviour, hence the perceptions and concerns that are voiced by adults about them.

## The changing context

As I remained hopeful, the development work had begun, relocating wildlife (and feral cats) from the Hackney Marshes, closing off the canal paths and erecting high-security fences along the perimeters of the site. Security guards were posted in sentry boxes along various spots on the canal side and the usual view across the canal and marshes was masked by hoardings and fences. For residents who had enjoyed views across the green landscape, their outlook became unrecognisable and those who cycled or walked along the canal were being monitored and observed via CCTV cameras or guards dressed in high-visibility garments.

As part of the outreach for Hub67, we had been discussing the possibility of identifying a space for young people with the young people themselves, both to establish what they thought about it and also to involve them in the process, encouraging engagement, participation and decision making. We did this by locating young people in their own chosen spaces, such as bus stops, around stairwells, outside shops and in shared green spaces. Youth work principles reside in the belief that connecting with young people on their terms (and in their spaces) engenders a basis for trusting and respectful relationships. We looked at other possibilities for a venue across the Wick and nearby. Centres which already existed outside of the area were not suitable, as parents and young people suspected there might be issues with safety amid gang and postcode disagreements. Hackney council were unable to offer resources at all; they were already overstretched and understaffed but recognised our concerns and needs. Any other space remotely possible was far enough from the centre of the Wick for young people to turn it down. We were in a frustrating situation which needed alternative strategies.

Continuing to work toward a suitable outcome and engaging with as many people as possible became the mission.

## Social cohesion

Urban planning often aims to reinforce social cohesion when designing public spaces. 'Groups are cohesive when group level conditions are producing positive membership attitudes and behaviours when group members' interpersonal interactions are operating to maintain group led conditions' (Friedkin, 2004, p 410) and more specifically when social interaction and social cohesion work together to reverse the decline of social capital, strengthening the notion of community (Katz, 1994). This is of course, when the concept of social capital is conceptualised as a set of norms and networks that support and motivate civic engagement (Putnam, 2000). Given that the 'set of norms and networks' might have been something we wanted to achieve for the young people in Hackney Wick we needed to think about what this entailed.

A sense of community had to be in our sights, a place in which members felt they belonged, mattered to each other and had a shared investment in being together. If we were aiming to increase young people's social capital alongside their sense of community, we needed to see bonding through trust and respect for each other emerging as social norms. Humans who feel socially supported are more likely to have good mental health (Hooper et al, 2020; Michalski et al, 2020) and this appealed greatly as a lasting outcome to the quest we were on. Young people are at risk globally of anxiety disorders and depression and if neighbourhood social cohesion can help to mitigate this, it must be something to aspire to. At the neighbourhood level, social cohesion can offer connectedness, solidarity, an absence of conflict and positive social lives and social capital.

## Working ethos

Having chosen the youth workers myself, I had a reasonably good idea of their attitudes and values around young people and their practice. Ethics, moral principles, and values strongly guide youth work in the UK, and it was necessary to establish clarity around how this impacted us and our future work with young people. As with any youth work provision, we were pleased to adopt the generic principles supplied by the National Youth Agency (NYA). These principles offer a clear framework for ethical youth work in the UK. However, applying them in community contexts such as Hackney Wick is not always straightforward. As practitioners operating in the context of regeneration, social tension and mistrust of youth, we found that while the NYA principles guided our intentions, putting them into practice

**Table 4.1:** National Youth Agency generic principles

| Principle (NYA) | How it is applied to practice |
|---|---|
| Treat young people with respect, valuing each individual and avoiding negative discrimination. | Applying unconditional positive regard – accepting the young person irrespective of their actions/background. Working with them without prejudice. |
| Respect and promote young people's rights to make their own decisions and choices, unless the welfare or legitimate interests of themselves or others are seriously threatened. | Be mindful of the Rights of the Child and Civic Rights. Encourage young people to make informed decisions and choices. Making it clear that should they be in serious threat of harm or be causing others serious harm this will be shared with relevant authorities – otherwise honouring confidentiality. |
| Promote and ensure the welfare and safety of young people, while permitting them to learn through undertaking challenging educational activities. | Ensure that all activities and opportunities you make available to young people are risk-assessed and professionally sound, all equipment is in good working order and professional staff is available at all times. |
| Contribute toward the promotion of social justice for young people and in society generally, through encouraging respect for difference and diversity and challenging discrimination. | Working with and encouraging young people to adopt tolerance and understanding of difference and power relationships and to challenge this appropriately. |

often involved complexity, negotiation, contextualisation and exercising of judgement. Table 4.1 outlines how we initially interpreted and intended to apply each principle – but it's important to critically reflect on the gaps between these ideals and the practical realities.

It is important to note that while we sincerely and enthusiastically adopted these principles, it was inevitable that tensions would emerge when putting them into practice and faced with realities. For example, while promoting respect and autonomy is a central value, our attempts to do so were challenged by community attitudes toward young people. Residents saw youth as being untrustworthy and even dangerous, which, at times, held back progress or meant more time needed to be spent on building trust. Similarly, our commitment to confidentiality and trust was challenged by the perceived need for surveillance and security protocols from venue managers. These experiences highlighted how professional principles can be compromised – not through lack of intention but due to constraints that emerge in lived experience.

As well as adhering to these guiding principles, we wanted to ensure that young people developed feelings of trust, honesty, openness and respect in the relationships they had with the team. We aimed for a sense of community and belonging, not only as part of the activities we offered but also in the wider context. As a team, we spent a great deal of time discussing the working principles that we agreed to adopt. These related specifically to the development of Hub67 and were overwhelmingly supported and encouraged by those we engaged with. Table 4.2 identifies the working principles which were applied to Hub67.

As far as working principles, our aim was crucially to encourage young people to learn about themselves, their options, actions, attitudes and chances via self-awareness and self-respect – a place from which all other aims in this strategy could develop. The working principles we developed for Hub67 were grounded in the NYA framework but also went beyond it. Where the NYA focuses on individual rights and safety, we also wanted to foster place-based belonging, intergenerational dialogue and visibility in regeneration processes. Hub67 was built not just as a safe space but as a political and symbolic space – a site where young people could belong, resisting their growing exclusion. While the NYA model provides ethical scaffolding, it is often silent on how to work relationally with power and space, especially in contested, regenerating areas like Hackney Wick.

At the inception of Hub67, once the working ethos and direction of intended youth work had been agreed in accordance with the aforementioned principles, a programme was implemented to discover what young people were doing in the Wick, what they wanted to do and how they felt about the

**Table 4.2:** Hub67 working principles

| Working principles | How these are applied |
|---|---|
| Encourage collaborative relationships between all members of the community. | Include young people in meetings, consultations and local developments. Open opportunities for intergenerational exchange and learning. Advocate for young people. Recognise different agendas and perspectives. |
| Increase young people's self-awareness about their lives, their problems and opportunities. | Work with young people to identify their attitudes and values, aspirations and needs. Encourage young people to value themselves and their potential. Encourage and practice congruence and unconditional positive regard. |
| Increase young people's self-sufficiency. | Work with young people to increase their skills, knowledge and potential. Encourage young people to develop confidence, positive relationships, and the capacity to take action. |
| Encourage young people to live safely and securely. | Increase young people's knowledge about being safe and respected, and respecting others, space and time. Ensuring safeguarding is featured as a strength in all activities. |
| Increase young people's social capital. | Encourage young people to learn about their neighbours and their community. Build geographic knowledge and appreciation of the area's strengths and opportunities. |

options available to them. A distinctive outreach took place three evenings a week in two shifts: one immediately after school and one into the evening up to 11 pm. We learnt how many young people there were, where they were and what their motivations were.

Looking back, I see our use of the NYA principles as both empowering and, at times, insufficient. They gave us a shared language and anchored us to important ethical principles. However, the principles alone cannot account for the daily ethical decisions required when youth workers are placed between the demands of the community, young people and resource scarcity. Hub67's practice evolved in the space between professional guidelines and lived values, balancing principle with the ability to be responsive and pragmatic. This was a reflection of its embeddedness in real, imperfect, relational youth work practice.

## Outreach

Outreach work with young people is a familiar practice in the UK and has a history in social work thought to have originated with the Salvation Army (Andersson, 2013) as 'friendly visitors' (Andersson, 2013, p 2). The context has a performative nature in that 'reaching out' to young people and making contact is central (Acland et al, 2004, p 14). It is also known as 'street-based', 'preventative' or 'detached' work. It offers a unique way of connecting with young people where they are rather than inviting them to a venue. There are contextual and safeguarding issues related to this way of working, which needed to be explored and managed before outreach was undertaken. Outreach is a highly reflective activity which gives prominence to flexible interventions and personal engagement. The youth workers engaged in it need to 'think outside the box' and respond to individuals or groups in extraordinary situations and locations. In fact, 'engagement is key in outreach' (Erikson and Erikson, 1998, p 1) and the process of outreach and engagement 'is an art, best described as a dance' (Erikson and Erikson, 1998, p 1), during which the outreach workers need to 'become artists of sorts' (Erikson and Erikson, 1998, p 264). In a sense, outreach is rather more about an attitudinal style of working than a method. Rather than refer to it as a dance I would suggest that at times it can be awkward – meeting people on the street or in a park is not necessarily the most comfortable location – open to the elements with none of the usual props like chairs, tables and so on. The informality in this case can seem 'romantic' (Erikson and Erikson, 1998, p 2) However, outreach was a necessity and presented a potential opportunity to develop strong, street-based relationships with young people.

Having determined where they were most likely to be, the outreach aimed to make contact with young people to identify their needs, find out what they would be interested in taking part in and what they would want from a youth-orientated provision. It also aimed to discover any issues or concerns that might arise from the interactions, such as gang-related activity, drug misuse, homelessness or other risky behaviours. Not having anywhere to signpost them to we made information packs with details of services, charities and therapeutic services that they could approach if needed. The local police were informed on each occasion the team outreached and they carried mobiles for emergencies. The fundamental purpose of outreach is to begin a process of social interaction between youth workers and young people and is usually associated with those who are deemed 'hard to reach' (Mikkonen and Vadén, 2009, p 15), although in this case, the young people were difficult to engage. Over four months, the outreach workers met with around 80 young people, most of them at least twice. A small percentage of these were 'visitors' to the area not residents of Hackney Wick, but the remainder were locals aged between 10 and 19 years. Seventy-five per cent of them were male. Initial interactions were positive, and the idea of a youth-focused resource was welcomed. However, we were having difficulties in finding a suitable space for this to happen. Young people in community venues seemed not to be a natural fit in Hackney Wick. When available, venues had concerns about how young people would use the space and were generally suspicious about what they would get up to. Even the local church said:

> They might be drug dealing or even having a sneaky fag round the back – or even having sex, you can't leave them alone really. This building has so many nooks and crannies, you would need a football team of staff to keep an eye on all of them.

They already ran Brownies and Guides for girls and young women, not Cubs and Scouts 'as boys are too unreliable and have caused us all sorts of problems – we decided to put a lid on it'. This was an interesting take on things and not one we had any chance of changing in the short term. We discovered that this discriminatory view was echoed across the Wick and those who were open to allowing young people into their venues wanted enormous financial deposits to safeguard property, which we could not afford.

There were a few of the new and emerging venues based in old warehouses that were keen to include young people. The nature of their venues and the lack of secured space made these non-starters – sharing sessions with people drinking alcohol was just not going to work. It was encouraging that there was some support for young people though, and many offers eventually turned into workshops or activities which were exciting one-offs, such as art workshops, DJing, dance, parkour and all sorts.

Over this period of outreach, relationships were productive. There was rapport, trust and dialogue between the young people and youth workers about a new space and how to use it. However, after continuously having to report that we had drawn a blank as to a venue, young people began to lose interest. Quite rightly, they thought we had wasted their time and felt let down – trust was dissolving. They were keen to have their say:

Yaz:      Yeah, yeah, man if it happens, it happens but it ain't looking like it to me.
Jim:      I heard you, but we ain't that popular round here and so I ain't investing any more.

Yaz and his 'crew' of five felt they had given us enough of their time.
    Responses from younger people (10–13-year-olds) were more direct:

Mel:      So when is the youth club opening? I am getting fed up waiting.
Sue:      I told my Mum, and she keeps asking me when it's opening.
Jack:     Why are we waiting, we've been waiting too long now.

Trust plays an important part in any relationship and conversations that occur (Jeffs and Smith, 2005). In dialogue, we embody assumptions about people we encounter, and the primary objective in these outreach relationships was to develop young people's trust to provide a dialogue about how they would receive and utilise a youth space. It was inevitable, given that nothing had materialised, that the young people were questioning the youth workers' credibility, how truthful they were and how much they could be believed.

    Rogers claims 'being trustworthy does not demand that I be rigidly consistent but that I be dependably real' (Farber et al, 2001, p 119). The youth workers were indeed being 'real' in reporting how things genuinely were. Mindful of the place and context (Jeffs and Smith, 2008), the young people were beginning to feel 'let down'. The young people in the area had competing priorities: they were seeking independence from their parents and making formative choices about their lives at the same time as looking for new adventures. When young people lack social capital, they are less likely to have 'trusted adults' who are not their parents in their lives (Louie, 2012). The relationships with youth workers had made some differences in their platforms, providing some social capital and the opportunity to be vulnerable but supported, where chosen. A trusting rapport was developed through empathy and ongoing commitment. Young people responded to the relationship potential by appreciating being spoken with rather than spoken to in the process.

    Youth workers should be recognised by young people as genuine and not mocking or patronising (Goffman, 1969). As the young people began to withdraw from the relationships, they could well have felt patronised, like their expectations had been quashed. I do not doubt that the youth workers were completely congruent with them as they updated and appraised the situation, but it may not have been how the young people saw it. Conversations with young people before this were process-orientated (Kane, 2003) in that they were focused on acquiring a space where they could socialise. Once this opportunity had faded, the process element had almost become redundant and it seemed that there was no further purpose in the conversations. Relationships with the young people had become less effective and there was tension building. We needed to withdraw from outreach and regroup.

So too, were the youth workers feeling 'let down'. Having invested energy and professional integrity into this project they had 'failed' to achieve any significant movement in it. Relationships with young people had been built based on mutual respect and trust that a space would be available to them. The youth workers' professional standing had been undermined and young people had lost faith in them – if they were going to regain trust it was going to be difficult. The community had not been supportive, and opportunities were not forthcoming – this was devastating for all of us, but we carried on.

## Summary

This period had been exhausting and frustrating, with moments of temporary highs and longer spells filled with deep disappointment. There were certainly some negative nostalgic reflections on times during my career when young people seemed to be given an unfair hand, where their chances were thwarted seemingly due to adult and community prejudices and assumptions. Getting to understand what it was like for young people to live in Hackney Wick and how they were perceived and understood as residents was important and sometimes shocking. I recognised that there was some risk in allowing young people into a communal space, but most decisions encompass known or estimated probabilities and risk-taking always brings an element of uncertainty, judgement, and skill (Trimpop, 1994). However, it seemed that no one was prepared to take any risk at all. As practitioners, we were unprepared to compromise on safeguarding as regards the two buildings and, on reflection, this may have engendered a missed opportunity, one which we were professionally unprepared to take. I was hugely disappointed when I saw my community had let young people down. In some ways, we had not been believed. Residents did not believe that there could be a space that could benefit young people or that they would make positive use of it. The community groups which had emerged before and during the 2012 Olympic Games (Hackney Wick and Fish Island Cultural Interest Group, Leabank Square Community Association, Wick Award and Hackney Wick Festival) were still operational and engaged in development, negotiation and improvement, and I became even more determined to link with them and continue the campaign for a youth provision in the area. This led me to become further invested in community support and I endeavoured to continue to advocate for young people, visit as many community groups as possible and explain the disadvantages that young people were experiencing in the context of regeneration. I did this over eight months, which eventually led to the development of Hub67, which will be discussed in the following chapter.

Overall, in this challenging period, the strength of commitment to and advocacy for the project became even clearer. The dedication of the youth workers, their desire to make the project a reality and the way relationships with young people, however strong, can change and weaken rapidly when they perceive that their role in their community is being undermined were the painful but reflective results of months of outreach and community dialogue. Disappointed yet determined we carried on.

# The co-creation of Hub67

Whereas the previous chapter outlines what led to the development of Hub67, this chapter charts the final phase of actually setting up the hub and introduces the model. In doing so, it offers insights into what it takes to embed this kind of service into the community. It refers to the 12 months directly before the project was realised and discusses neighbourhood experiences, obstacles, opportunities and complexities which we encountered. It discusses how young people's participation was achieved and how adults (residents and parents) engaged in the development of the hub. The project design, realisation and launch are described in this chapter as are the perceptions and experiences of young people and residents.

Themes and sub-themes are presented and discussed. This chapter aims to analyse the lived experiences of young people in Hackney Wick over this period and identifies how these were influenced by the complexities of neighbourhood living and the impact of urban regeneration and a changing local environment.

## Trust

Erikson was the first to emphasise the importance of trust (in ourselves and others) in effecting our abilities to develop as individuals (Erikson, 1980), and Bowlby claims early childhood caregiving as being fundamental to our future attachment patterns and trust development (Bowlby, 1969). Healthy (or trusting) interpersonal connections and mutual support are indicators of low anxiety and non-problematic lifestyles (Betts, 2014). Trust in relationships between young people and youth workers is essential yet fragile and, as seen in this case study, losing trust can happen easily and with lasting effect. Rebuilding trust can be slow and complex. It is an obstacle to moving forward but must be evident in youth and community relationships, particularly where change and development are significant.

Trust and mutual respect are continual themes in good youth work practice and within neighbourhoods and community groups. In the context of regeneration, there is often a need to review and rebuild perceptions and relationships with an emphasis on trusting and respecting each other. In many ways, these are idealistic concerns, but with congruent and dedicated persistence, trust can be developed even with the most suspicious of people. Repairing relationships and understanding within communities requires dedication. It requires persistence in meeting with groups and individuals who might oppose or behave negatively toward youth work proposals. It is important to continue to show respect and trustworthiness in the community. In this case study, youth workers felt that they were being disrespected by some groups in the community, and young people were being disrespected and disregarded as well. However, over time and with the persistent development of cohesive relationships, agreeing to disagree where necessary but doing so respectfully, diverse groups did come together and were even able to appreciate the needs and approaches of each other in mutual trust and respect.

Trust is about the dependability and consistency of promises or commitments made by one to another and depends on how reliable and honest we believe people to be. In this case study, youth workers with genuine intentions entered into truthful communication. They had the young people's emotional wellbeing and interests in mind, maintaining confidentiality and safeguarding the young people. It is determined that trust operates across three domains: the cognitive/affective, behaviour-dependent and behaviour-enacting (Rotenberg, 2010). It is no wonder that when we lose trust in someone or something we feel let down and disappointed.

As discussed, there was a huge disappointment among the youth work team, but also among the young people in the neighbourhood when we were unable to identify a suitable space to set up the youth centre. Relationships between the young people and youth workers were friendly but tense. Based on mutual trust and respect, advocacy and honesty, the notion of positive 'association' had become simply about 'catching up' and had little focus since the discussions about 'the space' were fruitless. Without the said space there was a change in focus which meant talking about other things, other options, and, for some, this became tedious.

Association in professional relationships strongly supports open access youth work principles, and notions of habitus and field (Savage, 2005; Alanen, 2011). The fact that young people can opt in or out of the relationship without sanction, compulsion or judgement is what most youth work practitioners prize about the work (Batsleer and Davies, 2010; Davies, 2016; de St Croix, 2016). However, where young people assert their right to remove themselves, it significantly impacts developmental opportunities, and in the case of Hub67, had begun to dominate the progress of further work and presented potential risks.

[T]he nature of the relationship between youth workers and young people, unlike any other professional intervention, is purely voluntary – the young person can walk away at any time. This fact lays the basis for trust between the two. In most cases when dealing with this group the youth worker is the first professional, and possibly the first adult, that the young person will have trusted. The quality of this relationship will determine the success of the re-engagement and development that the young person then experiences. (Nicholls, 2014, p 41)

Resonating robustly with the youth workers was the idea that young people were expressing feelings of being 'let down' and 'lied to' – they needed more than reassurance that there was still hope of a space. Many had removed themselves from usual meeting places – they were no longer available for discussion or consultation. They were disgruntled and wanted to make this clear.

One of the youth workers said:

I feel really awful. I have made some really great relationships with those kids and they now literally hate me. They even walked away yesterday and just kissed their teeth at me – I have never felt so bad.

Another was less worried.

I think it will pass. You can't blame them; they have been let down, but they also know that we are on their side and so I am sure in time we will get things back on track. Listen, they are young people and where else do they get to protest and stomp about – good luck to them, after all, we all feel the same so why shouldn't they - they will come back on board, trust me.

In youth work, trust, confidence and familiarity are everyday parts of our work. However, working with humans, in any forum, often means there will be emotional and attitudinal conflicts, which require significant emotional management. Emotional management theories are generally associated with organisations and their culture, although Bolton (2005) and Hochschild (2003) have both described this in relation to the individual and their potential for emotional exploitation and control in caring relationships. Indeed, youth workers are expected to manage their emotions in complex ways, consider their professional expectations and remain credible, reliable agents of information and knowledge yet be 'able to consent, comply or resist and alter the balance of power' (Bolton, 2005, p 87). To think that emotions are easily detached from work with vulnerable, challenged or troubled young people is naïve. 'Emotion work', such as this, will be affected by multiple influences on personal, professional and global levels, but one of our skills is to manage this. Youth workers are often isolated and marginalised based purely on their commitment to work with young people who others perceive as being troublesome or unworthy of support or those whom everyone else has given up on. I recall two incidents which brought these to life for me.

First, when I set up a project many years ago in Marylebone. One evening in the local pub with my team I was asked not to pet the landlord's dog on account of me being a 'do-gooder'. On another, I was planning to take a group of young men on a residential retreat to address some of their anti-social attitudes and behaviours. I sat for hours with local police officers who challenged my decisions, saying that these terrible young people did not deserve a holiday. In both cases, I was clear about my intentions, which were unchanged. My emotional intelligence was heightened after these incidents, but I cannot say my feelings were not hurt.

Emotional intelligence is being 'able to motivate oneself and persist in the face of frustrations; to control impulse and delay gratification; to regulate one's moods and keep distress from swamping the ability to think; to empathise and to hope' (Goleman, 1998, p 22). Given the centrality of emotions in trusting relationships, not least those between young people and youth workers, it is necessary to contextualise notions of trust in practice and levels of emotional intelligence in reflection. Nussbaum and Sen (1993) refer theoretically to notions of human 'functionings' which determine and accrue human levels of wellbeing, such as the capacity for happiness and the freedom to achieve. These break down into wellbeing achievement, agency achievement, wellbeing freedom and agency freedom – when one or more of these are underachieved, there is a substantial loss of emotional 'happiness'.

Some evidence suggests that youth work can be measured in terms of happiness indicators and wellbeing indexes (Bradbury et al, 2013), and that not enjoying work as a youth worker should involve 'finding another job' (Robertson, 2005, p 31). Familial bonds are formed in most organisations to relieve anxiety, anger and emotion (Goleman, 1995; Bolton, 2005; de St Croix, 2016). So unsurprisingly, disappointment, disapproval or disengagement can lead to high emotional and psychological feelings of guilt and underachievement.

## Projection and purpose

In this period of deep professional reflection, there were many changes in the local dynamic. Committee members had resigned, new ones were recruited and two youth workers had decided to move on. Morale and energy were generally low at this time and supporters of the youth work programme were dissatisfied. One said:

> I'm gobsmacked by the inaction and lack of concern in this community for youngsters. It's obvious they need something to do, and they deserve it with all the ridiculous up and coming gentrification and endless investment in this area – there's no whiff of anything for them – I have

given up so much of my time to get something moving I just can't do it anymore, I am gutted.

Expressions of anger, disappointment and a lack of support to continue to engage in the development process became common where youth workers had expressed their feelings to each other, although not to the young people. They said:

You know, it's no wonder they [young people] are fed up, so are we – we just seem to be hitting brick walls. It is so disheartening and disappointing. I can't get my head round it at all, why isn't anyone supporting this? I just don't think I can do it anymore; I just feel like they are so set in their ways and judgemental. I feel that they are judging me even.

It felt as though the attitudes and values of the residents were fixed and, without a working space for young people, there was little opportunity to change them. One said, referring to the elders' group:

I know they have lived here all their lives and I realise that kids get a really poor press around here but there seems to be no way of getting them to think differently – it's like they just can't or won't, never mind don't want to. Every time I show up there, I really feel like I am patronised and just a pain. It's not a good feeling and I have really tried hard with them.

Another said about the general situation:

Look, kids and youth workers are always getting the rough end of things because what we do is not popular – and generally we put up with it. We know that part of it all is keeping the peace and making everyone happy and, in this case, we have got the whole damn gentrification thing which is all about money making and how somewhere becomes 'cool'. Kids are not 'cool' and so we are stuck with being on the other side of things. Kids are a threat to people who have no empathy, you know and some ways you have to call it a day and just get on with doing what you can for them – the kids.

It is interesting to hear what Kellerman explains as 'every environment is sending a subliminal message to us, indicating that we are either part of it or separated from it' (Kellerman, 2007, p 87). At the same time, other workers expressed clear desires to keep on track with the project and an intense commitment to it. In the same way, as we refer to the self-fulfilling prophecy – it is a wonder what young people receive in these messages – they are not worthy perhaps.

Other youth workers said, 'This is just an annoying blip – we will get there.' Another said:

> This is what happens … we get knock back after knock back and they hope we will give up, but we can't as the problem still remains and these kids need their own space. They are deserving of something out of all this, and we owe it to them not to give up.

The intensity of feeling and professional integrity invested in the project in a changing and challenging environment was often overwhelming and uncertain. But I for one was not ready to give up. de St Croix (2016) talks about grassroots youth work needing to be 'passionate', a strong emotion, and one which is often used to describe how workers feel about their work (Bradford, 2009; Davies, 2011; Batsleer, 2012). However, there is little written about how young people might feel passion in this situation. Working with young people can prompt strong emotions in those who work with them, stirring up anxiety, pain or stress (Briggs, 2009). Faced with the anxieties of personal and external change, young people can 'split and project on to others' (Briggs, 2009, p 104).

## Reconnecting

With new vigour and enthusiasm, the remaining youth workers honed the opportunity to rejuvenate action and invigorate the plan. A review of the situation was made, and the remaining individuals regrouped to take stock, evaluate and begin to set some targets for the future.

Evaluating where further work and time were needed, it was necessary to consider the experiences of young people throughout the process, particularly concerning trust and confidence. There can be confusion between feelings of trust and familiarity, according to Luhmann, in that 'trust is a solution for specific problems of risk' (Luhmann, 2024, p 4010). Familiarity may not always reflect trust but provides a sense of what we become used to. Trusting the youth workers would have required some emotional engagement on the part of the young people, in this case, perhaps based on the potential outcome being desirable and advantageous. Once the desired outcome was no longer an option, at least temporarily, there was nothing specific for them to continue to invest in. The associated advantages of relationships with youth workers had become less than they had expected and, therefore, they may have come to regret their choice to trust them.

Seligman suggests that:

> The emphasis in modern societies on consensus [is] based on interconnected networks of trust – among citizens, families, voluntary

organizations, religious denominations, civic associations, and the like. Similarly, the very 'legitimation' of modern societies is founded on the 'trust' of authority and governments as generalisations. (Seligman, 2004, p 14)

Young people made comments about the youth workers in different ways by using terms which separated themselves from them, confirming that they no longer viewed the youth workers as 'on their side' but more as members of the generalised 'authority' and related network. Moral norms and social values may also be considered dependent on association and representations of trust (Putnam, 2005). In short, once the potential of a youth space was removed from the equation, young people had nothing further to invest in; the relationships alone were not offering them anything tangible.

In considering the best way to proceed there were several elements which needed to be revisited and assessed to ensure some success in future engagement with young people, but also, and possibly more specifically, with the community. It was clear that relationships with young people were only likely to progress if we maintained our original working ethos and framework (as discussed in Chapter 4) and that the importance of the voluntary relationship remained fundamental to practice.

Young people continued to express frustration about not having their own space and were beginning to articulate their views about the youth workers' effectiveness. The youth workers, in response, vowed to make the space a reality and agreed that networking and advocacy needed to be focused and significantly stronger than before. We became regulars at all community meetings, consultations and events. We contributed to newsletters and websites concerning local issues and joined as many committees and forums as was physically possible.

Community means different things to different groups and has been identified by the participants of this study as being about a neighbourhood, estate, street or village. When discussing the changes and opportunities in the neighbourhood, residents described their community in several ways: as a place where they live, where they are from, where they share interests with others, or as an area over which they have some ownership or claim.

## Community buy-in and relationship building

At this point in the case study, there was a need to repair the community, build hope and develop new ways of engaging young people. It was important to gather the views and perceptions of the locals toward young people, the hub and what was going on in the neighbourhood. We needed to understand community concerns, agendas and needs so that we could develop their buy-in and continue to develop and maintain positive, supportive and trusting relationships.

In community meetings, young people were often described as being a nuisance, causing damage, engaging in petty crime, creating noise, gathering in public spaces and causing general disruption. Adults, as we have mentioned, find young people gathering in communal spaces disturbing. Assumptions are made about their intentions and the potential to cause damage or disquiet. Those who thought this were not in favour of a youth-orientated space. They felt that young people did not 'deserve' it, that they were likely to destroy it, and some felt that it would only lead to a no-go area for adults, where young people dominated.

In the minutes of one residents' meeting, the following was recorded:

> Older people don't feel safe. They can't go out when there are groups of yobs hanging about, because they don't want to get mugged or beaten up. They know what the risks are, and they would rather stay indoors and stay hungry than go out with all that noise and messing around. They are scared of them, and they shouldn't be.

In other minutes the following was recorded:

Resident A:     Too many youngsters are hanging about in the dark and acting suspicious. They are noisy and a general nuisance.

Resident B:     The kids are a pain you know, they are always just hanging around, making noise and leaving rubbish everywhere. I am sick of them and don't think they deserve a space of their own. Why do they have to take over the streets and bus stops and all?

In research carried out in 2022 young people in Holland were also considered a nuisance in their communities; 'their non-verbal characteristics, and namely: the clothes they wear [hoodies], the way they stand, the sometimes-aggressive gestures they make when they talk to each other, their incomprehensible language' (Fiore, 2024, pp 23–34). They also found that these characteristics along with throwing rubbish on the street and noise from talking loudly, having music turned up and driving scooters back and forth also annoyed residents. Residents were annoyed by the attitude of young people toward their neighbourhood, treating it like a garbage dump, taking up too much space and being intimidating. On being challenged they are prone to shouting, spitting, name-calling and vandalisation, especially after residents seek the support of authorities (Fiore, 2024). In research into rural environments, except for beaches and graveyards, young people are still seen to frequent parks, benches and bus shelters (Weller, 2007).

Community is used to articulate a range of concerns, aspirations, hopes and emotions which connect us to our relationships with others with whom we share space and territory (Wood et al, 2014). Giving us a 'sense of belonging in an insecure world' (Delanty, 2003, p 192) and providing a 'moral realm, which neither one of random individual choice nor government control' (Etzioni, 1993, p 254). Despite the very nature of the community being restricted by mobility and resources, young people are inherently 'local' (France, 2007) and are shaped by the moral indignation expressed by residents. Young people are often viewed with judgement and apprehension, due largely to the media coverage and representations of youth that permeate social narratives and community tensions (Pitts, 2008; Davies, 2011). This is particularly interesting as the more young people move away from the media and further into social media as points of information, it seems the more negatively the media report about them.

The news media misrecognise young people in their reporting because their focus is purely on the creation and promotion of moral panics, and young people are regularly made aware of this. The economic imperative to sell newspapers to gain readers is the driving force in manufacturing the content. The readers are used to stereotypical, stigmatising stories of young people who pose a risk to society and amplify moral panics – misrecognising young people globally.

Concerns about young people in the neighbourhood have become less locally explicit and more contrived thanks to national perceptions of gang enterprises, highlighting the shift in gang operations from postcode to the marketplace, where gang activity has become more economically focused and less emotionally and territorially charged (Whittaker et al, 2022). Young people are exploited in gang marketplaces, where county lines' networks tap into the night time economy of emerging neighbourhoods (Whittaker et al, 2022). Social disruption and disaffection have long been attributed to young people, based largely on their associated youth cultures, chosen music, fashion or leisure preferences. The media is often blamed for the 'effects' that they have on the identification and stereotyping of such youth cultures. Cohen, credited with theorising notions of moral panic claims that the media play a 'disingenuous game' (Cohen, 2002, p xvii) since they know that their message will be received with multiple meanings, responding differently to the same message. He also claims that the media consistently use the 'simple minded' (Cohen, 2002, p xvii) blaming of others to sell their stories, which often misrepresents young people, ultimately leading to national perceptions and fear for them and of them. Langford's (2024) idea of misrecognising young people fits perfectly amid this and asserts the tensions between truth, culture and selling newspapers.

## Boredom

Many observations from residents included young people being bored and lacking provision in the area. The notion of boredom has been linked to young people over many decades and is attributed to the 'storm and stress' of adolescence (Lang, 1999; Winkler et al, 2011; Cohen, 2002; Langford, 2024), and among young men in particular, it is claimed that boredom 'looms large in our culture' (Farnworth et al, 2011, p 1). There was some sympathy among residents who recognised that there was little or nothing to occupy young people outside of school.

Boredom strongly evokes negativity, inducing feelings of pointlessness and lack of meaning which can be associated with many psychological, social and physical health issues, underperformance and opting out of things (Eastwood et al, 2012). Youth boredom is associated with being uninterested in events and opportunities (Bryant and Zillmann, 1984; Pekrun et al, 2002; Vogel-Walcutt et al, 2012). Bourdieu (1984b) refers to capital as being the resources which might alleviate boredom or a lack of interest in activities, particularly when leisure activities are inaccessible to individuals (Wegner and Flisher, 2009; Baxter, 2011) and, inevitably, financial security makes a broader range of options available. Research has shown that young people from families with fewer financial resources practice fewer leisure activities and experience their leisure time more often as unchallenging and monotonous and as 'having nothing to do' (Harris, 2000). Material deprivation and leisure time are generally matched, although not all leisure activities are expensive, which suggests that other variables might contribute to boredom, including a lack of interpersonal relationships and networks or social capital (Bourdieu, 2011). It is estimated that young people spend around 30 per cent of their time with friends (Vodanovich and Watt, 2016).

Young people with a high degree of social capital will feel bored less often than those who have limited resources (capital) and capacity. It is difficult to define what boredom is, according to many scholars (Goldberg et al, 2011; Malkovsky et al, 2012; Vodanovich and Watt, 2016), yet they agree that it is largely associated with dissatisfaction with one's own experiences or circumstances (Pekrun, 2017) and disengagement from their neighbourhood (Goldberg et al, 2011). It may also relate to what individuals or groups perceive about their environment (or neighbourhood) and what the environment offers them (Mercer and Eastwood, 2010; Fahlman et al, 2013).

Boredom can be seen as an emotional state leading to dropout and delinquent behaviour (Vodanovich, 2003; Vogel-Walcutt et al, 2012), or 'an aversive state of wanting but being unable to engage in satisfying activity' (Eastwood et al, 2012, p 483). Others see it as 'an emotion that calls out for remediation and relief – a plea for assistance' (Velasco, 2019, p 9) which perhaps highlights young people's need to be relieved of boredom. In research undertaken in the US, it was found that unlimited to race, gender, ethnicity and socioeconomic status, 66 per cent of high school students and 58 per cent of junior school students considered themselves to be bored all the time (Macklem, 2015). Some psychologists interpret boredom as serving a purpose in letting us know when we should stop doing what we are doing and move on to something else and that it can fuel creativity unless there is limited access to new things or opportunities (Mann and Cadman, 2014). For the young people in Hackney Wick, boredom may well be intrinsic yet amplified by a lack of opportunity or advocacy toward creative new ideas and options and, indeed, by nothing being on offer to them. Social media, however, can, according to some, create boredom by dividing attention, elevating a desired level of engagement, reducing the sense of meaning, raising opportunity costs as well as serving as an ineffective boredom coping strategy.

## Distant parenting

A significant number of residents articulated their disapproval of parents who were disengaged from their children's education and actions. Strong statements about responsibility, neglect and poor or distant parenting were made along with demands on parents to make more time to provide activities to occupy their children. These residents felt that young people should spend more time at home, not on the streets, and that parental responsibility was to ensure children were polite, well-behaved and not a nuisance. They were not overly enthusiastic about a youth space but did seem to appreciate that having one might reduce the number of young people out and about in the area.

Statements made by this set of residents were judgemental and aggressive – they were in many ways saying that they knew how to parent, that they had been successful at it and that others should follow suit. In their minds, parents were not bothered, didn't care and didn't have the time for their children. Accusations of needing to be 'funded' and not wanting to work seemed to go hand in hand with having too many children – there was a very clear sense of anger about these families in the eyes of resentful residents.

Parental distance may reflect the negative processes of economic stress, low morale and low spiritual values, plus the impact of associated underprivilege . It demonstrates 'intellectual rigidity, proneness to conflict and the inability to communicate with people, alienation, irresponsibility and indifference to the fate of others, self-doubt' (Kostyunina and Valeeva, 2015, p 225). Such characteristics seem to be associated with how some of the residents described young people. There is certainly evidence that when young people talk to their families about their learning and experiences at school, it is beneficial to their continued learning (Goodall, 2022) and that parents who engage in the learning feel better understood and appreciated by their children (Mapp and Bergman, 2021). There are social scenarios which create barriers to parents being involved in what their children are doing, unsurprisingly, these include demands on their time, mental health, depression, caring for others, poverty and language barriers (Jeynes, 2015).

## Entitlement

The bulk of the residents who expressed feelings of entitlement were parents. They discussed the challenges of parenting, having to work long hours to make ends meet and not being available or able to look after their children outside of school. They presented narratives of living in poverty as single parents or parents with unemployed partners, with two or more children and varying degrees of mental or physical ill health. Many came from large or extended families across the neighbourhood and had additional responsibilities to parenting, such as caring for siblings or parents. Entitlement was articulated by expressions of frustration and the need for help with their children and their circumstances. They seemed certain that the 'authorities' should provide something for their children and that the 'authorities' needed to take responsibility for the way young people were behaving.

Many of the parents in the neighbourhood with teenage children fall into the Generation Y category. They have most likely instilled into their children the idea that entitlement is positive and that public assistance is favoured and supported. The idea of work among this generation has become something to reject while happily drawing on society's economic pool. Perpetuating the trend is a never-ending cycle of blame where young people refuse to identify the faults in the process, and those who do simply push the blame back on their parents. The fact that there is an inability to take personal accountability and reform these behaviours has become 'the disease' that we live with (O'Rourke, 2011, p 3). Condescending residents were those who were likely doing several jobs to put food on the table for their families in previous generations – or at least their testimonies suggested as much.

Parents were keen to share their views about a youth space and often contributed in meetings:

Parent A: I do the best I can, but I can't do as much as other parents. I am on my own. I look after my mum and I work part-time. I can only do what I can and sometimes that means I am not at home. I have to trust my kids to behave themselves. I can't do anything else. They need a youth club or something and deserve it. At least I could stop worrying.

Parent B: It ain't fair that all this building stuff is going on and there ain't nothing for the youths, nothing. If they wanna hang out then they gotta go to the park – well how is that a good idea, with all the nonces and that around? The council should be doing something about this, they just, really should.

Parent C:      Yeah … um … I agree with that. My kids are good kids, but they don't have much, they don't get the new stuff and all that … um … and there should be a place for them to be supervised and looked after.

Parent D:      When you're poor, man, they don't wanna know. It's like our kids don't count, cos we don't count. Yeah, sure the council should give them somewhere to go.

Parent E:      I know things are tough, but it is your responsibility to look after your kids – no options.

These extracts show vulnerability and feelings of being overwhelmed by reasonability. Many are clear about their limitations in monitoring their children and what they say is almost a cry for help, a demand for support in what appears to be an underresourced and underappreciated struggle. Most of these parents will be claiming Universal Credit, designed to simplify and incentivise the benefit system for those on low incomes. In many cases, the allowance fails to cover basic family essentials – clothing, food and fuel (Porter and Johnson-Hunter, 2023). We know that young people's life chances depend heavily on the resources of their families (Rivenbark et al, 2020; Popay, 2021) and low household income has strong correlations between poor mental health and cognitive and social development (Cooper and Stewart, 2021). Poverty puts strain on familial relationships, can erode mental health and lead to negative parenting (Bywaters et al, 2022). Registering the highest rates of poverty in the UK (Barford, 2023), it is unsurprising given its geography, that Hackney Wick's families are victims of their time.

## Perceptions of local young people

There were some distinct perceptions of young people and their families, which had been shared throughout the project and proved helpful in developing a local picture of young people from their neighbours' perspectives. The themes that developed out of these perceptions included seeing families as 'needy', under pressure and inactive in their children's learning. Low income was a common thread as was the fact that many families were large, with three or more children. A sense of a cry for help seemed matched with a call to action given that parents were verbalising their desire for help and support with young people's leisure time.

Older residents and those with children over the age of 25 tended to consider neglect an issue with parenting patterns as was inaction and disinterest in their children's lives. Considering the relationship between poverty and depression, it was interesting to note that no one seemed to consider this a feature of parenting distance. There was not a great deal of sympathy or empathy shown around issues of mental ill health whenever it was discussed – rather it was seen as a weakness, which surprised me.

Young people understood that they were considered a nuisance and that hanging out anywhere was not appreciated by their neighbours. These were not cherished perceptions, and most would rather not have acquired them. They felt wrongly accused and 'labelled' in the community and assured us that boredom was a key component of their lack of motivation and that having something interesting to be involved in would certainly change things.

It was becoming clear that both a cry for help and a call to action could be fully exploited to pursue the establishment of a youth space. For youth work practitioners it is essential that different agendas are recognised and that community members are engaged on their own terms. Practitioners are aware of opposition to young people and how perceptions and concerns emerge. Rather than working in defensive ways, it is preferable to work to acknowledge and navigate through the concerns, reducing tension and creating cooperative working partnerships.

## Working with different agendas

It is important to realise in communities that not everyone will hold the same views, experiences or needs and that working cohesively means not only acknowledging this but working with it. What I mean is that you actively acknowledge differences of opinion and utilise them as a means to an end. Instead of resenting those who think young people are deviant and unworthy, acknowledge that their way of seeing things may not be yours, but may have validity. Ask them what would make things better, more effective, easier to live with and less problematic for them and encourage dialogue to explore this. For example, if I had considered this at the time, I might have asked the senior residents group, who would not allow young people in their centre, whether they would let us use it for a couple of hours, with them or representatives who could see young people in action, or would they consider having some kind of joint session to get to know the young people, ask them about themselves and so on. It is possible that they wouldn't have wanted to do this but presented with the idea, it may have allowed room for negotiation. Potentially, they would see that their worst fears might not be realised. Most people want their concerns or ideas heard and by offering them options, they can see that this is happening and they are being taken seriously. Once people feel validated, there is potential for shifting attitudes and values which might otherwise be stuck in place.

Meetings and forums which involve different ways of thinking are always better served when everyone is welcomed and considered – even when this seems impossible. Giving people space to contribute in whatever way they want (obviously within reason) generates a respectful equity that may not draw easy conclusions but gives time and space to alternative views and remedies. Your role is not to agree with everyone but to give them the space to share and observe, listen and appreciate perspectives from all angles. You, after all, will feel more congruent and be able to acknowledge things at 360s, with fairness and rationality.

## Co-creation

After what seemed like a lifetime, we were offered a temporary piece of land, architects, resources from recycled buildings and funding to set up the centre. Following the convening of what seemed like endless meetings to interpret and contextualise the urban regeneration and development where young people were featured, representatives from the London Legacy Development Company (LLDC) approached me with a proposition. In response to the requests for a youth space and in recognition of the outreach and consultation work that had been undertaken, they offered a piece of land in Hackney Wick which could be developed into a community centre, managed and facilitated by residents. Buildings on the land had been demolished and partially housed the skate park. The building would be designed by architects and materials would largely come from the recycling of temporary buildings and resources left on the Olympic graveyard. This offer was received with huge excitement and appreciation, yet also came with the acknowledgement of the daunting task ahead.

The LLDC commissioned architects and tasked me with establishing a steering committee and series of consultations with young people and residents, over and above those which had already been undertaken. The space was to be a community space with dedicated times and opportunities for young people, and the designers wanted to know how people could make the best use of it. Over the following four months, residents were asked about how they would use such a space, what their expectations were and what would make it useful to them. Overwhelmingly, the responses returned with clear requests for a space for young people above any other group, signifying a shift in residents' attitudes regarding the project and indeed toward young people. A crèche for under four-year-olds also emerged as a key necessity. Older groups and those with creative interests did not seem to think that the space would be of use to them. The elders were particularly keen on retaining their exclusive centre on the village greens. There was also a wide interest in sports and fitness activities while recognising that the open space in the area was vast and underutilised.

The steering group was recruited from those residents who had been active in the months leading up to this. Not all of them shared the same views and not all of them were fans of young people, but all of them were invested in their neighbourhood and were committed to making a difference. In calling upon people to join the group it was important to represent different groups and agendas – we had to be sure that we were as diverse as the community we represented. The steering group needed to be strong and clear about the management and leadership responsibilities within – how regular discussion and decision making was needed and that commitment to this had to be full and dedicated. Strong leadership was needed as were internal and external strategies for engaging the community and young people as and when appropriate. People volunteering to steer the project were trained and inducted into the programme and were fully informed about the importance of the role they were taking on. In all training, volunteers were reminded of the Hub67 model – the necessity for community buy-in, trust, respect and congruence. As well as working through the details of this, the principles, values and beliefs of the model were reinforced and developed.

The immediate task was to re-engage with the young people to encourage them to participate in the planning and development of the space. A series of 'on the street' sessions were designed to update them and ascertain how they wanted to be involved. We recruited a small group of young people as a 'street team' who were prepared to be the representatives for the rest of the group and regularly meet with youth workers and others, inputting views and comments that they would have gathered from their peers.

The first series of meetings involved the LLDC and the architects who wanted to know from young people what they wanted out of the space and how they could get involved. Many discussions were had with young people themselves, their parents and residents about their aspirations for the space, which often proved unrealistic due to spatial and financial limitations. Youth workers met with the LLDC, Cultural Interest Group (CIG) and tenants' and residents' groups, as well as the Wick Award committee. They talked of sports pitches and large dance studios, recording studios and rehearsal space, all of which, according to the designers were not feasible. Given the dimensions, there was potential for one large 'room', a kitchen area, reception, toilets and smaller rooms. This was not what the young people wanted to hear and once their 'ideal scenario' was not an option they seemed to become less interested in the project. There was a sense that they once again felt let down as what was on offer was already predetermined. Of course, to a certain extent, it was, as the architects and designers had some clear ideas about the best use of the space and had drawn up plans. What they wanted to know from young people was what kinds of colours and arrangements they wanted, not how they wanted to use the space.

The street team were initially engaged and motivated to discuss developments with their peers. Peer-to-peer conversations had proved a challenge as they encouraged their peers to get involved in ideas and activities. Young people wanted to create a dream space, not be told that it had already been designed. It was a tricky situation, as we had promised them their own space, but adults had determined what this would be. Of course, this is not unusual – adults always design spaces and present them, but there was something about what we had been advocating for that felt different – a building that was quite literally coming out of rubble seemed to have more potential than it had. We had in many ways assured young people of autonomy yet not been able to deliver.

A mutual lack of empathy, trust and understanding between planners and the community is not unusual, and often singing from the same song sheet is difficult. Young people often have deep concerns about their environments, their enjoyment of them and being able to articulate a passion for what they value most, and they do not always want to see things change (Strachan, 2024). The young people were showing frustration and irritation and seemed to begin to distance themselves from discussions about the planning of the space. Opening the planning to the community and young people offers a social and participatory element to what otherwise would purely be physical. Meeting the basic needs of the community of users can satisfy aspirations and life improvements (Brundtland, 1989). Including young people in the planning process showed progressive and public-spirited mindsets, where ethical concerns for young people presented what was most desirable but also possible. To young people, this might have seemed tokenistic and pointless – given that most decisions had already been made.

## Community engagement

As we prepared to launch Hub67 as a real entity it seemed an exciting but fragile time. Young people were still hesitant to completely commit, and the community, or at least an element of it, were negative and apprehensive about the launch. Young people were rather distant in the preparation for the launch, interested only in the celebrity that was going to attend – there was little desire to plan or prepare anything. This was disappointing, but I saw it as a caution – they were still not certain that we were genuine, and they needed to bide their time.

We kept reminding the young people via ongoing outreach and when they came by that the space was for them and that these were (at least in our view!) very exciting times. We might have been seen as being overenthusiastic and indeed perhaps we were, but this had been a long time coming and we felt it was a significant achievement. We continued with patience and continual communication, listening and sharing what was said and felt about the situation. We continued to pursue and uphold what we were starting to identify as the model and to believe in the potential resource the community was about to realise.

## Continual communication and engagement

As the site was prepared, the skate park was moved inwards by two metres to make more room for the new structure, and builders were evident daily. Young people were aware of this and were interested to see activity and progress. Young people named it Hub67, which represented the number that the building previously was, the fact that it would be a hub of activity and no space between the two added an air of uniqueness and modernity. Having something to call the space made talking about it easier and its existence more realistic. A logo was designed by young people and youth workers and began to be used on paperwork and funding applications.

The architects invited community participation and we created and assembled recycled tiles for the outside of the building on wire mesh. They were mobile and noisy but interesting. The building itself was being created out of metal containers and the main open area was double height, bright and airy, but it needed some colour. With the help of the designers, the youth workers engaged groups of younger people (8-10-year-olds) in developing a community chandelier. They used images of the things they liked most about living in Hackney Wick which were enlarged and transferred to Perspex which was then hung centrally from the ceiling. It had an incredible impact on how the room looked. The images included houses, trees, industrial buildings, cars, hamburgers, rats, dogs, gardens and a few shapes which were not so recognisable.

## The launch

Hub67 was ready to launch. There was a programme of workshops, activities and demonstrations lined up for all ages. The building had been furnished with upcycled furniture (revamped by young people), and the street team of young people agreed to be networkers and welcome people to the space. An EastEnders TV actor agreed to open the event, which drew a crowd, and it was difficult to move once the launch had begun. Families filled the space and took part in painting, crafts, alternative arts, steel pan, recycling games, gardening, painting and upcycling furniture, jewellery making and food production. There was a definite 'buzz' about the place and the chandelier was met with cheers from the children who had made it. Two hundred residents came and went, and all seemed genuinely pleased with the building.

Apart from the street team, only 20 young people visited, which was disappointing, but in a sense unsurprising. They were expecting Hub67 to be 'their' space, so perhaps showing up to find residents of all ages in there may have been uncomfortable – yet another 'takeover' by adults or an invasion of their space. Families came with children (10 and under) and happily took part, and once people were in the space it seemed rather small. The seating was sparse, the lighting was harsh, the soundproofing nonexistent, and the microwave was far too small to compete with demand. Overall, though, there was a real sense of community, fun and belonging that I don't think I have experienced in quite the same way before. You could see that people felt heard, that the volunteer hours they had put in had paid off and that most importantly, they and their young people mattered.

Reflecting on the street team, all of them had come to the project either having referred themselves from faith groups or local associations, or they had been recommended to us by schools and the youth service. All of them were looking for volunteering and activism in their communities – they were not merely looking for a space to use. Public sociology would suggest that these young people were already engaged in public conversations, making themselves visible, negotiating boundaries and accruing social capital (Burawoy, 2004; Lipman, 2011). They were challenging traditional inequalities within their community (Bourdieu, 1999; Charlesworth, 2000; Skeggs, 2004). They were civically engaged – in other words, they were confident, articulate, responsible and familiar with associational relationships and networking. In this way they stood apart from the young people who we met during outreach – they had already decided there was value in their community and that they could contribute to it.

## Open access

Intense outreach was undertaken over the following two weeks to ensure that young people knew the hub was opening. There was some excitement and some ambiguity, but over the first two weeks of opening, young people came to see what it was all about. They generally came in small groups or with their parents or siblings. They were unimpressed by the recycled interior and seemed to think it was dull and needed more colour. They liked the open space and the comfortable sofas but wanted to know where the music system was and where they would do sports and dance. Generally, they noticed what we did not have as opposed to what we did. We asked for equipment to be donated and we gathered a substantial music system, TV and computer games, which were met enthusiastically by the young people.

Over the weeks and months, young people came regularly, most straight after school. Some helped to develop the small garden space with donated plants and trees and hand-crafted furniture made from tree trunks and wooden scraps. They added colour by painting the donated tables, chairs and bookshelves which, once finished, looked impressively bright and on-trend. There was a developing sense of the space being 'lived in' by young people and they seemed to be enjoying being together. They developed a computer corner and set their own rota for deciding how and when music and TV would be shared. Some groups simply kept to themselves, keeping to a particular area or sofa, but also shared resources and space when necessary. The ambience when young people were around was energetic but calm, friendly and fun.

## Summary

The lived experiences of young people during this crucial time in the development of the hub were explored and the perspectives of other residents and neighbours were considered. A significant number of young people benefitted from being part of the hub and they recognised it in themselves and their peers. There was a significant nod toward the development of social capital, particularly from members of the street team who talked about their role outside of the hub and in working with and being part of the wider community.

Awareness, self-belief and community link nicely to social capital, and Bourdieu's theories also help to understand youth work practice in these contexts and the element of the model which have a profound impact. Without too much intervention or project evaluation, the principles located in good youth work outcomes were seemingly finding themselves in the analyses of what and how young people perceived their involvement and development in the hub which led to further and deeper reflection on the model itself and the desired outcomes.

# The Hub67 model

This chapter sets out the theoretical and practical model developed at Hub67. It draws together the beliefs, values and practices that emerged through youth work, community dialogue and the development of the Hub. While the model is rooted in professional standards, such as those of the National Youth Agency (NYA), and theoretical principles, it is also shaped by context, tensions and lived experience. The following sections explain the key components of the model and explore how they worked in practice, including where aspirations aligned, and sometimes clashed, with reality.

This chart represents the Hub67 model as it was developed and delivered and suggests theoretical, psychological and educational elements which undermined the youth work team's beliefs, actions and motivations. Much of the discussion so far has touched on the key principles and values which underpin this model, but I will attempt to clarify these and how they work together in this chapter.

## Core beliefs and values

Discussion about the ethical and moral element of youth work was introduced in the late 90s when we began to consider more closely the conversations and relationships that youth workers were having with young people and where our standards and codes of ethics came from (Young, 1999). In many ways, this was a response to changes in society and the lives of young people rather than a particular concern about whether youth work was well placed to help young people develop morally and ethically. To contextualise this in today's mindfulness agendas, issues around ethics and morals provide us with opportunities to appreciate and understand what we do and why we do it. What can be confirmed generally is that all youth work practice would claim to be about doing, being and making 'good' for young people and communities. Table 6.1 identifies the core belief and values which were essential applications to the Hub67 model.

As an adult, I would argue that whether we do good things or bad things is something about our way of thinking and feeling – the way doing good makes us feel and what motivates us to do 'bad' things. I am not so concerned about this in terms of how we deliver youth work, but more about how aware we and young people are about how behaviour impacts others (as well

**Table 6.1:** The Hub67 model

| | | | |
|---|---|---|---|
| Beliefs, principles and values | The therapeutic nature of youth work. Equality in communities. Social justice. Self-awareness. Unconditional positive regard. Safety. | Young people must be:<br>– reflective<br>– included in decision making and outcomes which affect them<br>– heard and included in community development<br>– treated fairly and without prejudice<br>– encouraged to reflect on their actions<br>– encouraged to develop self-awareness<br>– encouraged to develop social capital<br>– be co-creators of open access youth work. | Everyone has a role to play in communities and all have the capacity to change attitudes and values. |
| Local knowledge and culture | Acknowledge local cultural identity and history. Acknowledge different agendas and needs. Prioritise fairly and appropriately. Encourage intergenerational links and programmes. | Young people:<br>– understand and appreciate the neighbourhood<br>– engage with adults and elders from other groups in the neighbourhood<br>– understand and acknowledge all roles in the community<br>– contribute to the culture and history of the neighbourhood. | Community is made up of those who live in it as well as those who once lived there and those who will come. Embrace the change and celebrate the difference. Find your purpose. |
| Professional practice | Team discussion and experience sharing. Outreach. Open access youth work. Networking. Key roles in community. | Continued professional development for youth workers and volunteers:<br>– upskilling, acquiring new knowledge<br>– regular supervision<br>– non-managerial supervision<br>– volunteering and participation<br>– collaboration and networking. | Open access youth work improves the lives of young people and communities. |
| Organisational context | Intergenerational and eclectic boards. Links across organisations. Professional sharing and decision making. Participation and engagement on all levels. | All community members are represented on boards and forums. Encourage relationships between young people and adults both in governance and in social activities. Youth work represented in decision making and development. | Bring the community in and aim for community buy-in. |

**Table 6.1:** The Hub67 model (continued)

| Young people | Self-awareness. Respect. Citizenship. Social capital. | Understand themselves, their impact on others and their community. Appreciate their community, the roles that they play in it and how to choose others. | Empower young people to use reflection to make personal change. |
| --- | --- | --- | --- |

as how we feel about it). Key to the Hub67 model is self-awareness – it is what we strive to fine-tune as youth workers and how we also endeavour to empower young people.

Vital to emotional intelligence, self-awareness is a skill for success which has permeated throughout history (Rhee and Sigler, 2024). Current psychological concepts understand self-awareness as the ability to focus on the self, making comparisons to standards of correctness in the environment (London et al, 2023). Focusing on the self, in other words, enables us to reduce disparities between our actions and our ideals (Rhee and Sigler, 2024). Self-awareness encourages and enables the elevation and evaluation of our strengths, behaviour, learning effectiveness, self-efficacy, self-assessment, resilience and overall performance if we are brave enough to delve into them.

What we want for young people is for them to know themselves, their behaviours, triggers, strengths, areas needing development, their relationships with others and the link between how they are perceived and how they fit into their peer, social, family and community groups. We do this by encouraging self-awareness, utilising the skills and benefits of emotional intelligence and personal reflection. I recall meeting a young man some years ago who was troubled by not getting on with the students in his peer group. In group tasks he was ignored and in social settings excluded. He had taken this to mean that no one liked him and that he would fail his course as no one was willing to work with him on group projects. By encouraging him to look closely and critically at himself and his role in these relationships he was able to identify and remedy, after some time, issues such as personal hygiene, negativity and punctuality – all traits which seemed to be impacting the desire of others to be involved with him.

In another situation, I remember a young woman who was isolated from her peers but who also felt consistently abused and let down by them. Again, by encouraging her to critique her actions and behaviours she was able to recognise that in her desperation to have friends, she was over-compensating and over-promising to others. She felt that people were taking advantage of her good nature, She was offering opportunities or events to others instead of friendship – she would give away her possessions and money in the hope that people would reciprocate in friendship but was then hurt and upset when they took the items happily without giving anything in return.

While unconditional positive regard was central to our practice (Rogers, 1961), it was sometimes difficult to sustain in environments where young people were distrusted or stereotyped by local institutions and community members. We had to rely not only on values but also on consistency with staffing and fostering community tolerance. In communities, simply enabling young people to identify and understand how they (and their behaviour) are perceived by their neighbours can lead to changes in behaviour and social identities. Smith has described the conversations between youth workers and young people as 'encounters of the emotions' (Jeffs and Smith, 2010, p 40) which encourages us to see our endeavours and practices as greater than the transaction of giving and receiving but more as potential for lasting and enriching change in the thinking and feeling young people do in youth work scenarios.

I referred to 'love' earlier in this book as being something that young people were said to have experienced from certain types of youth work practice – and did so rather judgementally. I maintain that it is an emotion best left for familiar relationships and not those in the professional domain. However, Rogers described what counselling clients receive from the therapeutic relationship as 'emotional warmth' and 'attitudes of caring' and 'love' (Rogers, 1961, p 32). So, this indicates something about the strength of emotion and commitment required for unconditional positive regard. It is not youth workers who struggle to understand how to apply this but rather those more concerned with young people's actions and how poor decisions might be judged or punished. For example, the group of young men who were on route for referral to various institutionalised futures when my team decided to take them on were not being rewarded for bad behaviour but were being offered the opportunity to look intensely into themselves and their values in ways that they would nowhere else be invited to do. This was only possible with the application of unconditional positive regard and the belief that we are all capable of change.

By now I hope you will have discovered that while I do consider youth work a tool for education, I do not think of it in formal educational terms – rather more one which makes way for the 'crafting of experiential learning' (Baldridge, 2020, p 751) made up of conversations in equal partnerships where power is equalised (between young people and youth workers). What is different about youth work (as opposed to formal education) is its spontaneity, unpredictability, having to think on your feet, and the in-the-moment opportunities for creative and current ways of learning, and dare I say, 'actualisation' (Habermas, 1987). The 'use of self' (Fusco, 2012, p 1) in youth work has proved key to successful and motivational conversations with and for young people and highlights the therapeutic potential of the work.

As with all youth work safety and advocacy almost go without saying – safeguarding and protecting young people must be the platform on which we stand as youth workers, and the only thing that has changed about this over the years has been the intensity of need and increasing scenarios which require attention. The model highlights this as a value, and, as such, the intention is to ensure young people are safe and secure physically, emotionally and practically.

## Local knowledge and cultural context

A neighbourhood is a place where people live and share amenities and infrastructure and where communities are found (Hatuka, 2024). Communities might be described as 'a place that functions as its centre, everyday facilities and services, internal and external connectivity, social diversity within it or an openness to its enabling, and a means by which residents can be involved in its affairs and speak with a collective voice' (Talen, 2024, p 4699) resonates in this model. Community is the place that helps form collective identity in neighbourhoods rather than anything else. In times when environmental change (regeneration) is dominant, new and collective identities may form and unite or divide depending on their positions.

Acknowledging that the neighbourhood in which you work is made up of a collection of communities is important in youth work – not least because it means there is much to learn but also because there is scope for the development of a 'youth work community' where advocacy and acceptance are key, and dialogue and development are ongoing. That is not to say that as youth workers we should isolate ourselves from others, but more that we gather knowledge and commonalities with them as and when possible, for example, calling on particular groups when interests align and keeping others updated when they perhaps do not. In practice, this means trying not to sentimentalise neighbourhood life but seeing it as 'elastic in time and space' (Hatuka, 2024, p 12).

In Hackney Wick, it was important to acknowledge all communities, however dominant or insular they seemed: from the community of families with children who attended the hub, to the small, four-person LGBT group who met once a month and kept themselves to themselves – the privilege of knowing and engaging with different groups is part of the richness of youth work in communities. Knowing the complexities of community dynamics in an area is something that can only add to the resources and culture that develop over time, enabling heritage and history to exist among what is and what will be. Extensive knowledge of how the neighbourhood is made up, what culture is shared and what potential there is can only help young people in making decisions about their futures and in feeling there is somewhere or something to belong to.

## Professional standards and practice

Adhering to national standards and professional guidelines must always be paramount in youth work practice, not least by way of ensuring we protect young people but also ourselves from adversity. Given the delicate nature of youth work, as professionals, we owe it to ourselves to ensure we are invested in good practice and that we are recognised as so doing. Earlier I identified the NYA professional guidelines and we stood by these in all elements of developing the hub. This model advocates for the very best of professional practice, even when it seems costly.

Practitioners are rarely overresourced these days and are often short on time. However, the Hub67 model was founded on strong youth work team building and strengthening relationships among volunteers and youth workers before anything else. Clear lines of communication between all members of the team are essential as is line management. Knowing how and when to report, share or suggest something in the appropriate forum is built from the delivery and management of an articulate vision and a practical and achievable mission. Transparency and dialogue are key to good teamwork and although I do not intend here to discuss what good management is, it is useful to know that no matter how small or insignificant a project might seem, if it is managed well, it will be much more productive that if it were not.

## Organisational structures and governance

As an organisation, our aim was for inclusive decision making for both staff and young people. Although we aimed for this, in practice it was not always easy to achieve. For example, not all youth workers felt equally empowered to challenge decisions – especially newer staff. We became aware of how internal dynamics could mirror wider power structures, despite our best intentions. Openness was central to addressing this tension – in both governance and team working. We strived to ensure that opinions were treated as equally valid, and decisions, as far as possible, were made collectively. Further, the goal of intergenerational governance met with friction. Older people were sometimes uncomfortable sharing power with young people, and young people often found governance processes inaccessible or tedious. We continue to explore more creative and flexible ways of making shared decision making meaningful.

There may be times when responsibility falls on a few to conclude or act on something, but if the rationale and purpose behind this are shared and understood (not necessarily accepted), there can be no confusion about the outcomes of these scenarios. In other words, we might play different roles concerning power in our working relationships, but if we are aware of and transparent about how this works, we are likely to feel less compromised in challenging situations. For example, whether they have more information or not, managers are always perceived as being more 'in the know' about one thing or another, given their status – this is one of the pitfalls, if you like, of a management role. We always assume our managers have privileged knowledge and control over things that we don't – going to lunch with your colleague who has recently become a manager usually stops once your roles are separated – not because either of you has become a different person but because one of you has moved into a different power level.

Human responses and dynamics are difficult to regulate but once we feel someone has something 'over us' we usually struggle to feel comfortable in the relationship. In this model the idea is simple, being congruent and transparent about things helps – so if you are feeling uncomfortable knowing more about the future than your team – tell them that you are and although it doesn't solve anything, it lets them know that you are suffering too.

## Youth participation and power sharing

When youth workers talk about participation and engagement what they mean is that they are aiming for people (young people or adults) to be 'actively involved in something' (Kellett, 2009, p 44), and in the case of the Hub67 model, this especially meant involvement in decisions that affected the community. Participation for young people is a right recognised in Article 12 of the UN Convention on the Rights of the Child, with numerous models of participation developed over the years, although relatively few consider the perspectives of young people (Hart, 2008; Adu-Gyamfi, 2013). Young people often see the world differently from adults and have varying degrees of being able to express ideas and influence decisions. In this model, intergenerational participation is a way of sharing control and equalising decision-making processes. Ideal scenarios indicate that having young people as board members is a characteristic that funders and supporters appreciate, but there is a fear that this can be tokenistic and impractical. Asking young people to attend a regular board meeting that looks at actions from the last meeting, how much loo rolls cost and which drain cleaner is needed for the changing rooms is generally going to hold little interest for them and few ways of being heard.

Rather than being fixated on young people's participation, it is best to think about the form that their participation takes. There are four different types of participation in this context. Nominal participation is when it is symbolically used to legitimise plans – as in suggesting that young people are involved in decision making. Instrumental participation is where the participation of a particular group is desired for a specific aim or development (as in the development of the hub itself). Representative participation is when members of a community are given a voice in decision-making processes by involving them in consultations and choices, and transformative participation results in the training and development of individuals to change the structures and institutions responsible for marginalisation and exclusion. Youth workers can find creative ways of including young people in decision making, involving anything from running workshops which gather feedback in a variety of forms, operating rotating representatives in meetings (changing personnel regularly), utilising online functions and forums or creating 'speed dating' type events where information is exchanged and gathered. However, when participation is enabled and voices are being heard, it is key to keeping things fresh, creative and inspiring.

Putnam (2000) refers to community participation as a process that strengthens social ties and promotes trust and cooperation, and Freire (1996) sees it as a liberating process in which people become aware of their situation and work together to implement change: taking control of their lives and neighbourhoods with collective aims. Youth participation requires a high level of commitment by young people to their community challenges and is based on the premise that their opinions are important to the improvement of communities. This model encourages understanding the value of young people's opinions and the importance of seeing them as a resource. It abandons apathetic ideas that they are a threat to their neighbours and other community dwellers.

## Outcomes for young people

This model has embedded emotional intelligence and self-awareness as foundations for effective living for young people. Acquiring the skills to recognise and manage emotions, develop emotional competencies, establish positive relationships, make responsible decisions, handle challenging situations effectively, and have concern for others in communities is what we all want for young people, yet these are not skills learnt in schools. When this 'list' of attributes is covered, so too is an individual's potential for good health, citizenship, motivation, achievement and aspiration – happiness. In the next chapter, I provide some evidence that these acquisitions are possible in open access youth work scenarios.

## Limitations and learning

The Hub67 model was built on a strong foundation of theoretical insights, values, community engagement and professional standards. However, we are also aware of its imperfections. The desire to meet every principle sometimes exceeded our resources. There were times when power sharing was challenging or even impractical and other times creative solutions were hard to come by. Some aspects of the model, such as increasing young people's social capital, require long-term engagement that remains challenging in the face of short-term funding and staff turnover. Practitioners continue to reflect on these limitations so that we can continue to improve practice over time.

## Summary

This chapter has outlined the Hub67 model – its principles, practices, values and goals, showing how youth work values such as unconditional positive regard, self-awareness, emotional safety, voice/advocacy and community participation were embedded into everyday practice. At the same time, we have acknowledged where the model encountered challenges or contradictions, especially in negotiating the political context, institutional power and community assumptions about young people. Hub67 offered a flexible and reflective framework, requiring dynamic engagement with its core principles when put into practice.

# The impact and potential of open access youth work

As the Hub became fully functioning and we started seeking funding and permanent support this meant that we were potentially in competition with other agencies and groups in the area and clarity about where I positioned myself was important. I resigned from all boards other than for the Hub. There was some significant movement in terms of ensuring that the project was maintained and sustainable. A centre manager was appointed and tasked with the programme and staff, finance and resource management. A regular timetable of events and opportunities was on offer and young people knew exactly when they could access the Hub. In the context of this burgeoning stability, we were able to see the impact that the hub was having. This chapter draws on data from focus groups and interviews that explored how young people, parents and community members experienced and contributed to Hub67. The sections that follow outline six key themes – maintenance, obligation, freedom of choice, self-belief and awareness, co-creation and community engagement – and how they reflected the young people's experiences in relation to youth work principles, social capital and urban regeneration.

Thematic analysis was used to interpret participant accounts, acknowledging that themes do not simply 'emerge' but are shaped by the researcher's own positionality and perspective (Braun and Clarke, 2006; Bazeley, 2009). As Bazeley (2009) argues, thematic analysis is not neutral but interpretive; it reflects the researcher's own frameworks, assumptions and values. This chapter's thematic structure therefore emerges not just from what was said but how it resonated with the broader context of open access youth work, urban regeneration and my understanding of the power dynamics shaping these conversations.

## The needs and experiences of young people

Focus groups were encouraged with young people in the early stages of Hub67 being open access. This was essentially so that we could find out how they felt about the space, how it was benefitting them and what else could be done to make it a success. There were various responses, largely positive, about the space and especially about the opportunity to be with peers outside of school. However, there were also learnings. Several themes emerged from these sessions which were worthy of exploration.

## Maintenance

This theme centres on how young people identified emotional wellbeing and physical nourishment – especially through food – as key to their ability to function, feel supported and build resilience. This connects to the ethos of holistic care in youth work and reflects structural issues of food insecurity and economic marginalisation, which can limit access to the capital that supports development and engagement. This emerged as a theme when young people were talking about how positive or negative they felt, what contributed and why, and when they felt good about themselves, and things in general. Bourdieu (1964) may well liken these feelings to the wider concepts of social capital such as sociability, social networks, community and civic engagement, social support, trust and reciprocity. However, the maintenance, referred to here is that of functionality, patterns of competent behaviour and effective functioning (Blum, 1998; Morrow, 1998). In other words, it was concerned with their emotional wellbeing and is used as a marker for effective functioning and self-maintenance. Garmezy says 'functional adequacy (the maintenance of competent functioning despite interfering emotionality) is a benchmark resilient behaviour under stress' (Garmezy, 1991, p 403).

To elaborate on this, most of the young people talked about how food was important to them and how it helped them 'function' well. They explained that they could identify when they were hungry by changes in their mood. The food available at Hub67 was not extensive and included snacks, crisps and fruit. There was only a small kitchen and a microwave available so anything more was difficult to arrange.

A group of 12-year-old friends who 'hang out' together in Hub67 explained how they are separated at school, which proves stressful for them. They also talked about how food would improve their experience at Hub67. They explained:

| | |
|---|---|
| Josh: | Well, at school we don't do much together. We are separated all the time. |
| Tez: | Yeah, we are always separated so we don't have jokes. |
| Josh: | Teachers don't like jokes. |
| Jiggy: | Yeah, we not bad, we just like jokes man, and they can't take it – it stresses them out man, and we get stressed all the time. |
| Tez: | They should have some jokes man and they wouldn't be so stressed. |
| Researcher: | So, do you feel differently about the youth workers? |
| Mo: | Yeah, I guess [look at each other] they know how to laugh innit. |

| | |
|---|---|
| Tez: | Nah and yeah. |
| Pete: | They here to help us I guess, like get things ready and stuff. |
| Mo: | Yeh, and get us the food and stuff. |
| Tez: | Ain't no hot food man. |
| Pete: | Nah not really. |
| Tez: | Need chips. |
| Researcher: | So, you would like to get hot food here? |
| Pete, Tez, Mo: | Yeah [×3] |
| Josh: | For sure we do. |

In this extract, the group suggested that their teachers are stressed by their behaviour. They offer the information that they are separated at school, although they are in the same class, and it appears that their teachers see their banter and friendship as 'stressful'. This behaviour is significantly different from that experienced with the youth workers who seem to be unstressed and open to some fun. They also considered hot food as a particular benefit and seemed rather disgruntled that there was none available for them in the Hub.

In this extract, Will explains how he feels about food and in particular hot food:

| | |
|---|---|
| Researcher: | Is there anything that you would like to see here that doesn't go on at the moment? |
| Will: | No, not really, only food. I would really like hot food, like McDonald's or something. It's better to have hot food isn't it. |
| Researcher: | Why do you prefer hot food? |
| Will: | Well, its proper food isn't it, you know like makes you feel good. |

Toni explains here how hot food would improve things:

| | |
|---|---|
| Toni: | I think they should have food here, like hot stuff. Hot stuff makes you feel better and warms you up, you know, like if you have a sandwich at home it's not so much cheery as hot foods. |
| Researcher: | What would hot food mean to you if you could get it here? |
| Toni: | Just happy, you know, inside. |

In these extracts, food plays a dominant role in how young people feel about themselves, they claim that food, particularly hot or 'proper' food makes them feel happy and would enable them to enjoy the Hub more. Regularly evidenced in films, literature and on television, food brings people together, and given this importance and the perceived social nature of food in everyday lives, it could be part of further community formation. There could also be some level of food insecurity that exists within this wider community where concerns are transferred to the young people.

Food became a regular topic of general conversation in Hub67, or rather the lack of it. Young people were strongly identifying and articulating their need for food, not only as nourishment but as something which improved their mental health. Making clear key links between food, nourishment and good feelings might be connected to living in low-income households where food is limited or unavailable, and feelings of being 'unmaintained' or insecure about where their next meal is coming from. Being used to food insecurity works below the consciousness and beyond the control of the will, offering sufferers a sense of how they should respond in everyday life with self-preservation (Bourdieu, 1984b, p 466).

Struck by this comment from Batsleer (2016, p 5): 'laughter and joy are often there somehow when the miserable way things are is being challenged as well as good food to eat', I was encouraged to think about the social and comforting element to food and how it brings people together in doing something enjoyable. This meant that strategies needed to be put in place to accommodate the young people's needs and try to provide hot 'proper' food at least for some of the sessions. Luckily, we were surrounded by willing and entrepreneurial food vendors who helped enormously with weekly deliveries of pizza, pasta, chicken, chips and burgers. We realised this was not sustainable, but at least we had a temporary solution.

## Obligation

This theme explores how young people experience a sense of duty, often arising from hidden caring roles and educational pressure. It links to Bourdieu's concept of doxa (Bourdieu, 1998b) – what is taken for granted within social structures – and offers insights on the idea of constraints in relation to agency. Young people used Hub67 as a space for respite from the obligation and caregiving responsibilities that were limiting their access to capital. Many young people described obligations as being constructed out of their sense of responsibility both institutionally and within their families. A good number (over half) had specific responsibilities. A fair number of these were carers but were not identified as such. Some looked after siblings while their parents worked, some overnight, and others took over responsibility for elders once they returned from school. It seemed that Hub67 had provided some respite for these young people who had heavy care-based schedules.

Young people make positive social contributions which manifest in beliefs and the way we live with others (Kohlberg and Candee, 1984; Berman, 1997;

Gallay, 2006). Obligation or responsibility implies accountability for actions and decisions, being reliable and dependable to others. Active social responsibility is rather like acting on prosocial grounds, with moral, cognitive and identity development in values and actions (Wray-Lake and Syvertsen, 2011).

If your parents need you to take on responsibilities for example, many young people will do so as recognition of their place and importance in the family. Bourdieu considers doxa as a 'taking for granted' (Bourdieu, 1990, p 68) of the world and habitus clive as the tugs at the habitus in which we are involved. This, he says may cause unsettledness.

It is possible that young people who feel obligated also feel torn or conflicted by the two worlds they inhabit, the one which makes requests of them, and the one which enables them to be young. Many of the issues young people raised were related to having to act within others' expectations of them, such as their teachers, parents or neighbours.

Sue, Jon, Sonny and Leo (11–13 years) described their caring familial roles in relation to their availability to attend Hub67 and how it effects their friendships and activities.

| | |
|---|---|
| Researcher: | I see. Is there anything that you do here, at the Hub, that you don't or can't do at home or elsewhere? |
| Sue: | Yeah and no. I can do the same things at home, but my house is so busy that I'm never alone – it's not very peaceful. I have to get involved with looking after my sisters and my nan. Sometimes it's ok, but mostly it's stressful. I can't really make friends cos I can't be there for them – you know - I usually don't know what I am going to be doing next. |

The following young people talk about the Hub and what encouraged them to attend:

| | |
|---|---|
| Researcher: | How often do you come here? |
| Jon: | As often as I can, but I look after my mum, so can't always be here. It depends how she is feeling. I always hope she will be ok. |
| Sonny: | I haven't joined anything regular cos I look after my mum and my sister, and I can't be reliable, but they don't mind, you know. I can just show up when I can. I like it if I can get involved in something, but I just like to come and relax, you know. |
| Leo: | I come here when I stay with my aunty. She's not well and I have to look after her. I take her to church and that. |

Brian and Carl talk about their schoolwork obligations and how they feel about having to put that first:

Brian:    I come when I haven't got any homework to do. I have to get it done cos I get detentions and I hate it. It's not really fair cos some people come here all the time. It's like the school rules you.

Carl:    They do man, like your whole life is down to them. They even stopped me doing karate cos I didn't do some project. It's dread man.

One young person was clearly feeling the pressure of obligation and found Hub67 a haven from it: 'I'm a carer in my family and I know I have to do it but I hate it sometimes. I can't be me or do stuff that I want to. I come here to be free for a while – no one knows I'm here you know – it's where I sort of hide when it gets pish.'

There had been no suggestion from community groups that there was such a significant number of young carers in the neighbourhood, and these comments about young people's responsibilities came as something of a surprise. The idea that young people felt obligated to their families and their teachers (or education) suggests that they must place some value on this. Lowe et al (2016) argues that there is limited agency when one feels obligation above agency and in our 'duty of care' (Miller, 2012, p 45) toward pleasing or caring for others. Kant (1996) refers to allowing individual agency as supporting an individual's 'true needs' (Kant, 1996, p 14). Therefore, there is obligation and duty, as in attending school, and on the other hand, the need for agency and perhaps choosing not to attend school. In many cases, where people feel obliged to behave in a particular way, it implies that the obligation itself has either 'sanction or incentive' attached (Schopenhauer, 1988, p 129) and provides social enforcement of right and wrong (Boeker, 2023). Korsgard (1996) insists that in order to have or achieve agency, we must first believe that there is some value in it and appreciate it as a human right and a social and developmental tool rather than being something they are not entitled to.

I was pleased to know that young people were choosing to use Hub67 as something of a 'get away' from responsibility and that they had the agency to do so, but I also acknowledged that more needed to be done to help them navigate the pressures and stresses that they endured and that perhaps these were areas beyond Hub67's potential. This was not a failing but a very important learning experience.

## Freedom of choice

This theme highlights the importance of leisure and self-directed activity in identity formation in young people. It demonstrates how young people value autonomy and the freedom to explore who they are in a non-pressured setting, which is central to the practice of youth work in supporting the development of self-efficacy. Considering engagement in Hub67 as predominantly leisure time, non-formal and without specific curriculum, we hoped that it would provide young people with the relative freedom to explore new experiences and access opportunities not always available or possible in other environments. Leisure time itself provides space in which to discover, form, define and position identity, either as an individual or as part of a group, and psychologists have ascribed this to how individuals flourish (Gable and Haidt, 2005; Layland et al, 2018).

Sim and Joe (siblings) talked about what motivated them:

| Researcher: | So, your time at the Hub has been motivating for you? |
| Sim: | Yep, very. |
| Joe: | She didn't have much confidence when she was little, and my mum says she has really come on since she has been coming here. We have all noticed a difference in her. |
| Sim: | Shut up. |
| Researcher: | What differences have you noticed? |
| Joe: | She seems happier and more confident and more talkative – she used to be very shy. |
| Researcher: | What about you? Do you think you have changed? |
| Joe: | No not really ... well maybe. I am more confident at speaking out and telling people what to do, but I am older so I should be. I feel good coming here and never get into rows or anything. People are happy to be here, and it seems like you can just be yourself. I get a bit stressed at school and stuff, but it doesn't happen when I'm here. |

In this extract, there is an assertion that Sim's confidence and ability to speak out has improved because of being at the Hub, although it is interesting that it is her brother who describes this and not Sim herself.

| Researcher: | Ok, and what is your favourite thing about the Hub? |
| Jem: | It's fun and no one tells you what to do. Well, I mean not in a bad way. |
| Researcher: | So, what things might they tell you to do? |
| Jem: | Oh, you know, get involved in things, like the activities. But you can just hang out as well. |
| Researcher: | What do you mean by 'hang out'? |
| Jem: | Oh, I mean just sit around and hang with my friends. |

| Sue: | Mmmm, it's nice and welcoming I guess, and everyone is friendly. It's quite organised and there is always stuff to do like making things and art which I like and no one really gets on your nerves. |
| Researcher: | So, do you like doing things on your own? |
| Sue: | Yeah mostly. People get on my nerves. They want me to do things with them, but I don't want to, so they go on until they make me mad. I am best being on my own. |
| Researcher: | And is that something that happens here, are you able to get on with things on your own. |
| Sue: | Yeah mostly. The helpers try and get me to get involved in stuff, but I just go home. |
| Researcher: | So, when you are encouraged to get involved in group activities you go home? |
| Sue: | Yeah. But sometimes I just go and get some food and then come back. |
| Researcher: | Food from home? |
| Sue: | No from the shop. Chips and that. |

This extract demonstrates that the ambiance, or atmosphere, in the Hub is relatively relaxed, and while there are activities on offer on a regular basis, there is no pressure to undertake them, or judgement for not getting involved. There is a culture of being able to 'hang out', which seems to be a popular way of spending time with friends. Even Sue, who admits that she sometimes leaves the Hub to go home to get food, identifies the freedom with which the young people can come and go.

## Self-belief and awareness

This theme focuses on young people's growing ability to reflect on their emotions, behaviours and relationships. It aligns with Freire's notion of critical consciousness (1985), where individuals begin to recognise their agency within structures. This increase in emotional literacy is key to acquiring social capital as it supports trust building, participation and resilience. The theme of awareness came from responses from young people which indicated their awareness and recognition of their feelings and what stressed them. Generally, they demonstrated that they were comfortable talking about themselves, their emotional and psychological experiences and their thoughts. They also showed the ability to be self-reflective, which increased their self-awareness.

| Nin: | I'm in the arts crew and so I get involved with the arts and making sessions – it's really good cos I feel like I have a job [laughs] but I don't get paid [laughs]. People |

always call me bossy you know but I'm assertive, not bossy – don't mean no harm, just know what I need.

In another extract:

Cal:        I used to have racist feelings towards the Romas and those ones who live on the canal. I've gotten to know that it's not right and not true – I ain't a racist I just didn't get it. I do now and I know I'm not the same as them but it don't matter does it, we all gotta jog along.

Some comments from members of the street team:

I never thought I would be doing stuff like I am. I am always doing something for the Hub, like I go to meetings and speak to people. I made a presentation before about how much we need to keep it going and that. And I met with the politicians from Hackney and Newham and talked to them about, the place and that. I have got so much more confident, and I don't feel shy or nervous about speaking. I was, like, shy at school cos I don't like the people and all that but here I feel different.

I have some responsibilities here you know, and I like it. It makes me feel a bit important, like not in charge or anything but like I have things to do and look after, you know. It stops me being bored and I feel good about it.

My mum can't believe that I do all the stuff I do here. She says I have changed so much and got so much confidence now. I suppose I have.

Oh, I do loads of stuff. I'm quite important. I joined the street team and that means I have a lot to say. I go and tell people about the Hub and tell them what we do here and all. I come along to see my friends as well, but I am also one of the team and so I get to do a lot of interesting stuff. I talk to loads of people all the time. I never used to be like that.

These young people have grown in confidence. They say that this makes them feel good about themselves. It also shows that they have developed skills and interests, which they would not otherwise have done. Positive psychology is a way of improving the wellbeing of individuals, building on their signature strengths and increasing their happiness levels (Seligman and Csikszentmihalyi, 2000). There are five elements to wellbeing related to this method which include positive emotion, engagement, relationships, meaning and accomplishments. In breaking apart the comments from the street team there is evidence that they are finding their involvement and the consequential skills that they are acquiring positive and an improvement in their human condition.

## Co-creation

Here, we see young people exercising agency and participating as citizens in shaping their environment – critical dimensions of youth work that go beyond engagement into empowerment.

In one focus group, the subject of the Hub and its community was a significant topic.

| | |
|---|---|
| Researcher: | So, it sounds like you have a lot of support in keeping the Hub going and making things happen. What's it like living in Hackney Wick? |
| Pele: | Ok. |
| Gen: | Alright I s'pose. |
| Zac: | Difficult. It's not an easy place to live in there are lots of ups and downs. But it is becoming more wealth-like, and it will change in the coming years. |
| Tia: | It's a bit poor, but my friends are near, so I like it. My whole family live here, like my nan and grandy, my cousins and my mum's sister, my aunt. |
| Pele: | It's becoming better with the park and the Westfield. You can get anything there you know so it's not so bad. |
| Nic: | I heard it's gonna be the best shopping place in London and with a Primarni superstore. |
| Gen: | Yeah, for sure I am going there. [pause] |
| Researcher: | So, Westfield and the Queen Elizabeth Park will make a difference to Hackney Wick do you think? |
| Zac: | It already does – it has made a big impact. |

These young people identify the difficulties and poverty in the area but are also aware of the changes that regeneration is making to the neighbourhood and they express this in positive terms. They speak affectionately about Hackney Wick and seem to be resolved to the life they live there. However, the advantages they suggest are coming to the area are not particularly local or indeed specifically for them.

Nin, Max and Cal:

| | |
|---|---|
| Nin: | It's changed a lot around here, and then it hasn't. The places where we live and that are the same, but the area is different and busy and seems to be somewhere that people like to be. I suppose it's the bars and music gigs and all that but it's for older people. In a way it's only the Hub that has changed for us, but that's ok. |

| Max: | Yeah, it has. I never used to be doing anything in the community but now I am really involved in it – it's like I am a part of the community, and they know me, like I have met so many people and I know all about what happens in the studios, and I didn't even know they were even there before. It's like I have a lot more knowledge now and can talk about the area and that. |
| --- | --- |
| Nin: | Yeah, I know what you mean cos I have met lots of people who are around here, and they come and do workshops and things and I know things about the area that I didn't know before, like the canal community and the studios and stuff. Some of the artists are quite famous and stuff. |
| Cal: | I saw some of them artists too. At first, I was like, what, but then I got to like them. |
| Nin: | Yeah, I was like that. |

Mia, Nid, Bea, Dan, Pria and Cid add by saying:

| Researcher: | So how do you feel about living in Hackney Wick? |
| --- | --- |
| Mia: | I love it. |
| Nid: | No different to anywhere else, I guess. |
| Bea: | It's alright really. There's always something going on and I know a lot of people. It's fine for me. |
| Dan: | It's got different now cos of all the new shops and bars and cafes and all that. It used to be quiet but now people come here to do stuff. I like it now, it's like it has livened up. My sister and brothers go to the raves and that and my sister says she wouldn't have gone out around here before. It is nicer now. |
| Cid: | Regeneration – it means that these things that are new make us richer but poorer at the same time. |
| Researcher: | Can you explain what you mean? |
| Nid: | It's like the rich people who are buying up the buildings and starting bars and businesses and stuff are going to get richer, but the rest of the people can't do it, so they will get poorer because they can't benefit from it. It's like economics and that. Like the politicians want this place to be a hipster place but people who already live here are just like normal. I don't know how to explain it, but I think I am right. |
| Mel: | Yeah, but that's why we are on the street team cos you get to talk to the politicians and the builders, and you |

can say what you think about it and they do listen. That's how we got this Hub because they realised that children and teenagers are part of the community and have some needs.

Cid: Yeah, but it's like a job and I come here to relax. I don't wanna be doing work and stuff.

Mel: No, responsibility and making decisions doesn't mean a job, it means taking part and trying to make differences.

Dan: Well, it ain't me. I got years of it when I get older, you know.

Pria: I think it's good that people do it cos it makes things better and keeps things going. If no one knows we are here, then we would get forgotten and it could be super boring. I might join a group myself and try and do something.

Nid: You should, you would like it [young person's name].

Pria: Ok. Tell me later.

Nic: K.

Belle: I don't mind trying as well.

Nic: K.

Researcher: So, you have a few new recruits. How will they be able to get involved and help?

Nic: Just come to a meeting. I will tell you when the next one is. It's about a sale we are having. We need clothes and toys and books, I think, that we can sell, and I think we need food, but I can find out.

Cid: I think my sister is doing that. She makes purses and earrings and that.

Dan: I asked my mum to make some biscuits and sweets, but I don't know if she will. But that's what you need right?

Ben: I could ask my mum; she does paintings and cups and all that stuff. She sells it in Dalston, but she could sell it here, I think.

This sums up what the others are saying by suggesting that there is little of beneficial change for young people specifically, other than the Hub, and they clearly feel that the redevelopment and changes are for others. On the other hand, there is a distinct community spirit in the way in which they discuss raising funds and activating support for fundraising. They also make some suggestions about how their interactions with the community can help support the Hub and how their engagement has an impact.

They also show signs of educating or challenging each other, suggesting they can change their attitudes and actions toward the community and participation in it. This and the subsequent extracts respond to all the key themes, community, awareness and self-belief, therefore it is important to include them here.

Fi, Gen, Trish, Zella and Pam:

| | |
|---|---|
| Researcher: | Is there anything that you would say is good about coming to the Hub? |
| Fi: | No stress, no one stresses. |
| Gil: | Relaxin'. Yeah, it's cool and you don't have to do anything if you don't want, but also the things are intrestin', so you want to do them. |
| Trish: | It's good because it's all about us and what we want to do, also we get to do things that you wouldn't expect, like making decisions and being part of what's going on. I don't know how to say it, but it's like being active and aware of the community and that. |
| Zella: | It's called community involvement and it means have an equality say in what goes on. Some of us are joined to teams and we go out to meet managers and business members and discuss what they're doing and sometimes we go to MPs and church leaders and such. We made or joined a street team and that's what I do. I represent all of the kids and talk to people about what we want. |
| Gen: | It's not just him. We all do it. It's not just you [name]. |
| Zella: | I know, but you weren't saying it. |
| Gen: | We all get involved and so we belong to different groups, like the arts crew, the street team and the activities crew, and we do things to support each other and decide on what to do, and because of all of the developments and that around and about we [um] get to meet with developers and [um, um] builders and people to find out what they are doing and so we can add some ideas and say what, [um] young people want. |
| Trish: | It's important to be included and if we are here when we are adults we will understand where it all came from. |
| Fi: | Cos the buildings and developing will happen anyway it's not like we make any changes, you know, but it sort of means we can be included in it. |
| Researcher: | Well, this all sounds rather important. Do you all have different roles and responsibilities, or do you all pitch in? |
| Gen: | Depends on what team you join. Like, if you are street team you go around more and if you arts crew you mainly stay here. |
| Zella: | It's about us building skills as well, like in presenting and speaking. Like I weren't that good at public speaking |

|            | out, but I am cool with doing it now. I do it all the time and I know it will help me getting employment and a better job. I was talking to the Mayor of Hackney before and all of the people that works with him. I dint think I would do that, like. |
|------------|---|
| Researcher: | So [young person's name] are you the spokesperson for the group? |
| Gen: | No, he's not, he just always speaks first, before anyone else. We all do speak and that. |
| Pam: | [enters with can of drink] I'm back… |
| Trish: | Did you get me one? [points to can] |
| Pam: | Nah sorry. |
| Niv: | No one's in charge of the groups, but we all have to commit to them, like if you are in the arts crew you have to come to meetings or say that you can't. But you don't have to join a team, you can just be a member, like. |
| Researcher: | What do you get for being a member? |
| Niv: | Nothing, well I mean you do, like you can come here and join in, but you don't, like do the meetings and stuff. |
| Researcher: | Is that ok then, that some people come but don't do the meetings? |
| Niv: | Yeah. |
| Trish: | Yeah, cos even if you don't belong to a group when something's happening, everyone has to help. |
| Pam: | What you talking about? Can we go now the music is gonna start? |
| Researcher: | Yes of course, thank you so much for talking to me. |
| Pam: | Ok. |
| Trish: | No probs. |

The comments made are significant in how the themes were identified and in the perceptions of the young people as they freely and quite comfortably narrated their feelings and experiences. I also felt that the way in which they were able to quickly respond to a new activity in the Hub was encouraging and demonstrated the way in which they were keen to engage but also relaxed enough to assert themselves.

## Community buy-in

As a practitioner, I have had various inclinations about the involvement of parents in young people's experiences of youth work. Young people invariably recognise and value youth centres as places away from their parents, as a place to be themselves, unjudged and free of familial expectations and obligations. There is a dilemma for me about the controlling role that parents have as decision makers and directors of their journeys. As a youth worker, I want this role to be played by the young people.

Virtually no research into youth and community work includes the perspectives of parents or guardians (DuBois et al, 2002b; Phillips et al, 2004; Keller, 2008; Spencer et al, 2011). Parent and community involvement in formal education, on the other hand, garners significant attention as a pivotal factor in enhancing educational and social development. The multifaceted dynamics of partnerships between parents, communities and educational institutions encourage a holistic approach to young people's academic journeys (Eden et al, 2024). Effective parental involvement encompasses various elements of educational progress, and it is heavily documented those parents of young people who are actively involved in their education exhibit better performance, attendance and social development than those who do not. It is believed that parental involvement cultivates a supportive home environment that encourages learning, reinforcing the schools' efforts.

Community engagement in education has been documented in research, but it often extends beyond parental involvement for wider societal participation in education.

> Local communities play a crucial role in supplementing educational resources, providing mentorship opportunities, and facilitating experiential learning initiatives. Collaborative partnerships between schools and communities enrich the educational experience by bridging the gap between classroom learning and real-world application, thereby nurturing well-rounded individuals equipped with the skills necessary for societal contribution. Furthermore, fostering strong partnerships between schools, parents, and communities serves as a catalyst for social improvement. By promoting inclusivity, diversity, and mutual respect, these partnerships contribute to the creation of cohesive and resilient communities. (Eden et al, 2024, p 3)

Parental involvement is considered a cornerstone for holistic development and broader societal wellbeing (Li and Zhang, 2023). The significance of such involvement, researchers insist, cannot be overstated as it blends the work of the classroom with community fabric (Hamm et al, 2021). Collaboration between parents, communities and educational institutions is celebrated as a way of nurturing the skills and values necessary for meaningful societal contribution (Cordova, 2024). Parents are actively encouraged to engage in their children's educational journey and are criticised and judged when they fail at this (Hsu and Chen, 2023).

There is an argument to support community engagement in education which extends beyond the family unit, enriching the educational experience through diverse perspectives, resources and opportunities (Kelty and Wakabayashi, 2020). However, there is no similar argument to support parental engagement in youth work specifically. This case study in no way attempts to respond to this as the contentions and questions are too wide. However, I will say that parents as community members and resources were not simply incidental in the development of the Hub model. Being part of the engaged community and in, as it were, victims of ensuing regeneration, it was impossible to ignore the parental perspectives on the Hub and their children's participation. I also wanted to understand how they perceived youth work, what they thought about it and how it impacted them as parents and family members.

In this case study then, parents were not only important in terms of their relationships with young people but also as community members, and for this reason their perceptions and experiences were included as monitors of community and young people's progress. For this reason, we recorded parent and carer focus groups and the outcomes were considered in the development of the model.

In a sense, this chapter focuses on the experiences and involvement of the adult community members that were involved in the Hub – namely youth workers and parents and carers. As with all of the focus groups, the data was analysed and categorised into a number of significant themes.

## Satisfaction

Satisfaction was identified as a common theme which emerged from the data, in which the language and descriptions used by the adults addressed issues of fun, affection, young people's (and adult's) morale and activities. In the focus groups, parents were complimentary about the Hub and how their children had experienced it. In these extracts, they describe their children's 'love' of the place and the activities.

Ivy:            They love it here; I can't get them to come home! [laughs]

Ness:           Yeah, mine too, my daughter is besotted with the place, she has become so busy with things and is always up to something. She's done a lot of really interesting things, like visiting places and talking to people and she goes around to council meetings, and I think she is even doing a presentation somewhere.

Dan:            I think my kids love coming here – they just seem to have so much fun.

Ben:            … they have a great time they love telling me what they've done and what's coming next – it seems like they have a new set of fun things to do.

| | |
|---|---|
| Susy: | They are really into it – they love coming and I think they can just get stuck into things, you know, no pressure kind of thing. |
| Petra: | Oh, they love coming, they are always full of it. |

These parents witnessed their children showing affection and fondness for the Hub, activities, events and opportunities. Their children told them about what they had done and showed them examples of things they had made and learnt. There appeared to be enthusiasm coming from the young people as they reported it to their parents, they were keen to talk about new friends and different activities, as well as things they were looking forward to, what might happen the next day or the next week.

The parents indicated that, unlike at school, the young people were pleased and determined to tell them what they had been involved in, as opposed to having to be asked 'how was school today'. During the focus group, this extended a sense of community in that what the young people did in the Hub was an extension of home life and leisure. In addition, the parents made reference to their own feelings about the Hub as being 'welcoming', fun-filled and having a good atmosphere.

The use of positive emotive language in these extracts signifies a strong bond with the Hub and a sense of enjoyment and pleasure. Implying that their children's 'love' in their participation in the Hub is a robust example of pleasure and enjoyment as well as affection for the activities and individuals with which they were involved. The extracts are taken from a focus group in which the parents took part and, overall, the atmosphere was fun, relaxed and jovial. There was laughter and lots of smiling.

Satisfaction as a theme captures not only what was perceived as being how the young people feel about the Hub (and discussed with their family and friends) but also how the parents relay this, and indeed how they describe their feelings toward it. The indications of satisfaction shared by the parents are best described as 'evaluative' and 'descriptive' (Sen, 2009, p 77) since they indicate that resources and conditions influence their levels of satisfaction in this case, and that the Hub is a resource. Nussbaum (2009) suggests a strong relationship exists between capability and wellbeing or level of life satisfaction. Sen and Arneson imply that an individual's capabilities and resulting satisfaction are connected to equality of opportunity (Arneson, 1989; Sen, 2009) and may help to understand the perceptions of parents in this instance, since their children had been offered an opportunity to develop capabilities and learning on an equal level, thus improving levels of life satisfaction.

From a psychological perspective, the pursuit of wellbeing and the achievement of happiness are fundamental enquiries and include expressions of emotional, positive affect and judgements of life satisfaction (Seligman and Csikszentmihalyi, 2000; Seligman, 2002). While happiness is not consistently defined, in literature happiness is associated with various meanings where positive affect, satisfaction and pleasantness are identified as key indicators of overall quality of life (Diener and Diener, 1995). Therefore, it is not unreasonable to consider that the parents' levels of satisfaction were influenced directly by their children's levels of satisfaction and in the sense of contentment or pleasure that this derives.

## Connection

Connection as a theme came from common elements which emerged from the data, which imply links or relationships with others: peers, the community or indeed with themselves, in terms of self-awareness and development. In the following extracts, the parents demonstrate their pleasure in the Hub being located within their neighbourhood and the connections that this has enabled, be it in proximity or in the way they can link with neighbours. Some of the comments from parents demonstrate their feelings about how their children benefitted from participating in the Hub.

| | |
|---|---|
| Petra: | There is a sense of community here. I have noticed that a lot of people pop in, and during the day there seems to be loads going on – I quite fancies the yoga but haven't got here yet, but I know my neighbour does some sort of craft thing. |
| Susy: | My daughter has made so many friends here. At one point I had eight of them coming to collect her. It's been amazing for her. I am so chuffed. |
| Al: | I must say, from a friendship side of things, they have developed a stronger bond with each other and also made new chums too. They have always played with our neighbours, but they have also met new ones and it seems to have grown. It's great, I am all for it. |
| Yasmin: | A bit like me, I live on the canal and so although we do move around a lot, we always end up here because we love it – there is a real sense of community and energy and I'm just always happy when we are here. It bothers me that my kids don't always make firm friends as we are on the move all the time, but the Hub has given them a kind of base and they have a network of mates, which is lovely. |
| Bes: | I work a lot so don't get around here much and that, but my missus has met up with people and that and yeah, my kids have loads of kids they know now. |
| Ivy: | Yeah, but kids are kids, and they don't really see things like we do, do they? They play around with their |

friends, they go to school together, they either get on or they don't. The kids I know around here all rub along together good. But you see all of the new-fangled clubs and pubs around don't relate to them and so they don't get it. But for the adults, it cuts them off even more – I can't afford to go to these bars, and I wouldn't feel comfortable in them either, but the kids don't see it. They just like being part of something.

Susy:  I am happy living here; I like the diversity and the open space is amazing, there is so much to explore and learn and I really like the creative vibe and the colour. I'm a dog walker and so for me it's perfect. I don't think I would feel the same without the people that I know here, and I guess it's the same for the kids.

Researcher:  Do you think the Hub has made a difference to your children?

Eva:  Yeah, they do like coming and getting involved in things, they seem to push, or encourage them to do things, you know, like take part in meetings and all of that, they seem to include them in what they are doing and not just tell them what to do, if you see what I mean. The make networks that way, if you know what I mean.

Ivy:  Oh yes, it has. It's made a big difference to them, they come together and learn things and get to know about where they are, you know.

Susy:  I'd say so, it has given them inspiration, knowledge and ideas and new friends.

Nic:  Oh yes, I think so, they have some space and new energy, and people are interested in them and they like it. I think it's great to have youngsters involved in the community and in politics and what makes the world tick.

In these extracts, the parents are positive about the Hub and their children's involvement. They are pleased that their children have made or maintained friendships with local children and that they have a deeper connection with their peers. In the focus group, the parents talked warmly about the sense of community that they felt emanated from the Hub and said they had met and conversed with neighbours and other community members on many occasions while meeting their children before and after sessions. They also liked that the Hub was conveniently located close to their homes and workplaces. In addition, they were keen to note that their children had developed socially and had added to their social networks, as had some of the parents. They also commented on the sense of isolation that living in the neighbourhood can create, as it lacks resources and is set away geographically from the rest of the borough. They expressed their relief that Hub67 had made some differences to this in that there was a greater community connection and network as a result of its existence.

One of Putnam's key themes concerning social cohesion is voluntary association and the development of social networks (Putnam, 1993). The parents' narratives suggested that trust was a significant factor in how they perceive their children's involvement in the Hub, since they are clear about the benefits, especially those which demonstrate a relaxed and optimistic way, indicating there is little concern about the provision (Seligman et al, 2005).

One of Bourdieu's theoretical theories of class claims that socially effective communities put an emphasis on the function of power and conflict. Bourdieu maintains that social relationships increase an individual actor's ability to advance their interests and generate social capital as a resource in the absence of social struggles (Bourdieu, 1984a). A lack of social struggles might suggest that trust has been 'rewarded' by the positive development of communal relations (Newton, 1999, p 8) and benefits have been gathered because of past struggles and integrative values. Siisiäinen (1989, p 3) refers to this as 'brave reciprocity', when the short-term interests of a group are well functioning, based on generalised trust in voluntary networks and associations.

## Learning

Learning refers to individual, group and community learning. In the focus groups, the parents spoke about how their children had learnt because of participation in the Hub. They relayed scenarios and descriptions of how they had identified learning in their children's behaviour, activities and knowledge with enthusiasm, and were precise about the area of learning. This theme came from focus groups which evidenced four different areas of learning expressed by the parents. These included practical and skills development and in, say, crafting, but largely those which are evidenced by end products, such as paintings. Parents also discussed the acquisition of knowledge about local history as being a positive educational element of their time in the Hub and, indeed, of the wider community. In addition, the parents describe their children's confidence in speaking out as being a sign of advancing confidence and self-awareness.

The following extracts relate to how the parents considered their children's learning at the Hub:

Eva:        No worries, I was just going to say I see the staff encouraging them and working really hard to get them involved in things and it's great cos they do it with such passion and it rubs off on the kids. It's great. I think they learn a lot. My [young person's name] has gone all public speaking and super confident – she's a different person really - she used to be so shy.

Ron: I don't know if they learn anything and that, but they bring stuff home that they've made and that, you know, like paintings and all that. Oh, and they made T-shirts, I think.

Susy: Exactly that. Mine are so interested in everything that's going on around here now and they tell me stuff all the time. The other day they were telling me about the fact that rubber was invented here, I mean amazing stuff. I agree that they are more confident and seem to have grown up, I would say.

Ivy: I don't know much about politics to be honest, but my boys are learning about it, you know, like meeting the local ones and that and they are getting really interested in it. Good for them, I say.

Petra: I think that [young person's name] is getting more confident since she's been coming here and certainly is more vocal and talks for everyone. I think it's given her a sense of purpose in a funny sort of way.

Deli: Oh yeah, my kids take what they do here very seriously – they think it's important and they like to tell the other kids and us what's going on and what's changing and all kinds of random information – but they like knowing it and sharing it, you know.

Mic: I like, didn't really take a lot of notice, like, before but since they've been on the street team, my kids have like made me interested in it, like I look forward to hearing what they've been doing and finding out and like, they do talks and like presentations and I like, feel proud of them. They know more than me about this area than me, that's for sure.

Ivy: You see I speak my mind, and what you have always had here is the traditional east end, working-class families. Poor mainly, but content with their lot, you know. It's always been quiet and a bit cut off, but people have always known each other and looked out for each other. Now I've got nothing against all the artists and creative people, but at one time they were all working away, and no one really knew about them. Now they are all over the place and doing this and that, murals and all that and the new bars and clubs and all that is opening, and most people don't want it, you know, it scares them.

|       | They don't understand the hippy types on the canal, no offence, or the trending groups, and they feel like they are being ousted out because they are definitely not being included. But everyone wants to learn, you know, and then make choices. This place is a great thing, really and I want my kids to learn all the options and to make up their minds about stuff and learn all the time. |
|-------|---|
| Mel:  | You know I didn't think about the Hub as being educational, but you know, I think it is. They learn to do things and all that, but they learn about their surroundings and their neighbourhood, and I can't fault that. It's like a good way to educate them without all the hassles of school. |
| Blue: | I agree. I think there is so much learning you can do without school, at the end of the day, what you learn about yourself is the most important learning you can do. Schools are so stuffy and formal that no one ever gets anything out of them, but learning about who you are and where you come from serves you for life. |
| Petra: | My kids are so much more confident now. They literally talk to anyone and everyone and have become assertive and mature. I am not sure whether it wouldn't have happened if they didn't come here, but it definitely seems to have happened very quickly. |

These parents' responses provide even more evidence that they recognise the social educational elements of their children's involvement in the Hub. They mention practical skills and techniques which they have developed and changes in their interpersonal skills and behaviours. They talk in social capital terms about the acquisition of this without identifying what it is.

In 1943, research into British youth clubs declared them 'training places in the social art of citizenship' (Morgan, 1943, p 102), and some 70 years later they still maintain (those which have survived) an important place in civil society as the UK continues to focus on young people's citizenship education, moral fortitude and their leisure activities as part of a wider global context (Mills and Kraftl, 2014). Indeed, the National Citizens Service scheme, (previously discussed) declares informal education as being about the lessons that cannot be taught in schools. There is, undoubtedly, a diversity in definition and understanding of informal education since it refers to a number of everyday and spontaneous learning experiences that vary across contexts and should be a process of learning which flows from the day-to-day concerns of young people (Falk, 2009).

As the parents indicate, there is a reliance on positive associations around the Hub, which in turn is dependent upon dialogue and conversation and strong relationships between youth workers (educator) and young people (educated). Such relationships are founded on trust, affinity, respect and even affection (Jeffs and Smith, 2005), in an environment in which young people are encouraged to reflect on their lives in a supportive environment (Young, 2006), or rather where they are learning from life (Freire, 2008).

## Youth workers

The youth workers were key to the development of the Hub in the acquisition of funds and support, and in the associations and relationships they established and maintained with young people and the community. Although there were obstacles and challenges that had beset the project in what was at times a constantly interrupted and rarely simple trajectory, most of the youth workers were happy to continue work at the Hub. It was important to include their perspectives on the benefits to young people. We also include the perceptions and understanding of open access youth work as identified by the parents of participating young people.

## Reflection

It was important to have an idea of how the youth workers had experienced their interactions with young people at the Hub and how if at all, they believed they had seemed or made a difference in any way. The themes which emerged from the data were positive action, investment and reward. The following extract is from a focus group with the youth workers.

Researcher:     So how has it all been?
YW1:             It's been an uphill battle, from the start – never really knowing whether we were going to be able to do this or not. But it's such a relief and a pleasure that we have managed it and that the young people have had such a positive experience. I am so proud of them. They have been amazing, and I couldn't ask for anything more.
YW2:             It's been amazing, to be honest. I am so pleased with how it's gone and how the young people have responded and engaged, you know, they are such a great bunch, and they really seem to love it here.
YW3:             The young people are brilliant. I am so pleased with them and what they have achieved and how they've taken to this and all. You know, they have just got stuck in and really engaged with the place and the community. It's all been good fun and rewarding.

YW4: Yep, it's been good. They are great individuals and I'm really proud of them.

YW5: Yes, I agree, they've been brilliant, and I am so pleased to have been a part of it.

Researcher: So, you use positive words to describe the young people, like brilliant, great and your experiences similarly. Why do you think that is?

YW4: Well, I guess it's because that's how it's been. Everyone has had fun and engaged, and made connections, you know.

YW5: Yeah, I suppose it's about how we view the young people. They are full on when they're here, they are happy and interested and [um] I suppose that rubs off on us, in a way.

YW2: I definitely get a buzz being here and I know that comes from the young people, as they are always on a high when they are here and, yeah it rubs off.

Researcher: Are you saying that everyone is happy and having fun while they are here?

YW2: Well, I suppose most are. There's always someone who is a bit down or not engaged, I guess.

YW3: Mmmm, well not everyone has fun all the time, but it's not a problem if someone isn't on top of the world as they can just hang out, really, and just be whatever they want to be, really.

Researcher: But it sounds like you expect the default to be having fun, am I right?

YW4: Well yes, I guess we do, we want them to have fun and if they're not, there is other work to do, I guess, if you see what I mean. You gotta find out why they're not happy and try to help them to sort things out, I guess.

YW2: Sure, we want them to enjoy it here but if they don't, we don't judge them, we try and work out how to make it fun.

YW5: I think what we mean is that if they are down or not interested in something, that's ok, but we would look for ways of getting them involved or find something else for them to do, or just talk to them, find out what's wrong.

YW3: I think the fun thing is a bit misleading, I think what we want is for the young people to want to be here, whatever mood they're in and we do our best to work with them on whatever level they engage.

Researcher: You also talk about them engaging, what do you mean by this?

| YW4: | It means that they engage in relationships with us, they're happy to discuss and interact on a personal level, like on a one-to-one basis. |
| YW5: | I think it means that they engage in the process of youth work which involves respectful relationships based on trust and respect, mutual trust and respect. |
| YW2: | It's about them wanting to be here and developing relationships with us so that we can get to know them and work out how best to support or signpost them, as and when needed. It's also about them having a voice and being heard – like in real time. |

These extracts suggest that the experiences young people have, according to the youth workers, should be positive and fun-filled and that this, in turn, influences how they feel about their work. Engagement implies (according to their responses) that young people enter into adult-youth relationships willingly and voluntarily and that these engagements promote further development and association. The element of pride and pleasure that the youth workers articulate is somewhat vague in interpretation since it is challenging to understand how pride might be felt in environments which do not have some kind of membership or investment. Therefore, it is appropriate to suggest that the youth workers see what they do with young people as a genuine investment in the process and the relationships – leading to pride and pleasure when positive outcomes are observed.

Positive action through reflection essentially requires some objective reality (Bowling and Windsor, 2001) which is constituted by the social world (Graney, 2022). Positive action and reflection are interlinked in youth work practice. In reflective practice, we are encouraged to think about what we have done and how we have worked with young people to help us be the best we can be. Understanding the role that our personal and professional values play in our work is essential and helps us formulate our professional identity. Confident, competent work can be derived from reflection and learning from it.

To elaborate on the use of reflection, the links between reflection and practice must be seen as inseparable (Ghaye, 2010). Reflective practices help us to understand the links between our practice and how to improve our effectiveness (through practice). In other words, when we reflect on what we have done we can develop ideas about how what we did could be improved. Reflective practices also help us understand the links between feeling, thinking and doing. How we feel affects how we think, which affects what we do.

Reflection is often described as organised thinking. What do we think about? Perhaps feelings, as our work is influenced by emotions (how you feel and how those you are working with are feeling). Our work is also guided by what we are feeling and the context that we find ourselves in.

We understand our practice by looking backwards – but work is about looking forward. It is important to reflect on the here and now – how the context might have changed and what is to come, what happened or what we would like to happen. The power and potency of reflection help identify and amplify what we can do, not just what we can't. It is important to reflect on strengths. It is not always necessary to see reflection as being useful in problematic experiences. We must also reflect on our successes. This helps get rid of the negative feelings that might be associated with reflection (Ghaye, 2010).

Reflection is triggered by many things. We usually think of experiences as going well or not and, in practice, it would help us to draw upon the positive element of our internal queries, asking ourselves questions like 'How effective was I?', 'What is a better way of doing this?' and 'What do I want to happen next?'. Reflection-with-action assumes that we need to be clear about what particular kind of action we have in mind. Reflecting carefully on our work, who we are working with, and where and when can make prioritisation easier. We can usefully think about what we need to do immediately, as well as what can be left until later. Something else to consider is any distinction between what we feel is important and what others feel we should work on. It also enables us to distinguish between what we feel we can do and what must be done. The more specific we can be, the more likely we are to be successful in developing our practice.

## Investment and reward

In these extracts, the youth workers mentioned how and in what ways they felt the young people they worked with benefitted from open access youth work. They considered their work toward young people's development and what they had contributed in order to make it possible, hence the notions of investment and reward in this theme - reward being the advancements or achievements of the young people themselves.

They said:

YW2:    I think they get a lot out of being involved because they keep coming back. It's not just about us, it's also about them getting time to be with their friends and other young people and time to be themselves. You know, young people don't get much opportunity to be themselves without being judged or monitored in some way, do they?

YW3:    They don't, but I don't agree we don't monitor them cos that implies we don't, and we do – we watch how they behave and interact and develop all the time. If we didn't, we wouldn't know how well we were doing with them, or how well they were doing with themselves or others – if that makes sense.

YW5: Yeah, it does, but we do it in a way which is not judgemental or instructive – so their parents might tell them off for something, but we would talk to them about the same thing in a different but equal way – not as a parent.

YW1: Transactional analysis – we talk to them and deal with them on an equal, adult-to-adult level, that's why.

YW2: Sometimes that is harder than it sounds though, if they are not in adult mode then they are still acting like children, and you can't always get them to shift out of it. But I agree that's what we aim for.

Researcher: So, you think that talking to them as equals, or as adults, is beneficial to them, in what ways?

YW1: Of course, it encourages them to see people as equals and not adults making decisions about or for them, and they are able to rationalise, reflect and understand things, like how they impact other people through their behaviour, how they develop values and what they want to value and who and all. They can see things from a different point of view but also know that they are having an open and non-judgemental discussion or intervention with someone.

YW2: Yes, and they learn that thinking as people as equals and being equal to others is positive for their minds and behaviour.

YW4: It has to be of benefit, they don't experience it anywhere else, or it's unlikely that they do.

Youth workers often use transactional analysis theory in describing or carrying out their work (Merton et al, 2004; Davies, 2005; Ord, 2009a), particularly in relation to the period of development when young people are breaking away from their parents emotionally and psychologically (Biddulph, 2000). The way adults and young people see and interact with each other requires greater parity and process than most other adult/young person exchanges impose (Davies, 2005), and this often helps in defining the relational dynamic between youth workers and young people in professional settings (Ord, 2009b). Transactional analysis (Berne, 1964) models can be complimentary, successful and uncomplicated as well as mutually beneficial, yet when crossed or confused it can be antagonistic, not mutually beneficial and can break communication altogether.

Further extracts give some insight into how the youth workers perceived their experiences:

Researcher: What do you think young people have learnt as a result of their involvement in the Hub?

YW4: They've learnt loads, how to communicate better with each other, without cursing and cussing. They've learnt how to interact with people they don't know, appreciate people they don't know and not be so insular and protective of their space or environment.

YW2: I think they have learnt to be young people without fear of being called out or oppressed in some way. They are so used to being told to move on or shut up that it took them a while to work out that it was ok to be noisy or funny or just loud.

YW5: I think a lot of them have grown in confidence and realised that they can have fun, or ask questions, or just sit and chill without being judged and that what they say has value, they are important and people can listen and take notice, as well as have a positive relationship with them. I remember when we started here the number of them who expected me to tell them off or ban them or things like that, because that is what they were expecting. I think they've actually learnt that they can expect adults to be respectful to them and perhaps understand them.

YW2: They've gained a place in their community, I think. They were kind of silent contributors in a sense and certainly didn't have a space or place in it. The ways they have become active and involved in the community has been amazing. They know so many people and they get opportunities and invitations to learn and take part and even give advice on things and, you know, I am sure this would not have happened before, you know, it's like they are suddenly part of the community as opposed to being on the outskirts of it. They even tell us about things that are going on and places they've been and people they've met and all that – I feel strongly that it's made such a difference to them, definitely but also to the community – I can't really explain it, but it's like young people are seen now whereas before they just weren't. No one really cared what they thought or did and they definitely weren't, you know, asked to get involved in anything.

YW4:     Yeah, I agree with that too. They have given a lot back as well as got a lot out of it, and they are confident and assertive, and no one can boss them around anymore. They have a right to be here and they know it. They get invited to more things than we do, and they love it.

YW3:     I do too. The community is much stronger for them, I feel. They have brought such vibrancy and enthusiasm to things and people like to hear what they think and how they feel about stuff – they are confident and make decisions and speeches and all kinds of stuff that I don't think they would have done before. They are not scared to tell councillors what they think or what they need, and if people don't agree with them, they are able to argue in a way which makes people listen. I'm proud of them.

In these extracts, the youth workers identify the young people's progression and development as significant. They talk about their ability to interact with peers, adults and the community with confidence. They consider community engagement which has impressed and influenced as well as refreshed. In regenerated environments there is often aspiration for increased citizen participation and responsibility (Etzioni, 1996; Giddens and Pierson, 1998; Tam and Tam, 1998; Rogers, 2000) and 'community capacity building' (Duncan and Thomas, 2000, p 7), and it appears from the data that young people have indeed fulfilled this in part. This, given all we now know about social capital implies that they will also have gained a great deal of this within their neighbourhood.

Anti-social behaviour among young people is largely associated with neighbourhood disorganisation, dilapidation and limited resources (Lipsey and Derzon, 1998; Speer et al, 2001), along with a perceived lack of interest in politics on any level. Seen to be part of the condition of childhood (Buckingham, 2002), we generally expect that young people will not want to engage positively with their neighbourhoods. Civic virtue (Hart, 1992; Putnam, 1995) is a theory which could happily be entrenched in open access youth work philosophy as we refuse to exclude young people from democracy or political affairs. Young people engaging in civic education and action in the neighbourhood not only suggests a renewed or invigorated interest in their community but also empowers them to contribute and invest in it.

## Community feedback

This section offers insights into emergent citizenship where young people are contributors to social change and capable of bridging community divides.

As a final strand to the question of young people and their communities, I ventured into a previously unexplored area for the case study. The intention was never to evaluate young people's progress communally, nor did I deem it important at the beginning to gather feedback from members of the community who were not involved directly in the Hub. There was something that puzzled me about the negative and stereotypical comments and concerns that were shared earlier on in the case study where the elder community were fearful and resentful of resources being given to young people. I wanted to know more about this in relation to the provision of the Hub and credit it with more than what might be considered generational difference.

I decided to tackle this in several ways, first by revisiting tenants' and residents' groups to establish whether there had been any change in their experiences since the Hub had been in existence. Second, I decided, with the young people, to invite community members to the Hub to experience it as young people did. And finally, I wanted to attempt a kind of intergenerational skills exchange where elders could pass on skills and knowledge to the young people and vice versa.

In residents' group meetings there was an acknowledgement generally that young people hanging out and making noise had decreased since the Hub opened. There was apparently less litter and lower numbers of young people seen on the streets, at bus stops and outside shops, although this did still happen. I am not certain that I felt a softer style in responses from community members because I wanted to or whether it was real but there was absolutely a verbalised sense of relief and, dare I say, gratitude that young people had somewhere to go. If I am being honest, I heard what sounded like people being pleased to know where young people were most of the time.

Fred:          It's definitely quieter around my corner now and I hardly see any youngsters these days.

Iada:          Mine too – not as much litter either – it is better.

Manny:      It's good to know they've something to do, somewhere to go. Keeps your mind at rest I suppose.

In planning to invite members to the Hub, the young people wanted to have a tea and cake party, offering this as well as opportunities to take part in activities that they facilitated. I found it amusing that they wanted to have tablecloths, napkins, teapots and proper plates (not paper) for when their neighbours visited. So, we cobbled together a collection of these, and the young people set it all up. They had made posters as invitations and delivered them to shops and public spaces in the hope that many would turn up. They picked flowers to put on the tables, although I am not sure I want to know whose garden these came from! It did look lovely, and the young people were very proud of it. I was relieved to say the least when people started to arrive and seemed enthralled by the space and the young people in it. Some of the young people were visibly excited to be hosting and showed confidence, care and enthusiasm in sharing card games, arts activities and tea.

Others were quiet but focused on helping their visitors have a good time, checking when they wanted more tea or cake or whether they wanted to be shown around.

There was a lot of smiling going on, which felt good to me, and the elders left, I think, in a positive mood. It was clear that the young people had been pleased and proud to show off their space and to look after the elders. The elders too, I think, felt pampered and special and were able to engage with the young people without fear or stress and saw them as caring and interesting individuals. My hope was that these attitudes would prevail, and that on both sides of the generational stage, individuals would maintain a non-judgemental and open-minded approach to each other.

Intergenerational learning has been the informal vehicle within families for 'systematic transfer of knowledge, skills, competencies, norms and values between generations – and is as old as mankind' (Hoff, 2025, p 69). Typically, the elders share their wisdom in a valued role in perpetuating the values, culture and uniqueness of the family. This is often to keep new generations grounded in the history of their culture and to provide a link to the past. However, in more complex societies, intergenerational learning increasingly, occurs outside the family. I had been aware of primary schools developing project with elderly people in care homes but never heard of similar projects in youth clubs.

However, there is a wide and developing IG (intergenerational) community of thinking where older and younger generations engage in shared activities with the aim of improving social, psychological or health outcomes, such as relationships or attitudes between groups. It seems that IG programmes have encouraged older people to impart wisdom and positive social behaviour to young people at the same time as feeling useful (Webber, 2024). Older people also report increased confidence, a better sense of wellbeing and reduced isolation as a result of attending IG projects. Recent studies have recorded that older people have appreciated and benefitted hugely from contributing to what they perceive as the development and success of a younger generation (Lai and Burchett, 2021; Leek and Rojek, 2021).

For young people, the IG programmes offer opportunities to develop self-awareness and experience personal growth engaging with older adults who share a wealth of knowledge and wisdom. Young people, too, have reported heightened confidence in themselves. Social contact and the perceived acceptance of them by older people is reported to facilitate improved social and practical life skills for them (Forrester-Jones et al, 2004; de Souza Briggs, 2007). It is also reported that both older and younger people have welcomed the opportunity to debunk stereotypical assumptions about each other.

Setting up the IG group session was not as easy as it might have been. A group of young people were motivated by the idea, which was helpful, but I realised that the recruitment of the older people needed some planning. I was confronted by some (not many) of the elders who thought that they certainly 'could teach the young people a thing or two' and others who had skills and ideas to share – needless to say, the best people were those who came forward, and the session went ahead. Again, the young people played host to their neighbours and welcomed them into their space. There was a lot of sharing of ideas and some practical demonstrations (like knitting and woodwork), but overall, there was a sense of friendship, support and empathy. It was clear that if relationships were going to be strengthened, more of this time together was needed, but as a start it seemed fruitful. The young people enjoyed hosting and seemed to enjoy learning about the lives of the elders. The older people felt heard and seen and made some strong statements about the young people.

| | |
|---|---|
| Mary: | Well I've really enjoyed the day, thank you. I was pleasantly surprised that the youngsters were polite and kind and I have liked being here with them. |
| Ron: | I think the kids get fed up easily and so we couldn't finish what we were doing but that's just it, isn't it. They liked my workshop, and they'll remember a few things about the war and that. It has been a good day. |
| Chris: | I wasn't looking forward to this to tell you the truth, but it has been lovely. The children have been polite and kind and very keen to get to know me. They have been completely different to what I was expecting, you know, and thank goodness for that. I've enjoyed getting to know them and won't be worried about bumping into them again. |
| Dave: | My wife thought I was bonkers to come here you see and yet I have had a lovely time, you see, and I can't say better than that. I've found the youngsters to be so thoughtful and not at all noisy and rude, you see. I will go home and tell her they are not all bad at all, you see, and that's a surprise. |

## Reflections

There was a high degree of positivity from the adults, as to their feelings and appreciation of the work undertaken in the Hub, both from parents who have witnessed their children's development and from youth workers who have facilitated this development. Although older people described effective experiences with young people in the Hub, they did not associate this with youth work but more directly with the young people themselves.

The landscape of Hackney Wick had changed beyond recognition over the course of this case study, not so much in the context of social housing or in resources and amenities available to the working class community but in the number of luxury apartments, bars, cafes, restaurants, yoga studios, galleries, music venues, elite cycling stores, cultural interest companies creating high-priced recycled fashion and homewares, and vintage furniture 'salons' selling dining tables and table lamps featured in high end lifestyle magazines and platforms, all at astronomical prices. A new and vibrant night-time economy has emerged, attracting ravers, revellers and drinkers into the early hours becoming an emblem for Hackney Wick.

Apart from the promise of some concrete table tennis tables situated under the flyover, and a static outside gym on one of the public parks, there was little that had changed to improve the lives of those who could not afford the designer leather bags and cocktails on offer to new residents, nor was there much to enliven their day-to-day struggles.

The Hub had provided a space for young people and families to feel connected, to meet with each other without feeling misplaced or judged, and where they would be welcomed and made to feel comfortable, where the offer of a coffee and cake did not come with apprehension about the cost, and where, perhaps most of all, their children were not feared, deemed a nuisance or ignored. This comes amid a climate of concern about young people in public, and policy discourse among politicians and local authorities on the lack of youth and community work, devastating knife crimes and the rising concerns about children and young people being coerced into gang affiliation. The Hub provided an appreciated function in Hackney Wick. A safe and secure space where parents knew their children were occupied, respected and cared for. A space where young people did not have to be fearful of being in the wrong place at the wrong time, where they enjoyed making friends, being listened to and learning new things about themselves and their community.

At the start of this case study, the local dynamic included predictive poor social and psychological outcomes for young people based on stressful circumstances, poverty, familial complexities and being at heightened risk of adversity. I have also discussed the need for young people to experience conditions which enable them to function effectively in everyday life and maintain good mental wellbeing. Young people's development is generally measured by their ability to adjust and achieve at various stages of their life cycle. However, these are largely associated with their ability to establish and maintain friendships, follow rules of prosocial conduct, participate in extracurricular activities and crystallise a cohesive sense of self (Masten and Coatsworth, 1998).

Young people's self-awareness encompasses their ability to believe in themselves, think and develop individually, and recognise their mental health and wellbeing (Garmezy, 1993). Many studies identify resilience in young people as being enhanced by relationships with at least one caring, competent, reliable adult in social settings (Richmond and Beardslee, 1988; Resnick et al, 1993; DuBois et al, 2002a; Holloway et al, 2008; Miller and Coll, 2007). It makes sense that relationships with youth workers at the Hub were indeed enjoyed by young people and identified by their parents as essential to their participation and development in terms of their engagement and ongoing confidence.

## Summary

This chapter explored the lived experiences of young people and their communities through key themes identified in participant data. These themes, while rooted in participants' words, were shaped by my interpretive lens as a practitioner-researcher. Concepts such as obligation, freedom, co-creation and connection reveal the interplay between emotional wellbeing, social capital and structural conditions. Importantly, they show that youth work does not operate in a vacuum – it is constantly negotiating with community expectations, institutional pressures and regeneration politics. Hub67 offered a space for agency, connection, engagement, learning and even enjoyment, though not without its challenges. These reflections contribute to a deeper understanding of what open access youth work can achieve in shifting urban landscapes.

# What now for young people and youth work?

In this chapter, I will pull together the youth work model which evolved as a result of this case study and explore and identify important implications for open access youth work practice in the future. I have structured it in three parts: first, I summarise the key points from the study; second, I highlight the implications for youth work professionals; and finally, I summarise the contribution that this study has made to youth work practice and research to solidify the model. In pulling these strands together, I also draw on Regime Theory (Stoker, 1995) to explore how collaboration and power dynamics shaped the delivery of youth work within an urban regeneration context. Regime Theory highlights how coalitions of public, private and civil society actors come together to govern communities and steer development priorities. It draws attention to how decisions are made, whose interests are served and how power is distributed in urban contexts. In the case of Hackney Wick, regeneration decisions often excluded youth perspectives, a problem that Hub67 sought to address.

This case study set out to determine what the contribution of youth work was to the lived experiences of young people in a contemporary urban setting. The aim was to identify how open access youth work, its opportunities and challenges were characterised and conceptualised by young people and their community. To contextualise this, the origins of the study were set following the regenerative development following the London Olympic Games in 2012 but went far beyond this over eight years. The ever-emerging landscape of Hackney Wick provided the backdrop for the study as it changed beyond recognition amid a residential community with no choice but to endure it.

Considerable changes have been made throughout since the completion of the case study both locally and nationally around young people and youth services – not least a new government promising to put resources back into youth support. The local landscape has been almost completely reimagined. Hackney Wick has changed dramatically. Factories and derelict land have been transformed into blocks of luxury apartments and workspaces alongside coffee shops, restaurants, bars and fitness studios. The canal has barges and boats three deep, while the Canalside is littered with spas, cafes, bars and endless graffiti, alongside a new primary school. Ongoing developments and changes have been discussed in previous chapters, and the way young people responded to them was explored. Hub67 existed until early 2023 when the land it was built on was reclaimed by the land trust to develop more luxury housing and a newly designed train station, which stands where there once were factories. What is significant about this transformation is that there remain no services or amenities, apart from the Hub. Everything else is about personal fitness or entertainment. Eateries and bars are inaccessible to those on a low income and no free or subsidised activities are on offer anywhere.

## Researcher perspective

As my position as a researcher developed throughout this case study, I became more reflective and aware of the notions which led me to undertake this research and also what motivated me to engage with my community in the first place. I was already an active member in the community as chair of resident and tenant associations, and in fundraising for improvement and community projects. Over the course of the study, I was also chair and vice chair of local activist groups including the Cultural Interest Groups (CIG), the Hackney Wick Festival and the Wick Award, as well as a conduit between the London Legacy Development Company (LLDC) and local residents. My strong sense of justice and equality drove me to want to ensure that my neighbours were included in decisions and opportunities surrounding the Olympic Games and, based on my experience of their lack of participation and interest in the emerging creative scene in the area, I was aware that this would require dedication and influence. Most importantly, I was aware of and concerned by the lack of resources for young people in the area.

Having completed this study, it now seems both strange and obvious that I became the neighbourhood voice and advocate for young people. I was not planning on it but it became evident that with my experience and position, I was best placed to take it on the role. My roles and responsibilities changed throughout the study. The growing amount of work, time and action which was required as it progressed often felt intense and it would be disingenuous to say that these roles did not prove stressful at times, particularly since I remained a youth work professional overall. There were also moments when I queried my involvement, reflecting on my motivations and what might happen if I did not get involved. At times, I needed to stop and consider my intentions and admit that the challenge was inviting. At every juncture, I was certain of my commitment to young people and my belief in the value of youth work. I utilised the skills which I have developed and mastered over my career and was grateful for the experiences and learning that I had endured because of working with diverse groups and individuals over the years.

There were more than a few times when I felt personally and professionally isolated and alone in my pursuit, not least because generating support from residents proved so challenging – though verbally and notionally in support of the project, they were hesitant to appear in person at meetings or events. There were certainly tensions between my professional and private attitudes and values at times, and I was often especially torn as a resident of Hackney Wick when opportunities arose for me to take part in some of the unique experiences which I had enjoyed. However, on reflection, I viewed this as my social capital which I was able to activate and utilise for the benefit of the community. I was able to utilise these experiences by influencing those who I met, by continual advocacy for young people and assertively reminding them that young people exist. These opportunities did highlight for me, nevertheless, the exclusion that residents were subject to, and that if there was a pecking order, young people were certainly at the bottom.

Key to my reflective experience was indeed the highs and lows of volunteering and how ideas, opportunities and events were viewed. Limited attendance and participation in community activities can be demotivating, especially when the aims are well-meaning and designed to support and enhance lived experiences. However, it is necessary to acknowledge the different priorities and agendas which underpin people's day-to-day lives and make allowances for this. I have remained somewhat bemused, although sympathetic, to the divide that exists between the creative community and the residents, and feel frustrated by not having made more of an impact on this. It seems that a significant effect of regeneration is the isolation of resident communities when it does not relate to them or improve their living conditions or potential. To this end, the creative community still exists quite separately from residents who have been in Hackney Wick between 10 and 30 years. New residents, however, soak up the creative elements and have undoubtedly chosen Hackney Wick as a preferred destination.

Many of the frustrations, tensions and concerns I have had over my career about youth work and young people came to the fore in my reflections during this case study. The foremost is that youth work is poorly represented nationally, with few voices of note advocating and appreciating the professional potential of the interventions made with young people. But aligned with this is the consistent and relentless misunderstanding of what youth work is and what it has the potential to achieve. For the most part, I can reflectively apportion much blame for this to the service itself – not least because I fear that it has failed to position itself robustly enough within a distinct professional framework, at least not one which is readily transferable or translatable.

A strong and dedicated ethos and mission have survived and been drawn upon over the decades, but this has not been sustainable through the political and economic shifts which have dominated in recent times. Since other professions are immediately understood by their title, it would seem appropriate to ensure that the work that is done with young people is also understood by the nature of its title – youth work has not so far managed to do this. Job titles such as Coach, Counsellor, Trainer or Mentor are all decipherable but have dedicated remits – perhaps a 'Youth Worker' aims to cover too many things. What is being achieved with young people is not being translated into tangible positive outcomes and this is undermining its credibility. To adhere to current trends and aspirations, it might help if youth workers adopted a different title (there is no such thing as a 'children's worker' is there?). I suggest this in light of the limited understanding of the role and its purpose but don't claim to have the ideal suggestion.

Giving youth work a new image and brand might merely paper over the contentious 'cracks'. However, in creating brands, very often the 'product' needs to be differentiated, unusual and unique, which could be claimed as a characteristic of youth work. Most successful brands which we understand and trust as consumers have a clear and simple idea that sets them apart or encourages us to choose them, such as the preferred washing powder, the favourite teabags and the most attractive car. Branding experts insist that the key to a good brand is a focus on coherence, consistency and powerful emotion and or attitude – making something which people recognise and understand (Olins, 2005). Olins (2005) also advises that in launching or rebranding there needs to be clarity about the product quality. Rebranding is necessary when the existing brand perception, message and image is outdated and no longer aligns with business strategies, goals and priorities (Cheinman, 2012). If this is to be applied to youth and work, it could be the tool with which new positioning and platforms meet desired objectives and how youth work reconnects with its audience and inspires action.

## What did we find?

To conclude the case study and signpost youth work forward, there are two interrelated thematic clusters which emerged overall from the study and which respond directly to what is meant by youth work. The model presented in this book draws together the notions and practicalities of how open access youth work emerged and was delivered throughout this case study. As a result of this, there were several themes identified as findings from young people's participation in the Hub and evidence of positive and lasting outcomes which I intend to share.

Umbrella cluster themes emerged from gathering themes and identifying them through the analysis of data from the focus groups, meetings, interviews and conversations that were analysed and discussed in previous chapters. The clusters were identified by linking them with common concerns and themes over the course of the research. Civic engagement, for example, emerged as an umbrella term which encompassed all of the elements of entitlement, obligation, connection, positive action and community. Self-awareness was drawn from the links between themes, boredom, maintenance, learning, awareness and self-belief.

In previous chapters, I explained the difficulties that exist in understanding what youth work is, what it does and how it is understood, and made strong claims that it is not generally accepted as part of the educational curriculum as we know it. I consider that youth work does not have near enough potential for change without the engagement or recognition of the community and neighbourhoods. I hope that I have accentuated the need to include support and learning for young people who are marginalised and socially excluded or deemed to be 'at risk' (Sealey, 2015; Fung et al, 2007) and how this was relevant in respect to the young people in this case study.

We were fortunate enough to be able to include intergenerational activities where there was a better sense of enjoyment, and the ability to relax and have fun in a non-formal environment. It was agreed that mental health, self-confidence and the ability to participate equally on the part of young people were improved and encouraged in the Hub. In school, young people prefer to interact among themselves, 'mediating the teacher's message through informal groups' (Woods, 2021, p 24), which is often interpreted by teachers as 'deviant and to provoke censure' (Woods, 2021, p 24). Some of the young people alluded to this in their comments, as did their parents. Adults often hold negative memories of school and project these onto their children's experiences. There was no strong evidence of this, but it is certainly worth keeping in the back of our minds.

## Self-awareness

Self-awareness skills are linked to 'mindfulness' as a holistic teaching and learning technique, originally aimed at the relief of emotional suffering, to increase compassion and kindness and achieve peace and enlightenment (Armstrong, 2012; Kabat-Zinn, 2003; Coholic, 2011). Mindfulness encourages awareness to emerge because of paying attention to purpose and present non-judgementally, calmly questioning who we are and how we place ourselves in the complex world we inhabit. Defining mindfulness has proved challenging for many (Kabat-Zinn, 2003; Bishop et al, 2004; Grossman, 2011; Hick, 2009), although there is consensus around its 'aim of driving desirable change' (Kabat-Zinn, 2003, p 145).

There is evidence that mindfulness as an activity is acceptable and well tolerated by young people, particularly those who suffer from anxiety (Thompson and Guantlett-Gilbert, 2008), and that behaviour, stress and emotion regulation follow participation in self-awareness-focused programmes (Hayes et al, 1999; Bogels et al, 2008; Coholic, 2011). Significant improvements in behaviour problems, stress and attention deficit have been improved in young people when self-awareness techniques are introduced, as are their notions of life focus, purpose, and social and emotional resilience (Birnbaum, 2008; Semple et al, 2010; Napoli and Day, 2024).

For young people (and indeed adults), a lack of mindfulness can lead to negative self-concepts and self-doubt. The relationship between self-esteem and mindfulness is especially strong in young people, influencing their psychological growth and general wellbeing. Mindfulness activities increase our capacity for self-acceptance and self-awareness, which in turn boosts our sense of self-worth. Developing mindfulness abilities during youth will help in overcoming obstacles with more resilience and self-assurance, promoting a positive sense of fulfilment and self-worth (Strömbäck, 2024) which flows into adulthood.

In a practical sense, mindfulness or self-awareness entails paying attention to the moment, our thoughts, feelings and experiences. Being 'in touch' with how we feel or experience things enables us to understand and lower stress, anxiety and despair, improving and managing our wellbeing. Those who are self-aware are better able to handle difficult situations by being calm and compassionate rather than acting on impulse. Ultimately, it means people can live more truly, developing a deeper sense of contentment and serenity (Strömbäck, 2024).

Self-esteem is the ability to personally assess our value and worth. It includes one's self-perception and beliefs, which impact interactions, feelings and behaviours. Providing a balanced view of our skills and shortcomings is essential to developing resilience and confidence, giving us the ability to make our voices heard, as well as deal with obstacles in our lives. In other words, self-awareness gives us a sensitive and relevant ability to understand what affects us but also, and possibly more importantly, how we affect others. Poor self-esteem and awareness can hinder wellbeing and personal development, increasing insecurity, self-doubt and negative self-talk (Strömbäck, 2024).

If young people are self-aware does it make them feel or behave differently? Imagine the young people described in the comments and observations made by residents during the case study – being a nuisance, loud and unruly. With self-awareness, the idea of making noise in public places, littering, feeling at odds with the world and so on, may not necessarily end but they would be aware of the impact these actions have on others. If hanging around outside a shop intimidated shoppers and annoyed the shopkeeper, they might think about moving on as the reputation that goes with this is damaging. If they are struggling with school attendance, being self-aware might help to identify why and enable them to seek appropriate help rather than being unhappy and labelled as difficult. Taking responsibility for behaviour and attitudes is not always easy, but it does clarify the roles and responsibilities of people in our lives generally and enables us to understand why things and situations evolve the way they do.

Young people living in impoverished, stressful and socially complex circumstances often have difficulty articulating their thoughts and modulating their affect. They are likely to have limited social skills, have trouble remaining grounded in the present and lack resilience (Larsen and Hansen, 2008; Webb, 2011). Low self-esteem, hopelessness and lack of optimism stunt emotional intelligence and the ability to manage stressful situations and interpersonal relationships. It is a common factor in young people's perceptions of their life experiences, particularly in low-income and underresourced families.

Trust and investment in the associational relationships which had developed between young people and youth workers in the Hub were challenged along the way by various obstacles. In some cases, this was interpreted as unfulfilled promises made to young people and the disappointment and frustration which came with having to wait for 'something to happen'. What has been significant in the responses from young people, their parents and the youth workers is the notion of the trusting relationships which were established and maintained, and how this made them feel, participate and develop throughout the case study.

A topic which was raised often during the case study was food. A lack of appropriate food was of concern to young people and parents and was perceived to be one of the failures of the provision in the Hub. Significantly, young people felt that they should have access to food, in particular hot food as part of what was on offer to them. It was uncertain as to why they felt that food was an essential element needed for their enjoyment at the Hub, but poverty and the consequences of overstretched families not having much food at home, not having anyone at home to cook, or simply the fact that food makes them happy and therefore would be an extension of fun. Hofstede suggests that the desire for food, and in particular favourite food, belongs to a collective programming of the mind (Hofstede, 1980) and has been described as a general process of spiritual, aesthetic and intellectual cultural contexts and phenomena (Williams, 1976). 'Tastes are founded on social constructs' (Fowler, 1996, p 3) and are centred around cultural phenomena (de Certeau, 1982; Wright et al, 2001). In Victorian Britain, poor families were advised to ensure they ate bread and tea each day, and sweet, filling and fatty foods were seen as 'a taste of necessity' (Bourdieu, 1986, p 252) arising from a lack of choice and providing a sensation of feeling full. The chips, burgers and fried chicken that young people craved, according to Bourdieu, indicate 'a taste for what they are anyway condemned to … the pretext for a class racism which associates with everything heavy, thick and fat' (Bourdieu, 1986, p 241).

Whatever the reasons behind young people choosing to eat 'fast food', what can be seen is their self-awareness. In many cases, young people identified themselves as having mood changes when they had not eaten or recognised that eating fast food made them happy and feel good.

Youth empowerment, as in the Cycle of Courage model (Brendtro et al, 2002), has been considered an essential part of positive youthful development and is a multi-levelled construct. Youth empowerment refers to the empowerment of individuals, families, organisations and communities in gaining mastery and control within their lived experiences to improve equity and quality of life (Rappaport, 1994, 1987; Zimmerman, 2000). Empowerment, whether it be individual or collective is always associated with health and wellbeing (Freire, 1970; Zimmerman, 1998; Rappaport, 1987). Rocha associated this with a continuum dimension (Rocha, 1997) in which the focus is on changing the individual and the community. On an individual level, this includes capacity building, integrating perceptions of personal control or simply having a proactive approach to life and the social environment (Zimmerman, 2000). Collective empowerment takes place within families or communities, enhancing skills and mutual support to affect change or improve wellbeing. A safe and welcoming space where young people feel respected, encouraged, valued and supported allows them opportunities to inhabit a community-like environment in which they can share feelings and opinions, be creative, take risks and try out new things. A sense of empowerment is experienced in an environment which is owned by the participants and where they can be safely challenged and supported to move beyond their 'comfort zone' (Messias et al, 2005; Jennings et al, 2006) where adults retreat into the background, enabling young people to be actors on the centre stage (Goleman, 1995; Jennings et al, 2006). A safe environment is one where young people experience success and failure without judgement and where negative outcomes do not lead to decreased self-esteem or confidence (Messias et al, 2005). Conducive to self-actualisation (Maslow, 1943), youth workers will be familiar with these analogies. In addition, a supportive environment promotes the positive achievements of young people in their communities (Cargo, 2003) where youth workers or other adults are in relative positions of power from which they can advocate amid an otherwise negative vision of young people (Royce, 2004; Jennings et al, 2006).

A lack of community education around the potential of youth work makes it difficult to understand how interventions support or enhance young people's social and personal development, rendering it difficult to convince them it has any value (Benson and Saito, 2001). It therefore becomes important, in an already deprived and struggling community, not to be complacent about young people and their needs (MacDonald and Valdivieso, 2001) and to remain open-minded about potential and change. Adult perspectives often expect young people to display adult behaviours, but the impact of 'yo-yo' transitioning (to adulthood), being unable to place themselves firmly on any particular biological or sociological spot, is confusing and complex.

The accessibility of school to open access youth work is worth considering since in the case of the Hub most young people arrived immediately after school for sessions. The subject of schooling came into the focus group discussions, not because of questions asked but by the young people themselves. They often compared their experiences at school with being in the Hub. Reflecting on this encouraged me to consider the contrast that young people encountered in the Hub, but also whether they were reminded of school because they still wore uniforms, albeit looking rather more dishevelled than they might have done earlier in the day, and with various alterations or additions. Only a few ever went home to change or brought a change of clothes with them. It is thought that a uniform influences individual and group behaviour, creating team-type affiliations while avoiding prejudice against unfashionable or worn-out clothing (Caruso, 1996). It could have enhanced the unity and belonging experienced by the young people where they saw themselves as part of the same group determining a level or standard of behaviour or participation in the activities and opportunities. For those joining on their own, the familiarity of others dressed in the same way probably proved helpful.

Bourdieu maintains that 'the habitus, the durably installed generative principle of regulated improvisations produces practices which tend to reproduce the regularities immanent in the objective conditions of the production of their generative principle' (Bourdieu et al, 1977, p 78), where different forms of capital are embodied in a person's habitus which is closely linked to how they act. Applying this to wearing a uniform, although perhaps unpopular, provides a platform for regulation and cultural commonality.

## Citizenship

Youth work is not a 'single experience' (Sherraden, 2001, p 8) but a collection of experiences which include being part of an organisation, meeting and working with new people and experiences, and developing new skills but not necessarily in any different way to other institutions, such as school and family. Young people who participated in this case study had significant adults in their lives in the form of parents, stepparents or grandparents, even when they were carers for them. The perspectives of parents around youth work are limited (Philip et al, 2004). There is some material focussed on the role of mentoring in youth work and the impact it has on improved effectiveness of programmes for young people as perceived by parents (DuBois et al, 2002b; Keller, 2005).

Marshall described citizenship as 'a status bestowed on those who are full members of a community' (Marshall, 1950, p 84). Hoxsey suggests that 'the promise of citizenship rests on a balance between rights and duties' (Hoxsey, 1990, p 17), but also that 'as social rights are advanced and society evolves, individual inequalities will disappear' (Hoxsey, 1990, p 18). In many ways, these assumptions are now outdated, since advanced thinking and globalised constructions of what it is to be a citizen have been analysed and reassessed (Taylor et al, 2002; Isin, 2013; Birrell and Healy, 2013). However, though defining citizenship may be contemporarily straightforward, determining whether citizenship is an entitlement or an aspiration is quite another thing. In diverse and shifting landscapes, there is so much which might influence the citizenship status of young people, not least the anger and resentment that they have begun to articulate around a lack of access to certain generational opportunities deemed to have been destroyed by their parent's generations, housing, politics, employment and so on (Jericho and Elliot, 2020). For the young people who participated in this case study, their resentment was articulated mainly around parental absence due to workloads, family dysfunction and the expectations associated with helping out, watching siblings, caring for relatives or taking responsibility for 'adult chores' which prevented them from participating in fun, youth-led activities.

'Citizenship deficit' has been described because of community-led responses to austerity and calls for individuals and families to make efforts to remedy this themselves and not expect to be entitled to citizenship participation and status (Walsh and Black, 2018). Advised that they should make lifestyle choices that take them out of poverty by relocation (Abbott et al, 2016). Constraints on family mobility, both social and financial, however, are clear indicators of the lack of options and tend to harness the notion that young people are indeed the 'problem' in the citizenship debate. Low socioeconomic communities are often politicised around citizenship and attempts are made to encourage initiatives aimed at redressing social and economic exclusion. Thus enabling local citizens to mobilise responses to the need for resources, improve situations and strengthen social and community ties (Smyth et al, 2013). Young people are expected to become active citizens through formal education, non-formal education and as community participants. Projects and programmes encourage them to 'make a difference' or 'do something great in their community', yet they are often in disenfranchised and marginalised neighbourhoods, where they are viewed as 'risky' citizens. On the one hand, they are seen as not conforming, acting out or opposing social norms, and on the other, as beacons of hope, possibility and reform. Citizenship can be a social rather than purely political process (Dean, 2013) which is encouraging to smaller and more isolated communities.

Throughout the case study, young people shared strong views about what should be happening in their local community and some were willing to engage in action at the community level. Their involvement may have been encouraged as they identified with their neighbourhood and it was easier for them to trust and conceive of ideas which would directly affect them (Vromen and Collin, 2010), or because they may have found the rewards were more relatable and immediate for them. They may have been more comfortable and confident enacting their citizenship in the 'everyday settings that are important to them' (Torney-Purta, 2002, p 208). The ability to engage with and achieve direct, visible and immediate outcomes concerning the daily issues of their lives may well have been seen as less a means to belonging and more a sense of place in their neighbourhood. 'Contrary to much popular government and media rhetoric on the position of young people as anti-social and breaking away from their communities … most young people are instead seeking membership and inclusion within them' (Hart, 2009, p 653).

Although communities have expectations about the citizenship behaviours and attitudes of young people, this comes with social expectations about how they cope on their own and become attached to a neighbourhood, essentially making desirable choices for both individuals and society. We expect transitions – independent living, employment and setting up a family, and so on, to follow each other in a certain order and at particular ages (generally speaking). However, we have perceptions about independence – when and how it is appropriated, driven mainly by our social and cultural ideas.

Young people perceive the social transitions and expectations placed on them to be navigated independently and responsibly (Kallio, 2024). These transitions are also considered to be the prerequisites for the status of full citizenship (Thomson et al, 2004; Furlong, 2017; Cuervo and Wyn, 2014). Achieving independence is a critical phase of life when young people build relationships with society as members and citizens. However, there are young people whose independence has not been realised following these norms and ideals, their experience of citizenship may be different, and it may also be variable depending on age and intellect (Kallio, 2024).

Young people's experiences of citizenship must be formed through encounters with other citizens and social institutions, such as the Hub, the community groups that exist in Hackney Wick and the examples given by their significant adults. Young adulthood can be interpreted as a societal status based on the cultural associations of independence and participation in society, although it is also important to note that citizenship can be a negotiable yet dynamic relationship between youth and community. Young people are often overshadowed by adults and defined as lesser valued citizens, and their everyday aspirations to function in their community, as well as their rights to do so, are unrecognised and unsupported in general.

Of course, this is where youth work comes in. Merely responding to the principles and guidelines that we work within we must ensure that young people's rights are upheld and that they are treated fairly and equally as members of their communities without patronising or pathologising them.

Respecting young people is fundamental to youth work ethos and being present in their lives is enabled as a result. If, as youth workers we can surprise them, we might be able to encourage them to surprise themselves.

## Social capital

Galster maintains that:

> although there has been a burgeoning literature on qualifying the relationship between various aspects of the residential environment and numerous outcomes for individual adults and children residing in that environment, comparably less attention has been given to uncovering empirically the causal mechanisms that yield these relationships. (Galster, 2001)

Many scholars have attempted to identify the causes of positive neighbourly connection (Atkinson, 2011; Booth and Crouter, 2001); and have often identified peer influences in low-income neighbourhoods to be evidence of negative behaviours (Case and Katz, 1991). Even more suggest that young people with positive role models in disadvantaged areas significantly affect peer interaction (Ginther et al, 2000; Oberwittler, 2004).

Parents in this study indicated that they trusted the youth workers with their children. They felt they presented positive role models and acted as potential confidants who would offer them opportunities and experiences which would broaden their sense of self and their prospects. These areas of trust and respect were demonstrated by the youth workers as they interacted with the young people, showing commitment, genuine positive regard, attentiveness and consistency. Indeed, a strong role model appears to be significant in research and discussion about what youth work offers and how it works (Batsleer, 2009; Davies, 2011; Smith, 2011; de St Croix, 2018). Healthy development and integration into communities of young people, however labelled, over the years has shifted focus (Small, 2004), with a primary function on 'keeping young people off the streets' and removing them from risk-based behaviour by encouraging active community participation (McArdle, 2024).

Community and family networks are crucial in young people's aspiration formation (Boeck, 2009) as are peer relationships in successful transitions to adulthood (Holland et al, 2007). Access to and the flow of information relevant to improving conditions and aspirations for poor families is often unreliable and limited (Gregg, 2010). The Hub undertook to improve this by providing a central resource for local information. Details of events, support and all local resources were stored or posted there. Youth clubs and centres are accepted as sociable sites. This makes asking for, acquiring and locating information and resources less intimidating. Young people seemed to be aware of events in the neighbourhood throughout the case study and they mostly knew where and how to acquire local information.

Aspirations for young people to be social or active in the community and shape a personal future are usually at their height in their adolescent years (Catts and Allan, 2012). In line with National Citizens Service (NCS) policy, involving them in volunteering at this stage may influence their future volunteering life choices. Young people seemed to join and attend the Hub when they had family or friends who also attended, or they followed recommendations from others. It seems that familial and neighbourhood networks were key to increased attendance and acted as a reference for good activities, illustrating that some social capital was available and accessed by young people in the area during the period of the case study.

The Hub provided territory for young people with distinctly different values and norms from the school environment. Young people embraced these norms and even policed the space to maintain it as their own. It provided a safe refuge away from anti-social street behaviour, as determined by residents. Behaviour in the Hub was largely similar to street behaviour in most cases, as it involved groups of young people being together, chatting, laughing and generally having fun. However, it is interesting how differently such behaviour is viewed in varying venues – on the street, laughing, chatting and hanging out appears to suggest ill intent and danger to many, whereas, in the Hub, this behaviour is 'normal' and accepted.

Bourdieuisian habitus is embedded in shifting combinations of contemporary working-class space and displaced communities who are 'getting by' amid deprivation of housing, employment, finance and other resources (Gunter and Watt, 2009; Kennelly and Watt, 2012). Threats to residential notions of social and spatial community and belonging were in abundance throughout this case study, as was a sense of ambiguity towards regeneration and 'not in my backyard'. Residents, including young people, recognised that social housing is routinely framed around high crime rates, anti-social behaviour and jobless families but also demonstrated a sense of place, neighbourly conviviality and pride in their homes and gardens. Fear of 'spatial alienation and dissolution of place' (Wacquant, 2008, p 201) were evident, although not in precise terms.

There was certainly a shared sense of belonging and indications that residents and young people felt they were part of a stable community, although it should be acknowledged that community feelings often gain traction when change or external threat is apparent (Somerville, 2011). It is when action groups and campaigns come into their own. 'Community' is a contested term and as I have previously noted, is a rhetorical concept applied to regenerative processes. Young people and parents acknowledged that gentrification was apparent in and around neighbouring wards and that this was partly due to the Olympics back in 2012. They were aware of the shifting of class relations and a rebalancing of sorts which did not and, thus far, has not included them. The social housing stock in Hackney Wick was unthreatened by 'displacement' (Davidson, 2009, p 226) as such. However, there was still a sense of insecurity and a feeling that the regeneration was not for everyone. The distinct symbolic contrast between the corporate affluence which was emerging and the deprived estates in the area was ever apparent.

Throughout this case study, it was the intention to engage and motivate young people to become aware of and involved in the regeneration processes in their neighbourhood, not least to ensure they had a voice, but also to encourage understanding and appreciation of what was going on around them. With critical reflection, it is evident that any participation young people had in the events leading up to and following the Olympic Games in and around Hackney Wick was largely driven by the interventions of youth work (as opposed to Olympic bodies). Often acting as the conduit between young people and others, youth workers were advocates for young people and reminders to include them.

The relationships which developed were predominantly between adults, who would offer input at meetings, events and opportunities on their behalf – and although this was translated directly to the young people, they were rarely invited to take the lead. Again, reflecting on when young people were involved, they were encouraged and welcomed, but patronised – no one really expected them to have anything to contribute and there was always a sense that their involvement was tokenistic.

The Hub was a feasible project and derived directly from the ensuing regeneration. It was a productive and positive experience for young people (and continues to be). In this experience, a significant number of young people were able to access and undertake opportunities which they would not have been able to previously. They developed skills, networks, friendships, opinions, individual and collective social capital, community focus and meaning. They felt valued and appreciated as a result and many were able to pursue activities and ideas that they may not have previously thought of. Overall, the experience was hugely positive for young people and residents and the funding and support received were invaluable. Yet without the intervention, consistency and determination of youth workers, I suspect that young people would have been completely alienated from the regeneration and development in the area.

Young people participated in the Hub around the time they were likely to be forming their social identities, marking significant areas of interest and resonance for them in music, fashion, religion, sports, entertainment and so on, and there was evidence that some had made new friendships after joining the Hub. New friendships invariably enable new networks, and these connections inevitably encourage young people to define their social capital via territory and connection. The Hub being managed and maintained by residents in turn furthered opportunity for social capital in family and neighbourhood networks through shared interest and familiarity.

Since social class is fundamental in understanding community (Shaw and Mayo, 2016), relationships and collective activity are best described as social capital (Putnam, 2000). The young people attending the Hub shared a similar social class, making competition or isolation less likely. In the UK, harsh levels of deprivation exist alongside extreme affluence, introducing the concept of 'communities of income' (Halpern, 2005, p 67). Hackney Wick has become consistent with this. Such affluence, however, does not include children and young people, since it is young singles, businesses or childless couples who are moving into the neighbourhood's luxury homes.

Social capital is perceived as an imperfect yet inherently 'good' practice with a 'dark side' (Field, 2003b, p 17) and can be a useful tool by which to explore social practices and processes. In most theoretical concepts, young people are passive recipients of social capital resultant of their family status (Coleman, 1993; Morrow, 2001; Holland et al, 2007). Bourdieu (1986) was concerned with social injustice and inequality and how social capital might bridge these elements of community relationships. There was evidence in the case study that young people were included more in community events, meetings and activities (some decision making) following the establishment of the Hub, which seemed to be due to more proactive sharing of information and opportunity. Certainly, theorists have collectively associated access to information as key to social capital development (Bourdieu, 1986; Coleman, 1993; Putnam, 2000).

We want young people to learn both personally and educationally, so rather than accepting that both areas will be distinctly different, collaborative methods which embrace and enhance young people's personal and educational growth should be acknowledged in both environments. If social capital is not readily transferrable, this may be the 'dark side' to which Field refers (2003b, p 19). In this case study, young people utilised their individual and group social capital in a variety of ways: by engaging in forums and creative activities with residents and business networks in the neighbourhood; by partaking in art workshops and exhibitions; and by being able to 'greet' their neighbours as they encountered them. In impoverished families, most family members are unable to support education and employment pathways or choices (Goodman and Gregg, 2010), making the unique opportunities available via other networks invaluable. The hub was best placed to provide information about and access to activities and ideas in the area, as well as promote the development of social and local supportive relationships between young people and youth workers and parents and youth workers.

Young people in Hackney Wick largely lack economic capital. They live in poverty and are marginalised from mainstream society, but I can assert that they can accrue a rich social currency of social capital which they can use to spend in whatever way they choose, to enhance or overcome the situations they are in – it is their agency. Young people in the Hub created or enhanced their own subculture. In a way, they became a group with their own cultural meanings, values, styles and behaviour. In her study of subcultures and social capital, Thornton introduced this as 'a means by which young people negotiate and accumulate status within their own social worlds' (McRobbie and Thornton, 1995, p 163). So, social capital and sub-cultural social capital can be found and utilised in groups of young people sharing a space (Tolonen, 2007). Bourdieu and social capital theorists have lent a great deal to this study, and in applying theory to youth work practice, however robust this case study was, there was a sense that there was a missing element, something that may bring further or enhanced understanding to this study.

As these findings reveal, the youth work at Hub67 was both embedded in relationships of trust and belonging and broader factors such as cooperation and negotiation among community actors, residents and institutions. This raises the consideration of whether such forms of collaboration can be understood using Regime Theory. This concept, typically applied to urban governance, illuminates how collective interests are pursued and sustained in environments that are undergoing significant change.

## Regime Theory

I have discussed the challenges encountered in the development of the Hub and how some residents responded negatively to both it and young people. I have also detailed how there was unyielding support for the project from many residents and the creative community. I do not want to introduce it in its entirety here but suggest it be considered in future research as it is interesting to consider how it applies to youth work in changing environments.

Considered more a concept than a theory, a regime is commonly understood as a set of 'principles, norms, rules and decision-making procedures around which actor's expectations converge on a given area' (Krasner, 1984, p 13). Regimes create the coming together of expectations, establishing standards of behaviour and a mutual obligation, mitigating the anarchy which may alternatively emerge, aiming to stabilise and structure relations which benefit the regime members. The concept acknowledges that regimes are significant in enabling and facilitating cooperation among groups and become capable of exerting influence on them (Bradford, Jackson and Hough, 2016). Often viewed as responses to collective action problems, regimes largely arise from self-interest among groups (Keohane, 1982). In other words, regimes are created because it is expected that the welfare of the creators will be enhanced. Negotiated regimes are those which involve explicit consent and bargaining on the part of participating actors (Young, 2002).

Regimes continue to persist despite experiencing changes. The cost and investment in development will be central to the participants' values and purpose. Communication across regimes can encourage learning and interaction which leads to cooperative behaviour and understanding, building trust and stability, paving the way for enhanced collaboration (Bradford, Jackson and Hough, 2016) and a shared sense of identity. Concepts of regime forming and theory can be applied to urban environments undergoing neighbourhood renewal and regeneration both in terms of feeling the need to 'hold on' to what they know and to mitigate unwanted or unwelcome change, or indeed to impact how the change will look.

It struck me that this concept could readily apply to how the Hub was achieved – strength in the belief that it was needed and feasible because youth workers, young people and residents worked together to ensure it was realised. I was also reminded of the theories of Rogers (1980) and Goleman (2001), how we are all actors in our specific worlds and whether the notion of Regime Theory in practice brings a metaphorical stage, audience and sponsors for our actions.

However perceived, social capital has both emotional and practical significance to vulnerable groups, particularly in non-formal groups. Social capital has little relevance in formal education settings since it has little value to teachers (Allan and Catts, 2012; Smyth, 2012) where it is replaced by passive acceptance of the norms of the school environment. However, given the positive experiences and actions young people have had in the Hub, there may be an opportunity to improve relationships and attitudes around school by systems of sharing young people's development and achievements in open access youth work via school settings. The collaboration between youth workers, residents, local governance and funding agencies to bring Hub67 into creation can be understood as an example of a negotiated regime, one that temporarily stabilised resources, agendas and expectations around youth inclusion. This regime was not institutionalised in the traditional sense but rather emerged organically from community need and as a response to youth exclusion. However, as Regime Theory warns, such alliances can be fragile and one continued aspect of maintaining Hub67 is to ensure continued commitment to its ends and to promote institutional protection of the community-based regime.

## Implications for practice

The hub presented an opportunity to remedy the 'problem' of young people 'hanging out' on the streets, responding both to residents who found this disturbing and to young people who felt they were being unfairly treated. For all the young people, there was a positive reason for drawing them to the hub, either activities or the opportunity to meet with peers or trusting adults. Particularly relevant in vulnerable groups, the importance of networks which hold trusted and shared norms is important (Barry, 2006; Allison and Catts, 2012; Smyth, 2012) and can be utilised to address injustices for young people.

There was evidence from the research that a youth space in Hackney Wick responded to parents' and residents' concerns about young people and, at the very least, provided somewhere young people could be and were known to be, dispelling misconceptions about their whereabouts and behaviour. Having focussed on young people's self-awareness and citizenship, it is recommended that these be the core components of youth work models, not only because they are fundamental to successful lived experiences for young people but because they can also be readily understood.

In short, self-awareness encourages the ability to understand motivations, aspirations, fears, obstacles, objectives, reflection, ownership, mental health, effects and responsibilities. When it is possible to reflect and identify emotional and cognitive personality traits and past issues, self-awareness becomes a useful tool for examining relationships, responses and opportunities. We can, at the same time, learn to take responsibility for how others see us and learn how to build on desires, skills and needs. Whether self-awareness is associated and developed therapeutically or educationally – it is empowering and life-affirming. Acquiring skills in self-awareness or emotional intelligence in youth must lead to reflective and responsive adulthoods with the ability to manage and navigate lived experiences which are of benefit, despite the disadvantages and obstacles encountered.

Citizenship is associated with political, social, cultural and economic life domains, yet it is also closely linked to rights, entitlement, identity, membership and belonging, which in themselves can relate to aspirational and motivational goals and ideals. I have discussed how a sense of belonging and purpose can prove helpful in encouraging young people to thrive and how being gifted with a voice is positive for them and their community. By citizenship I mean young people being part of and contributing to their community, not specifically politically, but culturally, by understanding what it is to be part of a wider group, acknowledging and tolerating difference, sameness and belonging. Young people should not be seen as nuisances or disagreeable but as an essential part of the neighbourhood. Young people would be required to take greater responsibility for themselves and their actions, but with better self-awareness this becomes complementary. The neighbourhood too, would need to take responsibility, and more considered care is needed to include young people in any future making.

More multifaceted ideas of what it means to be a citizen in ways which are genuinely meaningful to young people can involve formal and informal inclusions in decision making, activism and neighbourliness, to suit and focus on the distinct or indistinct characteristics of any one neighbourhood. Austerity and the erosion of rights in terms of education, housing, adequate standards of living, health and employment have pushed young people into hopelessness in many ways, yet being useful or proactive in communities can act as a counter to this.

As with all types of youth work, the focus should be on the young person, and citizenship programmes could be designed to uniquely respond to each individual. Youth workers will always assert that every piece of youth work they do is unique due to the individuality and uniqueness of the young people themselves. Rather like each haircut undertaken by a hairdresser or every tooth extraction made by a dentist – everyone is unique, although perhaps similar. Somehow when applied to these professions, we understand exactly what is meant. When we say the same about youth work, very few people seem to appreciate it.

Recognising that citizenship is about experiencing full membership of a community, warts and all, young people should belong and be included. Young people of most denominations and social statuses share similar dilemmas, including deferred adulthood markers, often being left in a 'state of limbo' which has actively replaced conventional adulthood (Honwana, 2014, p 2439). This leads society to examine what it wants for and of its young people and how it intends to address this – and this may mean making significant changes to how they are integrated.

Given the current popularity of advice and guidance around mental health and the need for everyone to be identifying and 'talking' about it, I consider youth work as being at a crossroads - one at which it can embrace unashamedly its therapeutic qualities and benefits to young people (and communities) or continue to battle with its contested, complex and sometimes controversial status and place within the education sector.

As this case study progressed and the findings were analysed, I was concerned that I was in danger of advocating for what some may call 'extinct practice' - harking back to the days when youth clubs existed as extensions of schools that every young person belonged to. I even feared that this rendered me being labelled a dinosaur and well past my youth work 'use-by' date. However, after some intense and often painful reflection, I am unashamed to say that this case study shows open access youth clubs are not only credible but relevant and essential. All forms of youth work are, but there can be no excuses left to explain why youth centres are not central to urban communities. This evidence shows that young people thrive in an environment entirely dedicated to them and their communities, such as Hub67. Claiming that youth work can therapeutically enhance the lived experience of young people is not unrealistic – if something makes you feel, behave and reflect better, it is therapeutic.

The key strength of this study is, I hope, the unique and extraordinary opportunity that it presented and the one-off experience for both me as a researcher-practitioner and for the young people involved. Taking place in an exceptional place and time in history for a significant area of London and also for open access youth work and the challenges and contested environment in which it exists.

Over years of working with or for young people, I have held similar attitudes and values towards youth work as well as changed some fundamental notions over time. Youth work is contested both as a tool for working with young people and also as a professional practice. It has and continues to be poorly articulated by those who undertake it as well as those who interrogate it, yet little has been done practically to address this. Like with anything, there is a fear of change, a reluctance to be bold and a tendency to be resentful when criticised. By this I mean that holding onto 'youth worker' as a professional title may not be optimal when it is so difficult to explain and understand. It may also be worth considering whether young people's engagement in conventional citizenship is relevant and that open access youth work can provide, particularly in areas of regeneration, radical and alternative change-making opportunities and help young people to become actively involved in the community development of their neighbourhoods.

Young people are having to navigate stormy seas; they are concerned about their future and their prospects as parents seek better lives for their children. Young people are experiencing responsibility earlier than ever before. Mindful, self-aware youth citizenship might prove a resolution to the ambiguity with which young people view their neighbourhoods. Taking account of their sociospatial and socioeconomic circumstances, their lived experiences become contextualised realistically and honestly.

Finally, this case study and the model within aimed to address and tackle head-on the difficulties and challenges that young people faced as a result of regenerative development in their neighbourhood and also generally. Advocacy and ethics were also challenged during the process, but youth workers remained firm in their professional beliefs and abilities to make what often felt like a distant dream a reality. The alignment of young people with the community via youth workers was fundamental in making Hub67 a safe, welcoming, productive and reflective space for young people.

This case study illuminated the transformative potential of open access youth work within the context of rapid urban regeneration. Across the case study, it becomes clear that youth work – when grounded in trust, participation and autonomy – can cultivate more than just engagement. It can nurture self-awareness, grow agency and activate citizenship. These three elements are critical to the wellbeing of young people and their prospects, as well as to building cohesive and resilient communities. Models like Hub67 show what is possible when young people are positioned as capable, reflective and civic actors. This study offers a hopeful contribution to debates about power and young people. Hub67 offered more than a space – it became a platform for young people to assert agency, form meaningful relationships and engage civically. The model developed here demonstrates the importance of relational practice, youth-led design and embeddedness within community life. Importantly, it also illustrates the fragility of such work in the face of shifting political and economic landscapes. Urban spaces are transforming through political and contextual factors toward neoliberal values, and, in the face of this change, there is a great need for youth work that resists exclusion. This study affirms that youth work, grounded in values of participation and care, must be safeguarded as a public good.

The findings from this case study point to several key implications for policy and practice. First, there is a need to embed youth voices not only within service delivery but also within the urban planning and regeneration processes that shape young people's environments. The Hub67 model offers a replicable framework that could be adapted to other urban settings facing similar pressures. However, this requires long-term investment, policy alignment and recognition of youth work as a professional, place-based intervention. Policies that integrate youth services within regeneration strategies – rather than treating them as add-ons – are essential to avoid displacement and exclusion. There is also scope for local authorities and housing trusts to collaborate with youth practitioners in securing protected community spaces.

The Hub67 model is less about replication and more about adapting core principles – relational engagement, youth-led governance and embedded community partnerships – to new contexts with care and integrity. It is intended that this study be useful to youth workers and communities in considering the value, purpose and potential of open access youth work, and I have included reflections and observations from my experience to spark discussion and critical thought. Of course, I do not claim to have solved every problem or answered every question, but I hope I have made some constructive comments. There is always room for more research, and this especially applies to youth work.

Open access youth work as undertaken by youth workers at Hub67, which contributed positive, distinct improvement to the lived experiences of young people in Hackney Wick by providing them with a space of their own where they could be uninterrupted and unjudged. They were able to reach out of the constraints of the formal education environment to which they were accustomed and enjoy the non-formal ambience of the space. They made new friends, developed respectful and trusting relationships with youth workers and learnt new things about themselves and their community. They developed in confidence and capacity and gained a better sense of their potential. They were proud of the new skills they had gained, the meetings that they had organised, and the relationships they had established and maintained, and they enjoyed the safe and considered freedom which the Hub provided. In a shifting and uncertain neighbourhood, they gathered a sense of value, both in themselves and in what they had to offer. They enabled themselves to move beyond their 'comfort zones' and were challenged by and interested in new experiences as well as just 'hanging out'. They gained the resources of local citizens, capitalised on them and were able to meet and greet each other, young and old, when and where they came across each other. What more can you ask?

# References

Abbott, P., Wallace, C. and Sapsford, R. (2016) *The Decent Society: Planning for Social Quality*. Routledge.

Adu-Gyamfi, J. (2013) Can children and young people be empowered in participatory initiatives? Perspectives from young people's participation in policy formulation and implementation in Ghana. *Children and Youth Services Review*, 35(10), 1766–1772.

Alanen, L. (2011) Capitalising on family. Habitus and belonging. In L. Alanen and M. Siisiäinen (eds) *Fields and Capitals. Constructing Local Life.* Finnish Institute for Education Research.

Alanen, L. (2012) Moving towards a relational sociology of childhood. *Kindheiten. Gesellschaften: Interdisziplinäre Zugänge zur Kindheitsforschung*, 21–43.

Allan, J. and Catts, R. (eds) (2012) *Social Capital, Children and Young People: Implications for Practice, Policy and Research*. Policy Press.

Alldred, P., Cullen, F., Edwards, K. and Fusco, D. (eds) (2018) *The SAGE Handbook of Youth Work Practice*. Sage.

Allison, M. and Catts, R. (2012) Youth club connections. In J. Allan and R. Catts (eds) *Social Capital Children and Young People: Implications for Practice, Policy and Research* (1st ed). Bristol University Press, p 77.

Altshuler, A.A. (1969) Transit subsidies: By whom, for whom? *Journal of the American Institute of Planners*, 35(2), 84–89.

Amin, A. and Thrift, N. (2002) *Cities: Reimagining the Urban*.

Andersson, B. (2013) Finding ways to the hard to reach—considerations on the content and concept of outreach work. *European Journal of Social Work*, 16(2), 171–186.

Anheier, H.K. (2005) *Non-Profit Organisations: Theory, Management, Policy*. Routledge.

Armstrong, A. (2012) *Mindfulness and Consumerism: A Social Psychological Investigation*. University of Surrey.

Arneson, R. (1989) Equality and Equal Opportunity for Welfare. *Philosophical Studies*, 56, 77–93.

Ashton, D. and Field, D. (1976) *Youth Workers*. University of California.

Atkinson, W. (2011) From sociological fictions to social fictions: Some Bourdieusian reflections on the concepts of 'institutional habitus' and 'family habitus'. *British Journal of Sociology of Education*, 32(3), 331–347.

Axford, N., Tredinnick-Rowe, J., Rybcyznska-Bunt, S., Burns, L., Green, F. and Thompson, T. (2023) Engaging youth at risk of violence in services: Messages from research. *Children and Youth Services Review*, 144, 106713.

Baldridge, B.J. (2020) Negotiating anti–Black racism in 'liberal' contexts: The experiences of Black youth workers in community-based educational spaces. *Race Ethnicity and Education*, 23(6), 747–766.

Barford, A. (2023) *January. Youth Futures Under Construction*. British Academy.

Barry, J. (2006) Resistance is fertile: From environmental to sustainability citizenship. *Environmental Citizenship*, 21, 21–48.

Batsleer, J. (1994) Silence in working across difference: Groupwork in a youth and community work training context. *Groupwork London*, 197–209.

Batsleer, J. (2000) Hidden from history. *Research in Social Care and Social Welfare: Issues and Debates for Practice*, 32.

Batsleer, J. (2008) *Informal Learning in Youth Work*. Sage.

Batsleer, J. (2009) Commentary 4: Methods and frameworks. In *A Handbook of Children and Young People's Participation*. Routledge, pp 215–217.

Batsleer, J. (2011) Voices from an edge. Unsettling the practices of youth voice and participation: Arts-based practice in The Blue Room, Manchester. *Pedagogy, Culture and Society*, 19(3), 419–434.

Batsleer, J. (2012) Dangerous spaces, dangerous memories, dangerous emotions: informal education and heteronormativity–a Manchester UK Youth Work vignette. *Discourse: Studies in the Cultural Politics of Education*, 33(3), 345–360.

Batsleer, J. (2013) Youth work, social education, democratic practice and the challenge of difference: A contribution to debate. *Oxford Review of Education*, 39(3), 287–306.

Batsleer, J. (2014) Against role models: Tracing the histories of manliness in youth work, the cultural capital of respectable masculinity. *Youth and Policy: The Journal of Critical Analysis*, 113.

Batsleer, J. (2016) Precarity, food and accompaniment in community and youth work. *Education and Ethnography Special Issue Education and Precarity*, 11(2).

Batsleer, J. (2021) Re-assembling anti–oppressive practice (1): The personal, the political, the professional. *Education Sciences*, 11(10), 645.

Batsleer, J. and Davies, R. (2010) *What is Youth Work*. Learning Matters.

Bauman, Z. (2003) *City of Fears, City of Hopes*. University of London.

Baxter, J. (2011) An examination of the characteristics and time use of those who have unfilled spare time. *Electronic International Journal of Time Use Research*, 8(1).

Bazeley, P. (2009) Analysing qualitative data: More than 'identifying themes. *Malaysian Journal of Qualitative Research*, 2(2), 6–22.

Belton, B. (2009) *Developing Critical Youth Work Theory: Building Professional Judgment in the Community Context*, BRILL.

Belton, B. (2017) Colonised youth. *Youth and Policy* [Online]. September. Available from: http://www.youthandpolicy.org/articles/colonised-youth/

Benson P.L. and Saito R.N. (2001) The scientific foundations of youth development. In P.L. Benson and K.J. Pittman (eds) *Trends in Youth Development. Outreach Scholarship* (Vol 6). Springer.

Berman, S. (1997) *Children's Social Consciousness and the Development of Social Responsibility*. State University of New York Press.

Berne, E. (1964) *Games People Play*. Penguin.

Bernstein, R. (1983) *Beyond Objectivism and Relativism: Science, Hermeneutics, and Raxis*. University of Pennsylvania Press.

Betts, R.J. (2014) *Data-Driven Decision Making: A Study of the Collaboration Between Literacy Coach and Teacher to Inform Instructional Decisions in the Classroom*, doctoral dissertation, Capella University.

Biddulph, M. (2000) Villages don't make a city. *Journal of Urban Design*, 5(1), 65–82.

Birnbaum, L. (2008) The use of mindfulness training to create an 'accompanying place' for social work students. *Social Work Education*, 27(8), 837–852.

Birrell, B. and Healy, E. (2013) *Scarce Jobs: Migrants or Locals at the End of the Queue?* Centre for Population and Urban Research. https://apo.org. au/node/35576

Bishop, S., Lau, M., Shapiro, S., Carlson, L., and Andersen, N. (2004) Mindfulness: A proposed operational definition. *Clinical Psychology Science and Practice*, 11(3).

Blum, R.W. (1998) Improving the health of youth: A community health perspective. *Journal of Adolescent Health*, 23(5), 254–258.

Boeck, T. (2009) Social capital and young people. In *Work with Young People: Theory and Policy for Practice*, pp 88–103.

Boeker, R. (2023) Locke on education, persons, and moral agency. *International Journal of Philosophical Studies*, 31(2), 202–210.

Bogdan, R. and Biklen, S.K. (1997) *Qualitative Research for Education* (Vol 368). Allyn & Bacon.

Bogels, S., Hoogstad, B., van Dun, L., de Schutter, S. and Restifo, K. (2008) Mindfulness training for adolescents with externalizing disorders and their parents. *Behavioural and Cognitive Psychotherapy*, 36, 193–209.

Bolton, S.C. (2005) *Emotion Management in the Workplace* (Vol 190). Palgrave Macmillan.

Booth, A. and Crouter, A.C. (eds) (2001) *Does It Take a Village? Community Effects on Children, Adolescents, and Families*. Lawrence Erlbaum Associates Publishers.

Botterill, G. and Carruthers, P. (1999) *The Philosophies of Psychology*. Cambridge University Press, Chapters 2–5.

Bourdieu, P. (1964) *The Attitude of the Algerian Peasant Toward Time*. éditeur inconnu, pp 55–72.

Bourdieu, P. (1973) Cultural reproduction and social reproduction. In R. Brown (ed) *Knowledge, Education and Cultural Change*. Tavistock, pp 71–112.

Bourdieu, P. (1984a) *A Social Critique of the Judgement of Taste*, Cambridge, MA.

Bourdieu P. (1984b) *Distinction*. Routledge.

Bourdieu, P. (1986) The forms of capital. In J. Richardson (ed) *Handbook of Theory and Research for the Sociology of Education*. Greenwood Press, pp 241–258.

Bourdieu, P. (1990) *The Logic of Practice*. Polity Press.

Bourdieu, P. (1998a) *Practical Reason: On the Theory of Action*. Polity Press.

Bourdieu, P. (1998b) *Practical Reason. On the Theory of Action*, Cambridge: Polity.

Bourdieu, P. (1999) *The Weight of the World* (Vol 217). Polity Press.

Bourdieu, P. (2011) The forms of capital (1986). In I. Szeman and T. Kaposy (eds) *Cultural Theory: An Anthology*, pp 81–94.

Bourdieu, P. and Nice, R. (1980) The aristocracy of culture. *Media, Culture & Society*, 2(3), 225–254.

Bourdieu, P. and Passeron, J.C. (1977) *Reproduction in Education, Society and Culture*. Sage.

Bourdieu, P., Passeron, J.C. and Nice, R. (1977) *Education, Society and Culture*. Trans. Richard Nice. Sage, pp 15–29.

Bourdieu, P. and Wacquant, L. (1992) *An Invitation to Reflexive Sociology*. University of Chicago Press.

Bowlby, J. (1969) *Attachment and Loss* (No. 79). Random House.

Bowling, A. and Windsor, J. (2001) Towards the good life: A population survey of dimensions of quality of life. *Journal of Happiness Studies*, 2(1), 55–82.

Boyatzis, R.E. (1998) *Transforming Qualitative Information: Thematic Analysis and Code Development*. Sage.

Bradbury, A., McGimpsey, I. and Santori, D. (2013) Revising rationality: The use of 'nudge' approaches in neoliberal education policy. *Journal of Education Policy*, 28(2), 247–267.

Bradford, S. (2004) The management of growing up: Youth work in community settings. In J. Roche, S. Tucker, R. Thompson, and R. Flynn (eds) *Youth in Society*, 2, 245–254.

Bradford, A. (2007) Regime Theory. *Max Planck Encyclopedia of Public International Law* [Online]. Columbia Law School. Available from: https://scholarship.law.columbia.edu/faculty_scholarship/1970

Bradford, S. (2009) *Universals and Particularism English Youth Work*.

Bradford, S. (2011) Modernising youth work: from the universal to the particular and back again. *European Youth Studies. Integrating Research, Policy and Practice*, 197–203.

Bradford, S. (2012) *Sociology, Youth and Youth Work Practice*. Palgrave MacMillan.

Bradford, S. and Byrne, S. (2010) Beyond the boundaries: resistances to school-based youth work in Northern Ireland. *Pastoral Care in Education*, 28(1), 19–31.

Bradford, S. and Cullen, F. (2014) Positive for youth work? Contested terrains of professional youth work in austerity England. *International Journal of Adolescence and Youth*, 19(1).

Bradford, B., Jackson, J. and Hough, M. (2016) Trust in justice. *The Oxford Handbook of Social and Political Trust, Oxford Legal Studies Research Paper*, 43.

Braun, V. and Clarke, V. (2006) Using thematic analysis in psychology. *Qualitative Research in Psychology*, 3(2), 77–101.

Breen, R.L. (2006) A practical guide to focus-group research. *Journal of Geography in Higher Education*, 30(3), 463–475.

Brendtro, L.K. (1990) Powerful pioneers in residential group care: A look at our roots and heritage. *Child and Youth Care Quarterly*, 19(2), 79–90.

Brendtro, L., Brokenleg, M. and Van Bockern, S. (2002) *Reclaiming Youth at Risk* (rev ed). National Educational Service.

Brewis, G. (2024) Humanitarian and youth activism across time and space. *International Review of Social History*, 69(1), 135–138.

Briggs, S. (2009) Risks and opportunities in adolescence: Understanding adolescent mental health difficulties. *Journal of Social Work Practice*, 23(1), 49–64.

Bright, G. (ed) (2015) *Youth Work: Histories, Policy and Contexts*, London: Palgrave Macmillan.

Brinkmann, S. (2014) 14 Unstructured and Semi-Structured Interviewing. *The Oxford Handbook of Qualitative Research*, p 277.

British Youth Council (2011) *Valuing Young Voices, Strengthening and Democracy*. Available from: http://www.byc.org.uk

Brundtland, G.H. (1989) Global change and our common future. *Environment: Science and Policy for Sustainable Development*, 31(5), 16–43.

Bryant, J. and Zillmann, D. (1984) Using television to alleviate boredom and stress: Selective exposure as a function of induced excitational states. *Journal of Broadcasting & Electronic Media*, 28(1), 1–20.

Bryman, A. (2016) *Social Research Methods*. Oxford University Press.

Buchroth, I. and Parkin, C. (2010) Theory and youth and community work practice. In I. Buchroth and C. Parkin (eds) *Using Theory in Youth and Community Work Practice*. Learning Matters.

Buckingham, D. (2002) *The Making of Citizens: Young People, News and Politics*. Routledge.

Bunyan, T. (2009) *The Shape of Things to Come*. The EU Future Group, Spokesman Books.

Burawoy, M. (2004) Public sociologies: Contradictions, dilemmas, and possibilities. *Social Forces*, 82(4), 1603–1618.

Burke, N. (2022) *Investigating the Income Academic Achievement Gap: An Exploration of the Roles of Mindfulness and Self-Concept Clarity in Low-Income College Students*. Electronic Theses and Dissertations. Paper 4021. https://doi.org/10.18297/etd/4021

Butler, T. and Lees, L. (2006) Super-gentrification in Barnsbury, London. *Transactions, Institute of British Geographers*, 31, 467–487.

Butters, S. and Newell, S. (1978) *Realities of Training*. National Youth Bureau.

Bywaters, P., Skinner, G., Cooper, A., Kennedy, E. and Malik, A. (2022) *The Relationship Between Poverty and Child Abuse and Neglect: New Evidence*. Nuffield Foundation.

Caban, S., Makos, S. and Thompson, C.M. (2023) The role of interpersonal communication in mental health literacy interventions for young people: a theoretical review. *Health Communication*, 38(13), 2818–2832.

CABE Space and CABE Education (2004) Involving young people in the design and care of urban spaces. In *What Would You Do with this Space?*

Cahill, C. (2007) Doing research with young people: Participatory research and the rituals of collective work. *Children's Geographies*, 5(3), 297–312.

Campbell, M.M. (2011) *Youth Cultural Production in Practice and in Policy*. Library and Archives Canada (Bibliothèque et Archives Canada), Ottawa.

Cargo, M. (2003) *Empowerment as Fostering Positive Youth Development and Citizenship*. EBSCO.

Caruso, P. (1996) Individuality vs conformity. The issue behind school uniforms. *National Association of Secondary School Principals (NASSP) Bulletin*, 80, 83–88.

Case, A.D. and Hunter, C.D. (2012) Counterspaces: A unit of analysis for understanding the role of settings in marginalized individuals' adaptive responses to oppression. *American Journal of Community Psychology*, 50, 257–270.

Case, A.C. and Katz, L.F. (1991) *The Company You Keep: The Effects of Family and Neighbourhood on Disadvantaged Youths* (No. w3705). National Bureau of Economic Research.

Catts, R. and Allan, J. (2012) Social capital for young people in educational and social policy, practice and research. *Social Capital, Children and Young People*, pp 209–226.

Charlesworth, S.J. (2000) *A Phenomenology of Working-Class Experience*. Cambridge University Press.

Chapman, S.K. (2015) *The Role of Racial-Ethnic Identity and Family Socialization on Student Engagement: Latino Youth in Select New York City Independent Schools*, PhD dissertation, St John Fisher University.

Chauke, T.A. (2024) Skills learnt in youth work practice necessary for the digital age: A qualitative study of NEET youth. *Research in Social Sciences and Technology*, 9(1), 351–368.

Cheinman, I. (2012) Rebranding – the moment of truth. *Substance*, 151.

Cheinman, K. (2014) Creating alternative art libraries. *Art Documentation: Journal of the Art Libraries Society of North America*, 33(1), 41–58.

Chen, J., Yin, X. and Mei, L. (2018) Holistic innovation: An emerging innovation paradigm. *International Journal of Innovation Studies*, 2(1), 1–13.

Children and Young People Now (CYPN) (2023) Available from: https://www.cypnow.co.uk/content/news/budget-2023-key-announcements-for-children-and-young-people

Cieslik, M. and Simpson, D. (2015) Basic skills, literacy practices and the 'Hidden Injuries of Class'. *Sociological Research Online*, 20(1), 17–28.

Clarke, A. (2013) *The Sociology of Healthcare*. Routledge.

Coburn, A. and Gormally, S. (2017) *Communities for Social Change: Practicing Equality and Social Justice in Youth and Community Contexts*. Peter Lang, https://doi.org/10.3726/b11265

Coffield, F. (2024) *The Creative Art of Troublemaking in Education*. Taylor & Francis.

Coghlan, A. (2012) Environmental impacts of regenerative tourism. In *The Routledge Handbook of Regenerative Tourism*, Routledge, pp 239–251.

Cohen, H. (1972) Poverty and welfare: A review essay. *Political Science Quarterly*, 87(4), 631–652, doi:10.2307/2148200

Cohen, S. (2002) *Folk Devils and Moral Panics: The Creation of Mods and Rockers* (3rd ed). Routledge.

Cohen, S. (2011) *Folk Devils and Moral Panics*. Routledge.

Coholic, D.A. (2011) Exploring the feasibility and benefits of arts-based mindfulness-based practices with young people in need: Aiming to improve aspects of self-awareness and resilience. *Child & Youth Care Forum,* 40, 303–317.

Coleman, J. (1973) *Youth Culture*. President's Science Advisory Committee, Youth: Transition to Adulthood. Report of the Panel on Youth of the President's Science Advisory Committee, Washington DC, Resident's Science Advisory Committee, pp 112–124.

Coleman, J. (1990) *Foundations of Social Theory*. Harvard University Press.

Coleman, J.S. (1993) Rational reconstruction of society. *American Sociological Review*, 58(1), 1–15.

Coleman, J.S. and Hoffer, T. (1987) *Public and Private Schools. The Impact of Communities*. Basic Books.

Cooper, C. (2011) Imagining 'radical' youth work possibilities – challenging the 'symbolic violence' within the mainstream tradition in contemporary state-led youth work practice in England. *Journal of Youth Studies*, 15(1), 53–71.

Cooper, T. (2012) *Models of Youth Work: A Framework for Positive, Sceptical Intervention*. Open University Press.

Cooper, S. (2017) *Participatory Evaluation in Youth and Community Work: Theory and Practice*. Routledge.

Cooper, T. (2018) Defining youth work: Exploring the boundaries, continuity and diversity of youth work practice. In *The SAGE Handbook of Youth Work Practice*, 1.

Cooper, K. and Stewart, K. (2021) Does household income affect children's outcomes? A systematic review of the evidence. *Child Indicators Research*, 14(3), 981–1005

Cooper, T., Corney, T., Tierney, H., Gorman, J. and Sutcliffe, J. (2024) Talking about relational youth work: why language matters. *Journal of Youth Studies*, 1–18. https://doi.org/10.1080/13676261.2023.2298327

Cordova, T. (2024) *Developing Culturally Grounded Support for Parents: A Paradigm for Enhancing LGBTQ+ Acceptance in Jewish Families*, doctoral dissertation, University of Oregon.

Corey, B.M. (2021) *College Readiness: Rural High School Graduates*, doctoral dissertation, Walden University.

Corney, T., Marion, J., Baird, R., Welsh, S. and Gorman, J. (2024) Youth work as social pedagogy: Toward an understanding of non-formal and informal education and learning in youth work. *Child & Youth Services*, 45(3), 345–370.

Côté, J.E. (2014) Towards a new political economy of youth. *Journal of Youth Studies*, 17(4), 527–543.

Crabtree, B. and Miller, W. (eds) (1999). *Doing Qualitative Research* (2nd edn), Sage.

Crimmens, D., Factor, F, Jeffs, T., Pitts, J., Pugh, Spence and Turner, P. (2004) *Reaching Socially Excluded Young People: A National Study of Street-based Youth Work*. National Youth Agency.

Cuervo, H. and Wyn, J. (2014) Reflections on the use of spatial and relational metaphors in youth studies. *Journal of Youth Studies*, 17(7), 901–915.

Daly, M. and Wilson, M. (2001) *Risk-Taking, Intrasexual Competition, and Homicide.*

Davidson, M. (2009) Displacement, space and dwelling: Placing gentrification debate. *Ethics, Place and Environment*, 12(2), 219–234.

Davies, A. (2011) Youth gangs and late Victorian society. In *Youth in Crisis?* Routledge, pp 38–54.

Davies, B. (2001) Struggling through the past: youth service history. In R. Gilchrist, T. Jeffs and J. Spence (eds) *Essays in the History of Community and Youth Work*. National Youth Agency, pp 7–22.

Davies, B. (2005) Youth work: A manifesto for our times. *Youth and Policy*, 88. (Summer) National Youth Agency.

Davies, B. (2010) Policy analysis: a first and vital skill practice. In J. Batsleer and B. Davies (eds) *What Is Youth Work?*, Learning Matters, pp 7–19.

Davies, B. (2012) Negative for youth? Negative for youth work? In *Defence of Youthwork*.

Davies, B. (2013) Youth work in a changing policy landscape: The view from England. *Youth & Policy*, 110(May), 6–32.

Davies, B. (2015) Youth work: A manifesto for our times – Revisited. *Youth and Policy*, 114, 96–117.

Davies, B. (2017) Beyond the local auhtority youth services: Could the state fund open access youth work – and if so, how? A speculative paper for critical discussion. *Youth and Policy*, 116.

Davies, B. (2018) *Defending The Youth Service. Defending Youth Work. Youth Policy and the Deconstruction of the Youth Service in England.* Springer Publishing, pp 327–352.

Davies, B. (2019) Defending the youth service: defending youth work. In B. Davies (ed) *Austerity, Youth Policy and the Deconstruction of the Youth Service in England*, 327–352.

Davies, B. (2024a) *Youth Work Policies in England 2019–2023: Can Open Youth Work Survive?* Springer Nature.

Davies, B. (2024b) The impact of fourteen years of UK conservative government policy on open access youth work. *Youth*, 4(2), 492–508.

Davies, B. and Merton, B. (2009) Squaring the circle? The state of youth work in some children and young people's services. *Youth and Policy*, 103 (Summer), 5–24.

Davies, B. (2011) This is youth work: Stories from practice. In *Defence of Youth Work*.

Davies, R. (2003) *Education, Virtues and the Good Life*, DPhil, Oxford. Available from: http:// independent.academia.edu/RichardADavies/ Papers/851346/DPhil_Thesis_Education

Davies, R. (2016) Youth work and ethics: why the 'professional turn' won't do. *Ethics and Education*, 11(2), 186–196.

Davies, T. (2019) Religious education and social literacy: the 'white elephant' of Australian public education. *British Journal of Religious Education*, 41(2), 124–133.

Dean, J. (2016) Class diversity and youth volunteering in the United Kingdom: Applying Bourdieu's habitus and cultural capital. *Nonprofit and Voluntary Sector Quarterly*, 45(1_suppl), 95S-113S.

Dean, M. (2013) *The Constitution of Poverty (Routledge Revivals): Towards a Genealogy of Liberal Governance*. Routledge.

Dean, J. (2020) The kids aren't alright. The collapse of Kids Company. In *The Good Glow*. Policy Press, pp 97–120.

de Certeau (1982) *The Practice of Everyday Life*. University of California Press.

Delanty, G. (2003) The making of a post-Western Europe: A civilizational analysis. *Thesis Eleven*, 72(1), 8–25.

de Souza Briggs, X. (2007) 'Some of my best friends are...': Interracial friendships, class, and segregation in America. *City & Community*, 6(4), 263–290.

de St Croix, T. (2016) *Grassroots Youth Work. Policy, Passion and Resistance in Practice*. Policy Press.

de St Croix, T. (2018) Youth work, performativity and the new youth impact agenda: getting paid for numbers? *Journal of Education Policy*, 33(3), 414–438.

de St Croix, T. and Doherty, L. (2024) 'Capturing the magic': grassroots perspectives on evaluating open youth work. *Journal of Youth Studies*, 27(4), 486–502.

DeVilbiss, L.A. ( 1921) National health legislation of interest to women. *Public Health Reports (1896–1970)*, 519–523.

Dewey, J. (1916) *Democracy and Education: An Introduction to the Philosophy of Education* [Online]. The Macmillan Company. Available from: http://www.ilt.columbia.edu/publications/Projects/digitexts/dewey/d_e/chapter07.html

Diener, E. and Diener, M. (1995) Cross-cultural correlates of life satisfaction and self-esteem. *Journal of Personality and Social Psychology*, 68(4), 653–663. https://doi.org/10.1037/0022-3514.68.4.653

Dryden, P. and Greenshields, S. (2020) Communicating with children and young people. *British Journal of Nursing*, 29(20), 1164–1166.

DuBois, D.L., Holloway, B.E., Valentine, J.C. and Cooper, H. (2002a) Effectiveness of mentoring programs for youth: A meta-analytic review. *American Journal of Community Psychology*, 30(2), 157–197.

DuBois, D.L., Burk–Braxton, C., Swenson, L.P., Tevendale, H.D. and Hardesty, J.L. (2002b) Race and gender influences on adjustment in early adolescence: Investigation of an integrative model. *Child Development*, 73(5), 1573–1592.

Duncan-Andrade, J.M.R. and Morrell, E. (2008) *The Art of Critical Pedagogy: Possibilities for Moving from Theory to Practice in Urban Schools*, (Vol 285). Peter Lang.

Duncan, P. and Thomas, S. (2000) *Neighbourhood Regeneration: Resourcing Community Involvement*. Policy Press.

Eastwood, J.D., Frischen, A.M.J., and Smilek, D. (2012) The unengaged mind. *Perspectives on Psychological Science*, 7(5), 482–495. https://doi.org/10.1177/1745691612456044

Eden, C.A., Chisom, O.N. and Adeniyi, I.S. (2024) Parent and community involvement in education: strengthening partnerships for social improvement. *International Journal of Applied Research in Social Sciences*, 6(3), 372–382.

Eichsteller, G. and Holthoff, S. (2011) *The Social Pedagogy Development Network – A Grass Roots Movement for Professionals Working with Children and Young People in Social Pedagogical Ways* [Online]. Available from: www.social pedagogy.com.

Elgar, F.J. and Aitken, N. (2011) Income inequality, trust and homicide in 33 countries. *European Journal of Public Health*, 21(2), 241-246. https://doi.org/10.1093/eurpub/ckq068

Ely, J.W., Osheroff, J.A., Ebell, M.H., Bergus, G.R., Levy, B.T., Chambliss, M.L. and Evans, E.R. (1999) Analysis of questions asked by family doctors regarding patient care. *BMJ*, 319(7206), 358–361.

Eraut, M., Alderton, J., Cole, G. and Senker, P. (2000) Development of knowledge and skills at work. In F. Coffield (ed) *Differing Visions of a Learning Society* (Vol 1). Policy Press, pp 231–262.

Ervasti, H., Andersen, J.G. and Ringdal, K. (eds) (2012) *The Future of the Welfare State: Social Policy Attitudes and Social Capital in Europe*, Edward Elgar Publishing.

Erikson, E.H. (1980) *Identity and the Life Cycle*. W.W. Norton & Company (original work published 1959).

Erikson, E.H. and Erikson, J.M. (1998) *The Life Cycle Completed (Extended Version)*. W.W. Norton & Company.

Etherington, K. (2006) Reflexivity: using our 'selves' in narrative research. *Narrative Research on Learning: Comparative and International Perspectives*, 77, 92.

Etzioni, A. (1993) *The Parenting Deficit* (No 4). Demos.

Etzioni, A. (1996) The responsive community: A communitarian perspective. *American Sociological Review*, 1–11.

Evans, K. (2011) 'Big Society' in the UK: A policy review. *Children & Society*, 25(2), 164–171.

Fahlman, S.A., Mercer-Lynn, K.B., Flora, D.B. and Eastwood, J.D. (2013) Development and validation of the multidimensional state boredom scale. *Assessment*, 20(1), 68–85.

Falk, B. (2009) Supporting the education and care of young children: Putting into practice what we know. *Second International Handbook of Educational Change*, pp 933–951.

Farber, B., Brink, D.C. and Raskin, P.M. (2001) La psicoterapia de Carl Rogers. *Casos y comentarios*.

Farnworth, J.P.M.L., Rogers, T.B.H.S. and Prioletti, J.A.W.G.M. (2011) Crossing borders in correctional institutions. *Occupational Therapies without Borders-Volume 2: Towards an Ecology of Occupation-Based Practices*, p 235.

Farquhar, C. and Das, R. (1999) Are focus groups suitable 'Sensitive' Topics? In *Developing Focus Group Research*. https://doi.org/10.4135/9781849208857.n4.

Farrell, J.P. (2007) Community education in developing countries. *The Sage Handbook of Curriculum and Instruction*, 369–389.

Field, F. (2003a) *Neighbours from Hell: The Politics of Behaviour*. Politicos Pub.

Field, J. (2003b) *Social Capital* (1st ed). Routledge.

Field, J. (2008) *Social Capital* (2nd ed). Routledge.

Fiore, E. (2024) Navigating danger through nuisance: Racialized urban fears, gentrification, and sensory enskilment in Amsterdam. *City & Society*, 36(1), 23–34.

Flyvbjerg, B. (2001) *Making Social Science Matter: Why Social Science Fails and How It Can Begin to Succeed*. Cambridge University Press.

Flyvbjerg, B., Bruzelius, N. and Rothengatter, W. (2003) *Megaprojects and Risk: An Anatomy of Ambition*. Cambridge University Press.

Flyvbjerg, B., Landman, T. and Schram, S. (eds) (2012) *Real Social Science: Applied Phronesis*, Cambridge University Press.

Forrest, J. and Dunn, K. (2010) Attitudes to multicultural values in diverse spaces in Australia's immigrant cities, Sydney and Melbourne. *Space and Polity*, 14(1), 81–102.

Forrester-Jones, R., Jones, S., Heason, S. and Di Terlizzi, M. (2004) Supported employment: a route to social networks. *Journal of Applied Research in Intellectual Disabilities*, 17(3), 199–208.

Fowler, B. (1996) *Pierre Bourdieu and Cultural Theory: Critical Investigations*.

France, A. (2007) *Understanding Youth in Late Modernity*. McGraw-Hill Education.

Freire, P. (1970) Cultural action and conscientization. *Harvard Educational Review*, 40(3), 452–477.

Freire, P. (1972) *Pedagogy of the Oppressed*. Penguin.

Freire, P. (1974) *Education for Consciousness*.

Freire, P. (1985) *The Politics of Education Culture Power and Liberation*. Bergin & Garvey.

Freire, P. (1993) *Pedagogy of the City*. Continuum.

Freire, P. (1995) *The Pedagogy of the Oppressed*. Continuum.

Freire, P. (1996) *Pedagogia da autonomia*.

Freire, S. (2008) A look at inclusion. *Journal of Education*, 5–20.

Friedkin, N.E. (2004) Social cohesion. *Annual Review of Sociology*, 30(1), 409–425.

Fung, A., Graham, M. and Weil, D. (2007) *Full Disclosure: The Perils and Promise of Transparency*. Cambridge University Press.

Furlong, A. (2009) *Handbook of Youth and Young Adulthood: New Perspectives and Agendas*. Taylor & Francis.

Furlong, A. (ed) (2017) *Handbook of Youth and Young Adulthood*. Routledge.

Furlong, A. and Cartmel, F. (2012) Social change and political engagement among young people: Generation and the (2009)/2010 British Election Survey. *Parliamentary Affairs*, 65(1), 13–28.

Fusco, D. (2012) Use of self in the context of youth work. *Child and Youth Services*, 33(1), 33–45. https://doi.org/10.1080.0145935X.665323

Fyfe, I. and Mackie, A. (2024) Are you for real? Investigating authenticity in community-based youth work practice. *Journal of Youth Studies*, 27(1), 1–16.

Gable, S.L. and Haidt, J. (2005) What (and why) is positive psychology? *Review of General Psychology*, 9(2), 103–110.

Gallay, L. (2006) Social responsibility. In L. Sherrod, C.A. Flanagan, R. Kassimir, and A K. Syvertsen (eds) *Youth Activism: An International Encyclopedia*. Greenwood Press, pp 599–602.

Galster, G. (2001) On the nature of neighbourhood. *Urban Studies*, 38(12), 2111–2124.

Garmezy, N. (1991) Resiliency and vulnerability to adverse developmental outcomes associated with poverty. *American Behavioral Scientist*, 34(4), 416–430.

Garmezy, N. (1993) Children in poverty: Resilience despite risk. *Psychiatry*, 56(1), 127–136.

Gee, J.P. (1989) Two styles of narrative construction and their linguistic and educational implications. *Discourse Processes*, 12(3), 287–307.

Ghaye, T. (2010) *Teaching and Learning Through Reflective Practice: A Practical Guide for Positive Action*. Routledge.

Giddens, A. and Pierson, C. (1998) *Conversations with Anthony Giddens: Making Sense of Modernity*. Stanford University Press.

Gilchrist, A. (2019) *The Well-Connected Community: A Networking Approach to Community Development*. Policy Press.

Ginther, D., Haveman, R. and Wolfe, B. (2000) Neighbourhoods attributes as determinants of children's outcomes: how robust are the relationships? *Journal of Human Resources*, 35(4), 603–642.

Giroux, H.A. (1996) Democratic education and popular culture. *International Journal of Social Education*, 11.

Giroux, H. (1997) Rewriting the discourse of racial identity: Towards a pedagogy and politics of whiteness. *Harvard Educational Review*, 67(2), 285–321.

Giroux, H.A. (2003) Public pedagogy and the politics of resistance: Notes on a critical theory of educational struggle. *Educational Philosophy and Theory*, 35(1), 5–16.

Giroux, H.A. (2009) Youth in the empire of consumption: Beyond the pedagogy of commodification. *JAC*, 691–756.

Giroux, H.A. (2012) *Disturbing Pleasures. Learning Popular Culture*. New York.

Goffman, E. (1969) The insanity of place. *Psychiatry*, 32(4), 357–388.

Goffman, E. (1978) Response cries. *Language*, 787–815.

Goldberg, Y.K., Eastwood, J.D., LaGuardia, J. and Danckert, J. (2011) Boredom: An emotional experience distinct from apathy, anhedonia, or depression. *Journal of Social and Clinical Psychology*, 30(6), 647–666.

Goleman D. (1995) *Emotional Intelligence: Why It Can Matter More Than IQ*. Bloomsbury.

Goleman, D. (1998) *Working with Emotional Intelligence*. Bantam Books.

Goleman, D (2001) Emotional intelligence: Issues in paradigm building. *The Emotionally Intelligent Workplace*, 13, 26.

Goodall, J. (2022) A framework for family engagement: Going beyond the Epstein framework. *Wales Journal of Education*, 24(2).

Goodman, A. and Gregg, P. (eds) (2010) *Poorer Children's Educational Attainment: How Important Are Attitudes and Behaviour?* Joseph Rowntree Foundation, pp 76–92.

Gov.uk (2022) *Press Release: £368 Million Fund to Improve Youth Services in Underserved Areas Open for Bids*, 1 August 2022, Available from: https://www.gov.uk/government/news/368-million-fund-to-improve-youth-services-in-underserved-areasopens-for-bids?utm_medium=email&utm_campaign=govuk-notifications-topic&utm_source=5810cbc6-db3b-43f8-a5d0-dd5 5e78b15f6&utm_content=weekly

Gov.uk (2024) Available from: https://labour.org.uk/updates/press-releases/yvette-cooper-speech-at-labour-party-conference-2024/

Graney, K. (2022). *Empire and Belonging in the Eurasian Borderlands.* Cornell University Press.

Granot, Y. and Tyler, T.R. (2024) Adolescent cognition and procedural justice: Broadening the impact of research findings on policy and practice. *Social and Personality Psychology Compass*, 13(10), e12503. https://labour.org.uk/updates/press-releases/yvette-cooper-speech-at-labour-party-conference-2024/

Gregg, D. (2010) *Family Intervention Projects: A Classic Case of Policy-Based Evidence.* Centre for Crime and Justice Studies.

Grossman, P. (2011) Defining mindfulness by how poorly I think I pay attention during everyday awareness and other intractable problems for psychology's (re) invention of mindfulness: comment on Brown et al. (2011). *American Psychological Association*, 1040-3590/11, DOI: 10.1037/a0022713

Gunter, A. and Watt, P. (2009) Grafting, going to college and working on road: Youth transitions and cultures in an East London neighbourhood. *Journal of Youth Studies*, 12(5), 515–529.

Habermas J. (1987) *The Theory of Communicative Action Volume II: System and Lifeworld.* Polity.

Halpern, D. (2005) *Social Capital.* Polity.

Hamm, L., Maston, M., McLoughlin, J. and Smith, J. (2021) Educators responding to rapid demographic change in New Brunswick: 'It is not inclusion if they are just sitting in the desk'. *Alberta Journal of Educational Research*, 67(2), 178–201.

Hammersley, M. and Atkinson, P. (2019) *Ethnography: Principles in Practice.* Routledge.

Hamnet, C. (1983) The conditions in England's inner cities on the eve of the 1981 riots. *Area*, 15, 7–13.

Hancox, D. (2011) *Summer of Unrest: Kettled Youth: The Battle Against the Neoliberal Endgame.* Random House.

Harris, M.B. (2000) Correlates and characteristics of boredom proneness and boredom. *Journal Of Applied Social Psychology*, 30(3), 576–598.

Hart, R.A. (1992) Children's participation: From tokenism to citizenship. *Papers Inness*, 92(6), 43–60.

Hart, R.A. (2008) Stepping back from 'The ladder': Reflections on a model of participatory work with children. In *Participation and Learning: Perspectives on Education and the Environment, Health and Sustainability*. Springer Netherlands, pp 19–31.

Hart, S. (2009) The 'problem' with youth: Young people, citizenship and the community. *Citizenship Studies*, 13(6), 641–657. http://www.tandfonl ine.com/doi/abs/10.1080/13621020903309656

Harvey, L. (2003) Student feedback [1]. *Quality in Higher Education*, 9(1), 3–20.

Hatuka, T. (2024) Do neighbourhoods still matter? On our agency and (possible) future paths. *Built Environment*, 50(1).

Hayes, S.C., Bissett, R., Korn, Z., Zettle, R.D., Rosenfarb, I., Cooper, L. and Grundt, A.M. (1999) The impact of acceptance versus control rationales on pain tolerance. *The Psychological Record*, 49(1), 33–47.

Hawkins, R.L. and Maurer, K. (2010) Bonding, bridging and linking: How social capital operated in New Orleans following Hurricane Katrina. *British Journal of Social Work*, 40(6), 1777–1793.

Healy, K. and O'Prey, M. (2011) *Taking a Social Justice Approach to Community Development*. The Community Foundation for Northern Ireland.

Heath, S.C., Rabinovich, A. and Barreto, M. (2023) Exploring the social dynamics of urban regeneration: A qualitative analysis of community members' experiences. *British Journal of Social Psychology*, 62(1), 521–539.

Hennigh L. (1981) The anthropologist as key informant: inside a rural Oregon town. In J. Messerschmidt (ed) *Anthropologists at Home in North America, Methods and Issues in the Study of One's Own Society*, Cambridge University Press, pp 121–132.

Henze, R.C. (1992) *Non-Formal Learning, Implicit Learning and Tacit Learning in Professional Work*. Prospect Press, p 150.

Hick, S. (2009) *Mindfulness and Social Work Practice*. Lyceum Books.

Hochschild A.R. (2003) *The Commercialization of Intimate Life: Notes from Home and Work*. University of California Press.

Hoff, I. (2025) Raymond Williams and contemporary youth transitions: a cultural studies critique of social generational approaches in youth studies. *Journal of Youth Studies*, 28(1), 66–81.

Hofstede, G. (1980) *Culture's Consequences: International Differences in Work-Related Values*. Sage.

Holland C., Clark, A., Catts, J. and Peace, S. (2007) *Social Interactions in Urban Public Places: Public Spaces*. Policy Press.

Holland, R.G. (2008) Will the real smart city please stand up? Intelligent, progressive or entrepreneurial? *City*, 12(3), 303–320.

Holloway, S.D., Yamamoto, Y., Suzuki, S. and Mindnich, J.D. (2008) Determinants of parental involvement in early schooling: Evidence from Japan. *Early Childhood Research & Practice*, 10(1), p.n1.

Hookway, N. (2013) Emotions, body and self: critiquing moral decline sociology. *Sociology*, 47(4), 841–857.

Hooper, P., Foster, S., Knuiman, M. and Giles-Corti, B. (2020) Testing the impact of a planning policy based on New Urbanist planning principles on residents' sense of community and mental health in Perth, Western Australia. *Environment and Behavior*, 52(3), 305–339.

Howard, F. (2023) Youth work, music making and activism. *Youth*, 3(3), 1053–1062.

Howard, F. (2024) 'Radio is a blank canvas for youth work': communication, creative agency, compassion and empathy. *Journal of Applied Youth Studies*, 7(2), 137–154.

Hoxsey, S.Z.L. (1990) *The Relationship Between Family Environment, Self-Esteem, and Classroom Behavior of School-Age Children*, doctoral dissertation, Montana State University-Bozeman, College of Education, Health & Human Development.

Hsieh, C.C. and Pugh, M.D. (1993) Poverty, income inequality, and violent crime: a meta-analysis of recent aggregate data studies. *Criminal Justice Review*, 18(2), 182–202. http://dx.doi.org/10.1177/073401689301800203

Hsu, P.C. and Chen, R.S. (2023) Analyzing the mechanisms by which digital platforms influence family-school partnerships among parents of young children. *Sustainability*, 15(24), 16708.

Honwana, A (2014) Youth, waithood, and protest movements in Africa. In *African Dynamics in a Multipolar World: 5th European Conference on African Studies – Conference Proceedings*. Centro de Estudos Internacionais do Instituto Universitário de Lisboa (ISCTE-IUL), pp 2428–2447.

Hughes, J. and Batsleer, J. (2014) Looking through the other side of the street: youth participation in the arts in the edgelands of urban Manchester. In *Design in the Borderlands*. Routledge, pp 156–172.

Hunter, B.A. and Greenberg, A.G. (2016) *Social Capital and Community Well-Being: The Serve Here Initiative*, 199.

In Defence of Youth Work (IDYW) (2009) *Open Letter* [Online]. Available from: http://www.indefenceofyouthwork.org.uk

In Defence of Youth Work (IDYW) (2011) Available from: https://indefenceofyouthwork.com/

INFED (nd) *What Is Informal Education?* [Online]. Available from: http://infed.org/mobi/what-is-informal-education/

Isin, E.F. (ed) (2013) *Enacting European Citizenship*. Cambridge University Press.

Jamal, T. and Hollinshead, K. (2001) Tourism and the forbidden zone: The underserved power of qualitative inquiry. *Tourism Management*, 22(1), 63–82.

Jeffs, T. (2011) *Where Now? Youth and Policy* [Online]. Available from: www.infed.org/association/citizenship_youth_work_democratic_renewal

Jeffs, T. and Smith, M.K. (2005) *Informal Education: Conversation, Democracy and Learning*. Educational Heretics Press.

Jeffs, T. and Smith, M. (2008) Valuing youth work. *Youth and Policy*, 100, 277–302.

Jeffs, T. and Smith, M.K. (2010) *Youth Work and Practice*. Palgrave Macmillan.

Jeffs, T. and Smith, M.K. (2021) The education of informal educators. *Education Sciences*, 11(9), 488.

Jennings, L.B., Parra-Medina, D.M., Hilfinger-Messias, D.K. and McLoughlin, K. (2006) Toward a critical social theory of youth empowerment. *Journal of Community Practice*, 14(1–2), 31–55.

Jericho, M. and Elliott, A. (2020) Youth health in a digital world: approaching screen use in clinical practice. *Clinical Child Psychology and Psychiatry*, 25(3), 662–671.

Jeynes, W. H. (2015) A meta-analysis: The relationship between father involvement and student academic achievement. *Urban Education*, 50(4), 387–423.

Kabat-Zinn, J. (2003) Mindfulness-based interventions in context: Past, present, and future. *Clinical Psychology: Science and Practice*, 10(2), 144–156. https://doi.org/10.1093/clipsy.bpg016

Kallio, J. (2024) 'Basically, my only dream is to be a part of society'– young adults' negotiations for citizenship in the institutional system. *Journal of Youth Studies*, 1–18.

Kane, T.J. (2003) *A Quasi-Experimental Estimate of the Impact of Financial Aid on College-Going*. National Bureau of Economic Research.

Kant, I. (1996) *Metaphysics of Morals*. Cambridge University Press.

Katz, J.S. (1994) Geographical proximity and scientific collaboration. *Scientometrics*, 31, 31–43.

Kavanagh, N. and Lewis, C. (2024) Developing age-friendly communities in areas of urban regeneration. *Reimagining Age-Friendly Communities: Urban Ageing and Spatial Justice*. Policy Press, pp 100–117.

Keller, T.E. (2005) A systemic model of the youth mentoring intervention. *Journal of Primary Prevention*, 26, 169–188.

Keller, J. (2008) On the development of regulatory focus: The role of parenting styles. *European Journal of Social Psychology*, 38(2), 354–364.

Kellerman, A. (2012) Potential mobilities. *Mobilities*, 7(1), 171–183.

Kellerman, M. (2007). *Collaboration Assessment Guide and Tool*. United Way of Canada – Centraide.

Kellett, M. (2009) Children and young people's participation. In *Children and Young People's Worlds: Developing Frameworks for Integrated Practice*, pp 43–60.

Kelty, N.E. and Wakabayashi, T. (2020) Family engagement in schools: Parent, educator, and community perspectives. *Sage Open*, 10(4), 2158244020973024.

Kennedy, E. (2014) No childhood here. *Perspectives*.

Kennelly, J. and Watt, P. (2012) Seeing Olympic effects through the eyes of marginally housed youth: changing places and the gentrification of East London. *Visual Studies*, 27(2), 151–160.

Keohane, R. O. (1982) The demand for international regimes. *International Organization*, 36, 325–355.

Kiilakoski, T. and Kivijärvi, A. (2015) 'Youth clubs as spaces of non-formal learning: professional idealism meets the spatiality experienced by young people in Finland. *Studies in Continuing Education*, 37(1), 47–61.

Kobayashi, M. (2003) The role of peer support in ESL students' accomplishment of oral academic tasks. *Canadian Modern Language Review*, 59(3), 337–369.

Kohlberg, L. and Candee, D. (1984) The relationship of moral judgment to moral action. *Morality, Moral Behavior, and Moral Development*, 52, 73.

Kolb, D.A. (1984) *Experiential Learning*. Prentice Hall. Environment.

Korsgard, C. (1996) *The Sources of Normativity*. Cambridge University Press.

Kostyunina, N.Y. and Valeeva, R.A. (2015) Prevention and correction of juvenile neglect. *Review of European Studies*, 7, 225.

Krasner, S.D. (1984) Approaches to the state: Alternative conceptions and historical dynamics. *Comparative Politics*, 16(2), 223–46. https://doi.org/10.2307/421608.

Kynaston, D. (2011) *City of London: The History*. Random House.

Lai, A. and Burchett, R. (2021) Involving retired citizens in ESL education: Case study of a secondary school program. *Journal of Intergenerational Relationships*, 19(2), 249–271.

Lamb, S., Jackson, J., Walstab, A. and Huo, S. (2015) *Educational Opportunity in Australia 2015: Who Succeeds and Who Misses Out*. Available from: http://www.mitchellinstitute.org.au/wp-content/uploads/2015/11/Educational-opportunity-in-Australia-2015-Who-succeeds-and-who-misses-out-19Nov15.pdf

Lammy, D. (2011) *Out of the Ashes: Britain after the Riots*. Guardian Books.

Lang, S. (1999) Democracy is not boring. *Teaching History*, (96), 23.

Langford, B. (2024) *Intergenerational Conflict and Authentic Youth Experience: Adults Denigrating Young People*. Taylor & Francis.

Larsen, H.G. and Hansen, A.L. (2008) Gentrification—gentle or traumatic? Urban renewal policies and socioeconomic transformations in Copenhagen. *Urban Studies*, 45(12), 2429–2448.

Lather, P. (1992) Critical frames in educational research: Feminist and post-structural perspectives. *Theory into Practice*, 31(2), 87–99.

Layland, E.K., Hill, B.J. and Nelson, L.J. (2018) Freedom to explore the self: How emerging adults use leisure to develop identity. *The Journal of Positive Psychology*, 13(1), 78–91.

Lee, C.D. (2008) The centrality of culture to the scientific study of learning and development: How an ecological framework in education research facilitates civic responsibility. *Educational Researcher*, 37(5).

Leedy, P.D. and Ormrod, J.E. (1980) *Practical Research*, New York: Macmillan.

Leek, J. and Rojek, M. (2021) Project Reference Number: 2019-1-FR01-KA203-062506.

Lees, L. (2003) Super-gentrification: The case of Brooklyn Heights. *Urban Studies*, 40(12), 2487–2509.

Lees, L., Slater, T. and Wyly, E. (2007) *Gentrification*. Routledge.

Lefebvre, H. (1991) *Critique of Everyday Life. Foundations for a Sociology of the Everyday*, 2.

Lin, N. (2000) Inequality in social capital. *Contemporary Sociology*, 29(6), 785–795.

Lin, N. (2001) Guanxi: A conceptual analysis. *Contributions in Sociology*, 133, 153–166.

Lipman, P. (2011) Mixed-income schools and housing policy in Chicago: a critical examination of the gentrification/education/'racial'exclusion nexus. In *Mixed Communities*. Policy Press, pp 95–114.

Lipsey, M. and Derzon, J. (1998) Predictors of violent or serious delinquency in adolescence and early adulthood: a synthesis of longitudinal research. In L. Rolf and D.P. Farrington (eds) *Serious and Violent Juvenile Offenders: Risk Factors and Successful Interventions*, pp 86–105.

Li, Z.X. and Zhang, X.M. (2023) *'Good Kids' and 'Good Parents': Research on Parent-Child Tourism Interaction From the Perspective of Children's Education.*

London, M., Sessa, V.I. and Shelley, L.A. (2023) Developing self awareness: Learning processes for self-and interpersonal growth. *Annual Review of Organizational Psychology and Organizational Behavior*, 10(1), 261–288.

London Youth (2019) [Online]. Available from: https://londonyouth.org/wp-content/uploads/2018/09/A-Space-of-Our-Own-Final-Spread.pdf

Louie, V. (2012) *Keeping the Immigrant Bargain: The Costs and Rewards of Success in America*. Russell Sage Foundation.

Lowe, N.J., Stern, J., Bryson, J.R., Mulhall, R., Carolina, N. and Hill, C. (2016) Working in a new generation: Youth job creation and employer engagement in urban manufacturing. In *Association of American Geographers Annual Conference,* http://mfgren. org/wp-content/uploads/2015/10/Lowe-et-al-MC-Paper-2016. pdf

Lowry, L. (1960) Windows on the world. *English Journal*, 49(2), 115–117.

Luhmann, M. (2024) Long-term changes in well-being. In *Encyclopedia of Quality of Life and Well-Being Research*. Springer International Publishing, pp 4008–4011.

Lunneblad, J., Bengtsson, J. and Hammarén, N. (2024) Becoming a 'youth at risk': how professionals conceptualise risk among young people in disadvantaged urban areas in Sweden. *Critical and Radical Social Work*, 12(1), 75–88.

MacDonald, G.B. and Valdivieso, R. (2001). Measuring deficits and assets: How we track youth development now, and how we should track it. In *Trends in Youth Development: Visions, Realities and Challenges*, pp 155–186.

Macklem, G.L. (2015) *Boredom in the Classroom: Addressing Student Motivation, Self-regulation, and Engagement in Learning* (Vol 1). Springer.

Malkovsky, E., Merrifield, C., Goldberg, Y. and Danckert, J. (2012) Exploring the relationship between boredom and sustained attention. *Experimental Brain Research*, 221, 59–67. doi: 10.1007/s00221-012-3147-z

Mann, S and Cadman, R. (2014) Does being bored make you more creative? *Creativity Research Journal*, 26(26), 165–173.

Mannheim, K. (1952) The problem of generations. In P. Kecskemeti (ed) *Essays on the Sociology of Knowledge*. Routledge and Kegan Paul, pp 276–320.

Mapp, K.L. and Bergman, E. (2021) Embracing a new normal: Toward a more liberatory approach to family engagement. *Carnegie Corporation*.

Marshall, T. H. (1950) *Citizenship and Social Class*. Cambridge University Press.

Marshall, B.D., DeBeck, K., Simo, A., Kerr, T. and Wood, E. (2014) Gang involvement among street-involved youth in a Canadian setting: A gender-based analysis. *Public Health*, 129(1), 74.

Marshall, T.H. and Bottomore, T. (1992) *Citizenship and Social Class*. Pluto Press.

Marsiglio, W. (2008) *Men on a Mission: Valuing Youth Work in our Communities*. JHU Press.

Maslow, A. (1943) *Towards a Psychology of Being*. Nostrand Reinhold Company.

Mason, W. (2015) Austerity youth policy: exploring the distinctions between youth work in principle and youth work in practice. *Youth & Policy*, 114, 55–74.

Massey, D. (2005) The spatial construction of youth cultures. In *Cool Places*. Routledge, pp 132–140.

Masten, A.S. and Coatsworth, J.D. (1998) The development of competence in favorable and unfavorable environments: Lessons from research on successful children. *American Psychologist*, 53(2), 205.

Maton, K.I. (2008) Empowering community settings: Agents of individual development, community betterment, and positive social change. *American Journal of Community Psychology*, 41, 4–21.

Matthew, E. (2011) Effort optimism in the classroom: Attitudes of black and white students on education, social structure, and causes of life opportunities. *Sociology of Education*, 84(3), 225–245.

McAra, L. and McVie, S. (2022) *Causes and Impact of Offending and Criminal Justice Pathways: Follow-up of the Edinburgh Study Cohort at Age 35*. University of Edinburgh.

McArdle, R. (2022) Flexible methodologies: a case for approaching research with fluidity. *The Professional Geographer*, 74(4), 620–627. https://doi.org/10.1080/00330124.2021.2023593

McArdle, K. (2024) Impact, change and making a difference. In *Community Work*. Policy Press, pp 48–60.

McFarlane, C. (2011) Assemblage and critical urbanism. *City*, 15(2), 204–224.

McKee, V., Oldfield, C. and Poultney, J. (2010) *The Benefits of Youth Work*. Available from: http://www.cywu.org.uk/assets/content_pages/18779 9973_Benefits_of_youth_work. pdf (11 June 2017).

McRobbie, A. and Thornton, S.L. (1995) Rethinking 'moral panic' for multi-mediated social worlds. *British Journal of Sociology*, 559–574.

Mercer, K.B. and Eastwood, J.D. (2010) Is boredom associated with problem gambling behaviour? It depends on what you mean by 'boredom'. *International Gambling Studies*, 10(1), 91–104.

Merton, B. Payne, M. and Smith, D. (2004) *An Evaluation of the Impact of Youth Work in England*. DFES.

Messias, D., Fore, R. and McLoughlin, D. (2005) Adult roles in community-based youth empowerment programmes. *Implications for Best Practice. FAM Community Health*, 28, 320–337.

Michalski, C.A., Diemert, L.M., Helliwell, J.F., Goel, V. and Rosella, L.C. (2020) Relationship between sense of community belonging and self-rated health across life stages. *SSM-Population Health*, 12, 100676.

Mikkonen, T. and Vadén, T. (2009) The anatomy of sustainable open source community building the cultural point of view. In *Proceedings of the First International Workshop on Building Sustainable Open Source Communities*. Tampereen teknillinen yliopisto, pp 14–20.

Miller, R. (2012) *Teacher Absence as a Leading Indicator of Student Achievement: New National Data Offer Opportunity to Examine Cost of Teacher Absence Relative to Learning Loss*. Center for American Progress.

Miller, S.R. and Coll, E. (2007) From social withdrawal to social confidence: Evidence for possible pathways. *Current Psychology*, 26, 86–101.

Mills, C.W. (2000) *The Sociological Imagination*, Oxford: Oxford University Press.

Mills, S. and Kraftl, P. (2014) *Informal Education, Children and Youth: Geographies, Histories and Practices*. Palgrave MacMillan.

Mintzberg, H. (2009) *Managing*. Pearson Education.

Moore, H.L. and Woodcraft, S. (2019) Understanding prosperity in East London: Local meanings and 'sticky' measures of the good life. *City & Society*, 31(2), 275–298.

Morgan, A. (1943) *Young Citizen*. Penguin.

Morrow, V. (1998) 'If you were a teacher, it would be harder to talk to you': reflections on qualitative research with children in school. *International Journal of Social Research Methodology: Theory and Practice*, 1(4), 297–313.

Morrow, V. (2001) Young people's explanations and experiences of social exclusion: retrieving Bourdieu's concept of social capital. *International Journal of Sociology and Social Policy*, 21(4/5/6), 37–63.

Moustakim, M. (2012) Living contradictions in the professional practice of informal education. *Les dossiers des sciences de l'éducation*, 28, 43–56.

Murphy, C. and Ord, J. (2013) Youth work, self-disclosure and professionalism. *Ethics and Social Welfare*, 7(4), 326–341.

Muncie, J. (2006) Governing young people: Coherence and contradiction in contemporary youth justice. *Critical Social Policy*, 26(4), 770–793.

Nagar, R. (2002) Footloose researchers, 'traveling' theories, and the politics of transnational feminist praxis. *Gender, Place and Culture: A Journal of Feminist Geography*, 9(2), 179–186.

Napoli, M. and Day, D. (2024) Poetry as a vehicle to support social and emotional learning. In *Improving Mental Health and Wellbeing Through Bibliotherapy*. IGI Global, pp 301–319.

NCS (2018) [Online] Available from: https://www.gov.uk/government/publications/national-citizen-service-evaluation-report-2018

Neate, R. (2011) Soaring food prices will be devastating for the world's poor, *The Guardian*, 18 June, p 35.

Newlove, P.M. (2022) *A Diversity of Tactics: Exploring the Contexts, Negotiations, and Motivations of Teachers Doing Antiracist Work*. University of Colorado at Denver.

Newton, B. (1999) *The Urban Community: A World Perspective*. Henri Holt & Co.

Nicholls, A. (2014) November. London 2012 legacy: Olympic park waterways. In *Proceedings of the Institution of Civil Engineers-Civil Engineering*, 167(6), 40–45.

Nussbaum, M. (2009) Capabilities as fundamental entitlements: Sen and social justice. *From Employability Towards Capability*, 4(1), 15–30.

Nussbaum, M. and Sen, A. (eds) (1993) *The Quality of Life*. Clarendon Press.

Oberwittler, D. (2004) A multilevel analysis of neighbourhood contextual effects on serious juvenile offending: The role of subcultural values and social disorganization. *European Journal of Criminology*, 1(2), 201–235.

O'Carroll, J. (2016) *Identifying Barriers and Facilitators for Educational Inclusion for Young People who Offend*, doctoral dissertation, University College London.

Ocejo, R.E. (2011) The early gentrifier: Weaving a nostalgia narrative on the lower east side. *City & Community*, 10(3), 285–310.

Olins, W. (2005) Making a national brand. In *The New Public Diplomacy: Soft Power in International Relations*. Palgrave Macmillan UK, pp 169–179.

ONS (2019) *Young People not in Education, Employment or Training (NEET), UK: February 2019*, Available from: https://www.ons.gov.uk/employmentandlabourmarket/peoplenotinwork/unemployment/bulletins/youngpeoplenotineducationemploymentortrainingneet/february2019

ONS (2021) *Young People not in Education, Employment or Training (NEET), UK: November 2021*, Available from: https://www.ons.gov.uk/employmentandlabourmarket/peoplenotinwork/unemployment/bulletins/youngpeoplenotineducationemploymentortrainingneet/november2021

Ord, J. (2004) The youth work curriculum and the transforming youth work agenda. *Youth and Policy*, 43–59.

Ord, J. (2007) *Youth Work Practice – Creating an Authentic Curriculum in Work with Young People*. Russell House Publishing.

Ord, J. (2009a) Thinking the unthinkable: Youth work without voluntary participation? *Journal of Youth and Policy*, 103, 39–48.

Ord, J. (2009b) Experiential learning in youth work in the UK: A return to Dewey. *International Journal of Lifelong Education*, 28(4), 493–511.

Ord, J. (2011) 'John Dewey & experiential learning: developing the theory of youth work', *Youth & Policy*, 108.

Ord, J. (ed) (2012a) *Critical Issues in Youth Work Management*. Routledge.

Ord, J. (2012b) Planning for Outcomes: A youth work problem. In J. Ord (ed) *Critical Issues in Youth Work Management*. Routledge.

Ord, J. (2016) Defending youth work practice in an age of austerity. In *Youth Work Process, Product and Practice*. Routledge, pp 133–144.

Ord, J. and Davies, B. (2022) Young people, youth work & the 'levelling up' policy agenda. *Local Economy*, 37(1–2), 104–117.

O'Rourke, S.R. (2011) *Parent Factors Associated with Anxiety in Children with Attention-Deficit/Hyperactivity Disorder*. The University of North Carolina at Greensboro.

Oscilowicz, E., Honey-Rosés, J., Anguelovski, I., Triguero-Mas, M. and Cole, H. (2020) Young families and children in gentrifying neighbourhoods: How gentrification reshapes use and perception of green play spaces. *Local Environment*, 25(10), 765–786.

Packham, C. (2008) *Active Citizenship and Community Learning*. Learning Matters.

Pain, R. (2000) Place, social relations and the fear of crime: A review. *Progress in Human Geography*, 24(3), 365–387.

Palmer, D.K. (2001) Hillside Elementary, Our Research Collaborative, Gentrification, and TWBE in Texas. *Gentrification and Bilingual Education*, 1.

Pattillo, M. (2008) *Black on the Block: The Politics of Race and Class in the City*. University of Chicago Press.

Pekrun, R. (2017) Achievement emotions. *Emotions in Late Modernity*, 142. Taylor and Francis.

Pekrun, R, Goetz, T., Titz, W. and Perry, R.P. (2002) Academic emotions in students' selfregulated learning and achievement: A program of quantitative and qualitative research. *Educational Psychologist*, 37(2), 91–105. doi: 10.1207/S15326985EP3702_4

Petrocchi, S., Angelini, G., Levante, A., Lecciso, F. and Fiorilli, C. (2024) Exploring the relationships between extreme levels of trust on young people's view of the future. *Basic and Applied Social Psychology*, 47(1), 1–11.

Phillimore, J. and Goodson, L. (2008) Making a place in the global city: The relevance of indicators of integration. *Journal of Refugee Studies*, 21(3). doi:10.1093/jrs/fen025

Philip, K., Shucksmith, J. and King, C. (2004) *Sharing a Laugh? A Qualitative Study of Mentoring Interventions with Young People*. Joseph Rowntree Foundation.

Phillips, S.D., Burns, B.J., Wagner, H.R. and Barth, R.P. (2004) Parental arrest and children involved with child welfare services agencies. *American Journal of Orthopsychiatry*, 74(2), 174–186.

Pitts, J. (2008) Intervening in gang-affected neighbourhoods. In *Prevention and Youth Crime*. Policy Press, pp 21–40.

Pitts, J. (2013) *Reluctant Gangsters: The Changing Face of Youth Crime*. Willan.

Popay, J., Whitehead, M., Ponsford, R., Egan, M. and Mead, R. (2021) Power, control, communities and health inequalities I: Theories, concepts and analytical frameworks. *Health Promotion International*, 36(5), 1253–1263.

Poplack, S. (1988) Contrasting patterns of code-switching in two communities. *Codeswitching: Anthropological and Sociolinguistic Perspectives*, 48, 215–244.

Porter, I. and Johnson-Hunter, M. (2023) *Inadequate Universal Credit and Barriers to Work*. Joesph Rowntree Foundation.

Portes, A. (1997) *Globalization from Below: the Rise of Transnational Communities* (Vol 98). Princeton University.

Prilleltensky, I. (2008) Migrant well-being is a multilevel, dynamic, value dependent phenomenon. *American Journal of Community Psychology*, 42, 359–364.

Prilleltensky, I. (2014) Education as transformation: Why and how. In *Psychology in Education: Critical Theory Practice*. Sense Publishers, pp 17–35.

Putnam, R.D. (1993) The prosperous community. *The American Prospect*, 4(13), 35–42.

Putnam, R.D. (1995) Bowling alone: America's declining social capital. *Journal of Democracy*, 6(1), 64–78.

Putnam, R.D. (2000) *Bowling Alone: The Collapse and Revival of American Community*. Simon and Schuster.

Putnam, R. (2005) *The New Movement of Civic Renewal*. Public Management - Lawrence then Washington. 87(6), 7.

Quinn Patton, M. (2002) A vision of evaluation that strengthens democracy. *Evaluation*, 8(1), 125–139.

Quintanar, I.M. (2007) *Defining the Mobilization of Social Capital for Low-SES inority uth articipants in the Summer Bridge Program by Program Leaders*. University of Southern California.

Rappaport, J. (1987) Terms of empowerment/exemplars of prevention: Toward a theory for community psychology. *American Journal of Community Psychology*, 15, 121–148.

Rappaport, J. (1994) *Cumbe Reborn: An Andean Ethnography of History*. University of Chicago Press.

Rhee, K. and Sigler, T. (2024) Can you develop self-awareness? Only if you are willing. *Journal of Leadership Education*. https://doi.org/10.1108/JOLE-02-2024-0045

Resnick, M.D., Harris, L.J. and Blum, R.W. (1993) The impact of caring and connectedness on adolescent health and well-being. *Journal of Paediatrics and Child Health*, 29, S3-S9.

Rhodes, J.E., Schwartz, S.E.O., Willis, M.M. and Wu, M.B. (2014) Validating a mentoring relationship quality scale: does match strength predict match length? *Youth and Society*, 49, 415–437.

Richmond, J.B. and Beardslee, W.R. (1988) Resiliency: Research and practical implications for pediatricians. *Journal of Developmental & Behavioral Pediatrics*, 9(3), 157–163.

Richardson, L., Minh, A., McCormack, D., Laing, A., Barbic, S., Hayashi, K., Milloy, M.J., Huyser, K.R., Leahy, K. and Li, J. (2022) Cohort profile: the assessing economic transitions (ASSET) study—A community-based mixed-methods study of economic engagement among inner-city residents. *International Journal of Environmental Research and Public Health*, 19(16), 10456.

Riessman, C.K. (2008) *Narrative Methods for the Human Sciences.* Sage.

Rivenbark, J., Arseneault, L., Caspi, A., Danese, A., Fisher, H.L., Moffitt, T.E., Rasmussen, L.J., Russell, M.A. and Odgers, C.L. (2020) Adolescents' perceptions of family social status correlate with health and life chances: A twin difference longitudinal cohort study. *Proceedings of the National Academy of Sciences*, 117(38), 23323–23328.

Robbins, L.B., Ling, J., Pfeiffer, K.A., Kerver, J.M., Resnicow, K., McCaffery, H., Hilliard, A., Hobbs, L., Donald, S. and Kaciroti, N. (2024) Intervention to increase physical activity and healthy eating among under-represented adolescents: GOAL trial protocol. *BMJ Open*, 14(1), e080437.

Robertson, S. (2005) *Youth Clubs, Associations, Participation, Friendship and Fun.* Russel House Publishing.

Robottom, I. and Hart, P. (1993) Towards a meta-research agenda in science and enviormental education. *International Journal of Science Education*, 15(5), 591–605.

Rocha, E.M. (1997) A ladder of empowerment. *Journal of Planning Research*, 17, 31–44.

Rogers, C.R. (1961) *The Characteristics of a Helping Relationship.* pp 39–58.

Rogers, C. (1980) *A Way of Being.* Houghton Mifflin.

Rogers, C. (2000) Person-centred therapy. *Six Key Approaches to Counselling and Therapy*, 1, 98–105.

Rose, R. and Shevlin, M. (2004) Encouraging voices: Listening to young people who have been marginalised. *Support for Learning*, 19(4), 155–161.

Rotenberg, K.J. (ed) (2010) *Interpersonal Trust During Childhood and Adolescence.* Cambridge University Press.

Royce, S. (2004) *Hearing Their Voices: Using Photovoice to Capture Youth Perspectives on Empowerment.* University of South Carolina.

Sapin, K. (2009) *Essential Skills for Youth Work Practice.* Sage Publications Ltd.

Salazar, N.B. (2011) The power of imagination in transnational mobilities. *Identities*, 18(6), 576–598.

Salamon, K. (nd) *The New Identity of Social Work in a Sociological Perspective*, RADA NAUKOWA, 33.

Saunders, P. (1989) The meaning of 'home' in contemporary English culture. *Housing Studies*, 4(3), 177–192.

Savage, M. (2000) *Class Analysis and Social Transformation.* Open University Press.

Savage, S. (2005) Urban design education: Learning for life in practice. *Urban Design International*, 10, 3–10.

Schinkel, M. (2019) Rethinking turning points: Trajectories of parenthood and desistance. *Journal of Developmental and Life-Course Criminology*, 5, 366–386.

Schlichtman, J.J. and Patch, J. (2014) Gentrifier? Who, me? Interrogating the gentrifier in the mirror. *International Journal of Urban and Regional Research*, 38(4), 1491–1508.

Schön, D.A. (1983) *The Reflective Practitioner: How Professionals Think in Action.* Temple Smith.

Schopenhauer, A. (1988) Preisschrift über die Grundlage der Moral. In Lütkehaus, L. (ed) *Werke in 5 Bänden, Bd. 3: Kleinere Schriften.* Haffmans, pp 459–631.

Seal, M. and Frost, S. (2014) *Philosophy in Youth and Community Work.* Russell House Publishing.

Sealey, B.C. (2015) Protecting children from child abuse & neglect in Egypt: addressing neighborhood factors. *Egyptian Journal of Social Work*, 1(1), 59–77.

Searle, J.R. (1995) *The Construction of Social Reality.* The Free Press.

Seebach, M. (2008) Youth participation and youth work. *Youth Studies Ireland*, 3(2), 37–53.

Seligman, M.E. and Csikszentmihalyi, M. (2000) *Positive Psychology: An Introduction. American Psychologist*, 55(1), 5–14. http:/ www.freelogy.org/w/ images/d/dc/Sen85.pdf

Seligman, M.E.P. (2002) *Authentic Happiness: Using the New Positive Psychology to Realise Your Potential for Lasting Fulfilment.* Free Press.

Seligman, M.E. (2004) *Authentic Happiness: Using the New Positive Psychology to Realize your Potential for Lasting Fulfillment.* Simon and Schuster.

Seligman, M.E., Berkowitz, M.W., Catalano, R.F., Damon, W., Eccles, J.S., Gillham, J., Moore, K.A., Nicholson, H.J., Park, N., Penn, D.L. and Peterson, C. (2005) *The Positive Perspective on Youth Development.*

Semple, R.J., Lee, J., Rosa, D. and Miller, L.F. (2010) A randomized trial of mindfulness-based cognitive therapy for children: Promoting mindful attention to enhance social–emotional resiliency in children. *Journal of Child and Family Studies*, 19, 218–229.

Sercombe, H. (2010) *Youth Work Ethics*. Sage.

Sen, A.K. (2009) *The Idea of Justice*. Alan Lane, Penguin Group.

Setty, E. (2023) Risks and opportunities of digitally mediated interactions: young people's meanings and experiences. *Journal of Youth Studies*, 27(8), 1188–1206.

Sharbatiyan, M.H. (2011) The semantic components reflecting the link between social capital and the rate social health of the benefit of students of Payam Noor University, Mashhad. *Sociological Studies of Youth*, 2(5), 149–174.

Shaw, M. and Mayo, M. (eds) (2016) *Class, Inequality and Community Development*. Policy Press.

Sheridan, L.A. (2018) *Youth Participation Practice in North Ayrshire, Scotland from a Freirean Perspective*, doctoral dissertation, University of Glasgow.

Sherraden, M. (2001) *Assets and the Poor: Implications for Individual Accounts and Social Security*. Centre for Social Development, Washington University in St Louis.

Shipway, R. and Jones, I. (2007) Running away from home: Understanding visitor experience and behaviour at sport tourism events. *International Journal of Tourism Research*, 9(5).

Shipway, R., Holloway, I. and Jones, I. (2013) Organisations, practices, actors, and events: Exploring inside the distance running social world. *International Review for the Sociology of Sport*, 48(3), 259–276.

Siisiäinen, M. (1989) *Four Studies on Voluntary Organizations in Finland*. University of Jyväskylä,

Silbereisen, R.K. and Richard, L.M. (2007) *Approaches to Positive Youth Development*. TJ International Ltd.

Skeggs, B. (2004) *Class, Self, Culture*. Routledge.

Small, M.L. (2004) *Villa Victoria: The Transformation of Social Capital in a Boston Barrio*. University of Chicago Press.

Smith, A. and Seal, M. (2021) The contested terrain of critical pedagogy and teaching informal education in higher education. *Education Sciences*, 11(9), 476.

Smith, C.L. (2012) The impact of low-skilled immigration on the youth labor market. *Journal of Labor Economics*, 30(1), 55–89.

Smith, D. (2003) New Labour and youth justice *Children & Society*, 17(3), 226–235.

Smith, D.M. (1970) Adolescence: A study of stereotyping. *The Sociological Review*, 18(2), 197–211.

Smith, M. (1988) *Developing Youth Work. Informal Education, Mutual Aid and Popular Practice*. Open University Press.

Smith, M.K. (1999, 2009) Animateurs, animation and fostering learning and change. *The Encyclopaedia of Informal Education* [Online]. Available from: www.infed.org/animate/banimat.htm.

Smith, M.K. (2001) Ragged schools and the development of youth work and informal education. *The Encyclopaedia of Informal Education* [Online]. Available from: www.infed.org/youthwork/ragged_schools

Smith, M.K. (2002a) Youth work: An introduction. *The Encyclopaedia of Informal Education* [Online]. Available from: www.infed.org/youthwork/b-yw.htm

Smith, M.K. (2002b) *Transforming Youth Work: Resourcing Excellent Youth Services* [Online]. Available from: www.infed.org/youthwork/transformingyouthwork

Smith, M.K. (2011) Young people and the (2011) 'riots' in England – Experiences, explanations and implications for youth work. *The Encyclopaedia of Informal Education* [Online]. Available from: http://www.infed.org/archives/jeffs_and_smith/young_people_youth_work_and_the_2011_riots_in_england.html

Smith, R. (2017) *Diversion in Youth Justice: What Can We Learn from Historical and Contemporary Practices?* Routledge.

Smyth, L. (2012) *The Demands of Motherhood: Agents, Roles and Recognitions.* Palgrave Macmillan.

Smyth, J., McInerney, P. and Fish, T. (2013) *Culture and Society.* Taylor and Francis.

Somerville, P. (2011) *Understanding Community: Politics, Policy and Practice.* Policy Press.

Speer, P.W., Jackson, C.B. and Peterson, N.A. (2001) The relationship between social cohesion and empowerment: Support and new implications for theory. *Health Education and Behavior*, 28, 716–732.

Spence, J. (2008) What do youth workers do? Communicating youth work. *Journal of Youth Studies Ireland*, 2(2), 3–18.

Spencer, R., Basualdo-Delmonico, A. and Lewis, T.O. (2011) Working to make it work: The role of parents in the youth mentoring process. *Journal of Community Psychology*, 39(1), 51–59.

Spry, P.G., Johnson, C.A., McKendrick, A.M. and Turpin, A. (2001) Variability components of standard automated perimetry and frequency-doubling technology perimetry. *Investigative Ophthalmology & Visual Science*, 42(6), 1404–1410.

Stoker, G. (1995) Regime theory and urban politics. In D. Judge, G. Stoker and H. Wolman (eds) *Theories of Urban Politics.* Sage.

Strömbäck, C. (2024) Forecasting emotions: exploring the relationship between self-control, affective forecasting, and self-regulatory behavior. *Journal of the Economic Science Association*, 10(2), 472–484.

Strachan, C.D. (2024) *Voices of Bahamian Students: Using Student Voice to Leverage School Reform in the Bahamas*, doctoral dissertation, Morgan State University.

Sultana, F. (2007) Reflexivity, positionality and participatory ethics: Negotiating fieldwork dilemmas in international research. *ACME: An International Journal for Critical Geographies*, 6(3), 374–385.

Sweetman, B. (2009) *Religion and Science: An Introduction*. A&C Black.

Tam, H. and Tam, H. (1998) The challenge to build inclusive communities. In *Communitarianism: A New Agenda for Politics and Citizenship*, pp 247–268.

Talen, E. (2024) New urbanism. In *Encyclopedia of Quality of Life and Well-Being Research*. Springer International Publishing, pp 4697–4700.

Taylor, T. (2017) Treasuring, but not measuring: personal and social development. *Youth and Policy*. Available from: http://www.youthandpolicy.org/articles/treasuring-not-measuring/.

Taylor, C.A., Liang, B., Tracy, A.J., Williams, L.M. and Seigle, P. (2002) Gender differences in middle school adjustment, physical fighting, and social skills: Evaluation of a social competency program. *The Journal of Primary Prevention*, 23, 259–272.

Taylor, T., Connaughton, P., de St Croix, T., Davies, B. and Grace, P. (2018) The impact of neoliberalism upon the character and purpose of English youth work and beyond. In *The SAGE Handbook of Youth Work Practice*. SAGE, pp 84–97.

Terrion, J.L. (2006) Building social capital in vulnerable families: Success markers of a school-based intervention program. *Youth & Society*, 38(2), 155–176.

The Campaign for Youth Social Action (CYSA) (2013) *Scoping a Quality Framework for Youth Social Action*. CYSA.

The Children's Society (2011) [Online] Available from: https://www.childrenssociety.org.uk/sites/default/files/2023-08/GCR%202013.pdf

The Guardian (2015) *Are We Too Ready to Brand Teenagers as Yobs?* Available from: https://www.theguardian.com/commentisfree/2013/nov/12/teenagers-branded-antisocial-yobs-cleveland-chief-constable

The Guardian (2024) *Teenagers 'Crying Out' for Return of Youth Clubs in Englnd, Study Finds*, Available from: https://www.theguardian.com/society/article/2024/jun/30/teenagers-crying-out-for-return-of-youth-clubs-in-england-study-finds

Thompson, M. and Guantlett-Gilbert, J. (2008) Mindfulness with children and adolescents: Effective clinical application. *Clinical Child Psychology and Psychiatry*, 13(3), 395–407.

Thomson, R., Holland, J., McGrellis, S., Bell, R., Henderson, S. and Sharpe, S. (2004) Inventing adulthoods: A biographical approach to understanding youth citizenship. *The Sociological Review*, 52(2), 218–239.

Tolonen, T. (2007) Social and cultural capital meets youth research: A critical approach. In H. Helve and J. Bynner (eds) *Youth and Social Capital*. The Tufnell Press.

Torney-Purta, J. (2002) The school's role in developing civic engagement: A study of adolescents in twenty-eight countries. *Applied Developmental Science*, 6(4), 203–212. https://doi.org/10.1207/S1532480XADS0604_7

Trimmer-Platman, T. (2014) If you can name it you can claim it: Redefining youth work. *Research in Teacher Education*, 4(2), 34–38.

Trimpop, R.M. (1994) *The Psychology of Risk Taking Behavior* (Vol 107). Elsevier.

Trotz, D.A. and Peake, L. (2000) Work, family, and organising: an overview of the emergence of the economic, social and political roles of women in British Guiana. *Social and Economic Studies*, 189–222.

Turton, J. (2014) *Discover Society*. Essex University.

Tyler, K.A. (2009) Risk factors for trading sex among homeless young adults. *Archives of Sexual Behavior*, 38, 290–297.

UNISON (2016) *The UK's Youth Services: How Cuts are Removing Opportunities for Young People and Damaging their Lives*. UNISON.

van den Berg, M. (2013) City children and genderfied neighbourhoods: The new generation as urban regeneration strategy. *International Journal of Urban and Regional Research*, 37(2), 523–536.

Velasco, R. (2019) *Boredom Is in Your Mind*. Springer International Publishing.

Vodanovich, S.J. (2003) Psychometric measures of boredom: A review of the literature. *The Journal of Psychology*, 137(6), 569–595.

Vodanovich, S.J. and Watt, J.D. (2016) Self-report measures of boredom: An updated review of the literature. *The Journal of Psychology*, 150(2), 196–228.

Vogel-Walcutt, J. J., Fiorella, L., Carper, T. and Schatz, S. (2012) The definition, assessment, and mitigation of state boredom within educational settings: A comprehensive review. *Educational Psychology Review*, 24, 89–111. https://doi. org/10.1007/s10648-011-9182-7

Vonneilich, N. (2022) Social relations, social capital, and social networks: A conceptual classification. *Social Networks and Health Inequalities*, 23.

Vromen, A. and Collin, P. (2010) Everyday youth participation? Contrasting views from Australian policymakers and young people. *Young*, 18(1), 97–112. https://doi.org/10.1177/110330880901800107

Wacquant, L. (2008) Relocating gentrification: The working class, science and the state in recent urban research. *International Journal of Urban and Regional Research*, 32(1), 198–205.

Walker, J.S., Geenen, S., Thorne, E., and Powers, L.E. (2009). Improving outcomes through interventions that increase youth empowerment and self-determination. *Focal Point: Research, Policy, and Practice in Children's Mental Health*, 23(2), 13–16.

Walsh, L. and Black, R. (2018) *Rethinking Youth Citizenship after the Age of Entitlement*. Bloomsbury.

Wasserman, S. and Faust, K. (1994) *Social Network Analysis: Methods and Applications*.

Watt, P. (2006) Respectability, roughness and 'race': Neighbourhood place images and the making of working-class social distinctions in London. *International Journal of Urban and Regional Research*, 30(4), 776–797.

Webb, J. (2011) *Hearing Voices: Coping, Resilience and Recovery*. University of Leeds.

Webber, C. (2024) New ways of researching teen reading: Do the aims of reading research, policy and practice align with adolescents' priorities for reading? In *The Reading Lives of Teens*. Routledge, pp 209–229.

Wegner, L. and Flisher, A.J. (2009) Leisure boredom and adolescent risk behaviour: A systematic literature review. *Journal of Child and Adolescent Mental Health*, 21(1), 1–28.

Weisbrod, B. (1988) *The Nonprofit Economy*. Harvard University Press.

Weller, S. and Bruegel, I. (2006) Locality, school and social capital. *Families and Social Capital*.

Weller, S.C. (2007) Cultural consensus theory: Applications and frequently asked questions. *Field Methods*, 19(4), 339–368.

Wesselow, Ramos-Vidal, I. and de la Ossa, E.D. (2024) A systematic review to determine the role of public space and urban design on sense of community. *International Social Science Journal*, 74(252), 633–655.

Whittaker, A., Radcliffe, P., Chandler, A., Wincup, E., Carver, H., Finch, E. and Callaghan, J. (2022) *The Relations Study Data, 2021–2022*.

Wick, R.G. (2018) 'He was a friend of us poor men': Ida M. Tarbell and Abraham Lincoln's view of democracy. *Indiana Magazine of History*, 114(4), 255–282.

Wiley, C. (2012) Suicide prevention for counselors working with youth in secondary and post-secondary school. *Alabama Counseling Association Journal*, 38(2), 9–14.

Williams, B. (1976) *Problems of the Self: Philosophical Papers 1956–1972*. Cambridge University Press.

Williamson, H. (2015) 'Finding common ground', in presentation at the 2nd European Youth Work Convention [Online]. Available from: http:// bit. ly/2Rc6kn9

Williamson, H. (2020) Cornerstone challenges for European youth work and youth work in Europe making the connections and bridging the gaps. In *Proceedings of the 3rd European Youth Work Convention, Bonn, Germany*, pp 7–10.

Williamson, I., Leeming, D., Lyttle, S. and Johnson, S. (2015) Evaluating the audio-diary method in qualitative research. *Qualitative Research Journal*, 15(1), 20–34.

Winkler, D., Farnworth, L., Sloan, S. and Brown, T. (2011) Moving from aged care facilities to community-based accommodation: outcomes and environmental factors. *Brain Injury*, 25(2), 153–168.

Woods, A. (2021) Are we there yet? Research with and for teachers and children and the possibilities of schooling in a complex world. *The Australian Educational Researcher*, 48(1), 23–44.

Wood, J., Westwood, S. and Thompson, G. (2014) *Youth Work: Preparation for Practice*. Routledge.

Woodcraft, S., Izcue-Gana, J., Lorgat, R., Temple, W. and Jump, R. (2024) *Mapping Livelihood Insecurity in East London: A guide to Using Secondary Data to Measure and Map Livelihood Insecurity.* UCL Institute for Global Prosperity.

Woodman, D. and Wyn, J. (2015) Class, gender and generation matter: Using the concept of social generation to study inequality and social change. *Journal of Youth Studies*, 18(10), 1402–1410.

Woodman, D. and Wyn, J. (2018) How to support young People in a changing world: The sociology of generations and youth work. *The SAGE Handbook of Youth Work Practice.* Sage, pp 18–28.

Worpole, K. and Knox, K. (2007) *The Social Value of Public Spaces.* Joseph Rowntree Foundation.

Wray-Lake, L. and Syvertsen, A.K. (2011) The developmental roots of social responsibility in childhood and adolescence. *New Directions for Child and Adolescent Development*, 2011(134), 11–25.

Wright, L. and Nancarrow, C. and Kwok, P. (2001) Food taste preferences and cultural influences on consumption. *British Food Journal*, 103, 348–357. doi: 10.1108/00070700110396321.

Yamagishi, T. (2011) *War and Health Insurance Policy in Japan and the United States: World War II to Postwar Reconstruction.* JHU Press.

Yin, R.K. (2003) Designing case studies. *Qualitative Research Methods*, 5(14), 359–386.

Young, K. (1999) *The Art of Youth Work.* Russell House Publishing.

Young, I.M. (2002) Lived body vs gender: Reflections on social structure and subjectivity. *Ratio*, 15(4), 410–428.

Young, K. (2006) *The Art of Youth Work.* Russell House Publishing.

Zimmerman, B.J. (1998) Academic studing and the development of personal skill: A self-regulatory perspective. *Educational Psychologist*, 33(2–3), 73–86.

Zimmerman, B.J. (2000) Self-efficacy: An essential motive to learn. *Contemporary Educational Psychology*, 25(1), 82–91.

Zizek, S. (2011) *Living in the End Times.* Verso.

Zuchowski, I., Cleak, H., Nickson, A. and Spencer, A. (2019) A national survey of Australian social work field education programs: innovation with limited capacity. *Australian Social Work*, 72, 75–90. 10.1080/0312407X.2018.1511740.

Zuchowski, I., Braidwood, L., d'Emden, C., Gair, S., Heyeres, M., Nicholls, L., Savuro, N. and O'Reilly, S. (2022) The voices of 'At Risk' young people about services they received: A systematic literature review. *Australian Social Work*, 75(1), 76–95.

Zukin, S. (2010) *Naked City: The Death and Life of Authentic Urban Places.* Oxford University Press.

# Index

References in **bold** type refer to tables.

www.ingramcontent.com/pod-product-compliance
Lightning Source LLC
Chambersburg PA
CBHW070625030426
42337CB00020B/3916